Winning the SAFETY COMMITMENT

for Lowell

by ART FETTIG

FOR EVERYONE INVOLVED WITH SAFETY!

Art Fettig's
Growth Unlimited Inc.

36 Fairview
Battle Creek, Michigan 49017
Phone (800) 441-7676 (616) 965-2229
Fax (616) 965-4522 Web: www.IMASource.com
e-mail artfettig@voyager.net

Growth Unlimited books are available for bulk purchase
for educational, business, or sales promotional use.

Manufactured in the United States of America

Design, Layout and Typesetting
by Robbie & Robyn Fortner
616-962-9209

Library of Congress
Catalog Number 98-093334
Art Fettig

ISBN 0-916927-23-7

Table of Contents

Book I
World's Greatest Safety Meeting Idea Book

Book II
More Great Safety Meeting Ideas

Book III
Selling Safety

Book IV
The Quest Continues

About the Author....
Products and Services....

Books and Booklets by Art Fettig

Safety Books

Selling Safety In The 90's
World's Greatest Safety Meeting Idea Book
More Great Safety Meeting Ideas Book
*A Declaration Of Interdependence For Safety Booklet **
*A Personal Pledge To Safety **
*You Do WHAT While You Drive? **
How To Use The Book, "How Funny Art You, The Humor Game"
To Build Great Safety Teams
Winning The Safety Commitment

Sales Books

Selling Lucky
Selling Luckier Yet
*16 Great Lucky Selling Ideas **
World's Greatest Sales Meeting Idea Book
How To Follow-Up! For Greater Success In Sales
*Seeing Your Book In print **

Speaking Books

How To Hold An Audience In The Hollow Of Your Hand
*Anatomy Of A Speech **
Showtime
How Funny Are You?
*Speaking, Speaking **
Como Meterse Al Publico En El Bolsillo

Inspirational Books

*Reflection On Growth Booklet **   *The Platinum Rule*
*Self-Esteem Credo Booklet **   *Serenity! Serenity!*
Love Is The Target   *This Is It! **
Mentor: Secrets Of The Ages   *Songwriter*

Parent's Teacher's Books

It Only Hurts When I Frown
The Pos Parenting Book
The Declaration Of Interdependence For Excellence *

Children's Books

The Three Robots
The Three Robots Learn About Drugs
The Three Robots Find A Grandpa
The Three Robots Discover Their Possibilities
The Three Robots And The Sandstorm
Remembering
The Pos Activity Book
The New Just Say Yes Activity Book
The Santa Train *

Novels

Unfit For Glory
Success Rally

Business

Welcome To The 21st Century *

Verses

Army Memoirs 1952 *
A Single Man At Burnham Brook *
A Special Collection Of Verses For Seniors *
Best Verses Of Art Fettig And Friends *

For a complete catalog of Art Fettig Books and Tapes contact

Growth Unlimited Inc.

36 Fairview Ave
Battle Creek, MI
49017

Phone: (800) 441-7676
Fax: (616) 965-4522
Email: artfettig@voyager.net
Website: www.IMASource.com

Preface.....

I just had a call from the chairman of our 50 year high school reunion. Imagine that, 50 years since I received my high school diploma.

He asked if I would be their keynote speaker. Me, the fellow who spent more time in detention room than any other student in the school's history. A poor class clown.

I can imagine what my parents must have felt when they read that about their first son. Not very promising to say the least.

And now, some fifty years later they have asked me to be the keynoter. Not the doctors, not the lawyers, not the judges that have come from our class. No, not those who have made their mark in industry and accumulated millions of dollars along the way. They want Art Fettig as their keynoter.

"And what do you want me to talk about?" I asked. "Oh, why don't you just talk about a new book that you are currently working on or have just published.

Pretty daring of him. Who knows - I might be doing something vulgar. Who can tell what us dirty old men might be up to at the time.

I graduated in June of 1947 and after trying out a couple of jobs I wandered into the General Claims Department of the Grand Trunk Western Railroad where I began work on February 1st, 1948.

That is the real purpose of this book. On February 1st, 1998 I will be celebrating my 51st Anniversary of working in some way in the safety field.

That is a long time to do anything, even to stay alive,

by some people's standards.

50 years. Oh how the field of safety has changed in all of those years. And, oh, how many lives have been saved and how many injuries have been prevented in those 50 years.

In a way, this book is a celebration. It is a toast to all of the dedicated men and women I have come in contact with in those fifty years and for the passion we shared for the safety profession.

This book is a collection of my writings in the safety field.

We've upgraded all of the work and added a lot of new material throughout. *Book I* comes from my book titled, *World's Greatest Safety Meeting Idea Book*. I wrote this book for the attendees of the 1988 National Safety Congress in Chicago where I had the honor of being their early morning speaker on two consecutive days. We gave away some 3,000 copies of the book and it was an instant success. Some firms purchased as many as 1,000 copies for their own people.

Book II is a somewhat revised edition of my book titled: *More Great Safety Meeting Ideas*. We found that most of the people who had a copy of the first meeting book wanted the second, and so it was an instant success. *Book III* is a revision of my book titled, *Selling Safety In The 90's*. I suppose if we were to publish it alone now we'd call it, *Selling Safety in the 21st Century*. The ideas in this book are timeless. The fact is that safety must be sold on a continuing basis at all levels from the office of the CEO throughout an organization to include every employee, every contractor and everyone including the entire family of every worker.

Book IV is a collection of some of my other writings in the safety field. Some appeared in our popular newsletter and some are being published for the first time. We call it ,*The Quest Continues.* The title refers to our continuing quest for the golden goose egg. In many of my speeches I talk about that elusive golden goose egg and that, of course, is a zero that depicts zero accidents, zero injuries, zero incidents.

It is perfection and that is what everyone in the safety field dreams about and strives for.

Very few ever attain that level of excellence and still it is a wonderful goal to shoot for.

We truly hope that the sharing of many of the things that we have learned along the way might make your own journey more pleasant and successful.

If there is some way I might help you further then please give me a call.

This book is dedicated to the safety professionals who have touched my life. Without their continued support and sharing, my well of ideas would have run dry a long time ago. As it is, not a day passes that someone, some-where, some way doesn't call or write or in some way renew my own commit-ment and dedication to safety.

Their uncompromising commitment is a daily source of help to me.

BOOK *one*

World's GREATEST SAFETY MEETING IDEA BOOK

Finding a Commitment

Chapter 1

IF YOU HAD TO PICK ONE DAY IN YOUR LIFE when you really got serious about safety, what day would it be? Was there some turning point where you said to yourself that you were willing to commit a big chunk of your time and your dedication to saving people's lives and preventing accidents?

Most truly dedicated Safety People who I've met over the many years I've worked in the Safety field can point to one specific incident that changed their lives and their attitudes.

I've had hundreds of incidents during my long career where I became particularly excited, inspired, disgusted, enlightened, or what have you, when I took on a greater commitment to the field of safety, but one incident stands out in my life. I guess it's because that incident changed my job, my salary and my entire life.

At the time, I was employed as a claim agent for Grand Trunk Western Railroad Company at Battle Creek, Michigan. My records showed that I had been on the employee roles of the railroad for some 25 years, but two years of that I had spent in the United States Army.

In that 25 year span, I guess I had seen more death, more suffering, more horrible accidents than most people will ever see if they live to be a hundred.

I'd personally investigated decapitations and multiple amputations. I'd suffered long with the families of employees who were rendered vegetables and died a long suffering death. I'd investigated and negotiated claims where entire families were wiped out in an accident. I'd handled disasters such as a truck-train accident where a passenger train collided with a tractor-trailer loaded with steel and the train was tossed on its side down an embankment with dozens injured and others killed.

I'd seen it all. The deaths, yes, I'd investigated literally hundreds of death claims over that 25 year period.

Somehow I hung in there, year after year, and it certainly took its toll on my life, my marriage and my role as a father of four children.

Our train dispatchers were instructed to call me, no matter what the hour, the moment they learned of a serious accident.

I used to dread hearing the ring of our telephone because it meant that something was wrong. Someone was lying in a ditch alongside a railroad track, dead or near death.

I can still remember the call that changed my life. A trainmaster called me that night and said simply, "We've got a bad one, Art. You'd better get down here to the yard office right away."

I dressed quickly and when I got to the yard office, I learned that one of our firemen had climbed down from his engine to help make a fancy switching move to save a few minutes and somehow he was standing on a live track when they kicked some cars down that track.

It was dark and the cars hit him and passed over him and cut off two legs and an arm.

This fellow was a young man, younger than I was, and he had a wife and kids at home and it just made me sick.

I was to get a whole lot sicker that day.

Our safety man rushed down from his home about 75 miles away and we drove out to the scene of the accident together.

I hope you never discover this fact personally yourself, but there are a lot of sick people in this world. Some of them listen to police radio messages and when they hear the report of a gory accident, they immediately go to the scene. Nothing thrills them more than to see a dead body that is badly mutilated. When they arrive after the body is removed, they scour around the scene looking on the ground for signs of blood or flesh. You can actually see the saliva on the lips of these creeps.

Long ago I discovered these people and so I just got into the habit of kicking the gravel at the scene of such accidents to help cover up such signs following an accident.

That morning, as dawn broke, the safety supervisor

and I were at the scene of the accident and there was no kicking the gravel that morning.

There were big chunks of that man on the track and alongside the rail and I remember that I took a couple of sticks and I picked up those chunks and I dug a hole with the stick and I buried pieces of that man with my two hands.

That morning, I resolved that I would change my life.

I made a vow that day that I would no longer be just a claim agent. After twenty-five years of cleaning up the messes from accidents, I was going to do something to prevent those accidents. That day I dedicated my life to the Safety Movement.

Some time before then I had become a freelance writer in my spare time, whatever there was. I was beginning to sell articles and short stories and I'd been writing material for a professional speaker named Herb True.

I'd written a number of articles on accident investigation, too, that had been published in an Association of American Railroad magazine. In fact, I had won their Article of the Year Award twice--something no one else had ever accomplished.

I had made a number of efforts to use my special skills and talents on the railroad, but all my effort fell on deaf ears.

I began producing audio-visual shows for outside clients on sales and employee training, and was meeting with a measure of success.

Immediately following that triple amputation, I went to work in my attic producing an audio-visual program for Grand Trunk.

I did this with my own money. I wanted to do something to change the attitude of our employees and I titled the program "What's A *Grand Trunk?*"

I started shooting pictures and writing a script and I went so far as to record some words on top of a song and then I called John Burdakin, who was then Vice President of the Railroad.

Let me tell you, I had never even met a Vice President of our railroad, not in the twenty-five years I had worked for the company.

I said simply, "Mr. Burdakin, our triple amputation case is in the hospital at Kalamazoo. He has a terrific spirit and it looks like he's going to live. Could you come and visit him and tell him we love him and that we will stand by him and put his kids through college, and we'll try to rehabilitate him and keep him working for us?"

There was no hesitation. "Sure I will, Art," he said, and we immediately made a date.

He came to my office right on time and he asked me to drive his car as we went to Kalamazoo.

I figured that was as good a time as any to hit him with my idea. I told him what I had in mind and I had a little cassette player with me and asked him if I could play the sound track for the audio-visual program I was producing.

I got so excited playing it for him that I nearly smashed up his car. He laughed and suggested we just pull off to the side of the road while we listened to it. When it was done, he asked if I could make some additions and modifications and the next day he set up appointments for me with the two other Vice Presidents and the President of our Company.

I only had about five minutes with each of them to get their pictures for the slide show and to get their messages on tape, but I worked fast and I put it all together. A few weeks later, I had them all in a meeting where I showed my program and told them some of the ideas I had to make ours a safer and better railroad.

I'll never forget that feeling when the last slide popped on the screen and the music ended. I had a clear slide on the end so it came on sort of like a spotlight as the show ended. I walked in front of the screen and said, "Gentlemen, this is my thing now and either you let me do this sort of thing for the railroad or I am leaving to do it for somebody else."

I was scared to death. I had a wife and four kids to support. I had twenty-five years with the railroad and it was the only job I knew and I was laying it all on the line.

They took a few weeks to decide but they finally called me in and gave me a $5,000 raise, a new car and complete freedom to do what I thought should be done to save lives and improve morale on the railroad.

I worked at that job for ten years and during that period we went from a railroad that was losing millions and millions of dollars each year to one that made a good profit.

Our railroad had been consistently last or near last in the safety ratings for railroads of its size. During that ten year period, we went from last to first place and won a number of Harriman Safety Awards.

We produced slide shows and film strips that were seen by millions of students throughout the United States and if all my efforts saved one life or prevented just one injury, then I feel I have been amply rewarded.

Do you have a commitment? Have you dedicated your life, or at least a part of your life, to the exciting business of saving lives and preventing accidents? If the answer is no, then I invite you to "Just Say Yes!"

Working for Safety can be one of the most exciting and rewarding ventures you will ever experience.

Chapter 2

THE LATE GREAT SALES TRAINER AND motivator, Elmer Wheeler, was quite famous for his saying, "Sell The Sizzle, Not The Steak."

For a moment will you go along with me in your imagination? Just for a moment, picture a huge steak sitting in the super market with a thin plastic wrapping around it. The label on the package says, "Prime". How does that hit you?

Now, picture that same steak on the griddle, sizzling away with the fantastic aroma that only a sizzling steak can provide, wafting in the wind. That steak is just about right for you, medium rare with just a bit of blood running out of it and you know all the fixings are ready for a succulent meal.

Which of those steaks is more appealing to you? Of course, the sizzling steak has it all over the one in the store. Right?

Wouldn't it be a lot easier to sell that sizzling steak than the one with the plastic wrap? Of course.

Now you've got the job of selling the idea of safety to a group. That word "safety" might mean a dozen different things to a dozen different people but I'll just bet you that sizzling steak would appeal to a lot more people than the subject of safety. Do you agree?

Safety. What does it mean? Is safety something contained in a book of rules that you take out and point to after an accident has occurred?

Is the word "safety" usually mentioned with terms like should have, could have, ought to have?

Is safety a sign you hang on the wall?

Is safety a piece of equipment that people had better wear, or else?

Is safety just a slogan? Or is safety something else?

And what is a safety meeting? Is a safety meeting a place to threaten people? Is a safety meeting a place to really get tough--a place to lay it on the line to those clowns?

Is a safety meeting a place to instruct? To train? To inform? To inspire? To motivate? To praise, and celebrate and reward?

And what in the world could ever be done to really produce the World's Greatest Safety Meetings?

I guess more than anything it is a challenge. After Fifty years of working in the field of safety, I have come to the conclusion that safety is something that must be sold. It must be sold and sold again on a daily basis.

And I have come to the conclusion that it is important and vital and exciting and challenging and rewarding and worthwhile.

This little book is my attempt to make your job a bit easier. It has a few ideas that I've picked up along the way--ideas I truly believe will help you produce Great Safety Meetings.

I certainly don't have all the answers and I know that you have answers I have not yet discovered. If so, would you do me a favor? Would you take the time to write me and share your ideas on how to have better, more effective safety sessions? If you do send me ideas, and if I use them in my next book, I'll give you full credit and some kind of reward too.

Tell me how you make your safety sessions sizzle. Just send your ideas to Art Fettig, Growth Unlimited Inc., 31 East Ave. S., Battle Creek, Michigan 49017, or call me at 1-800-441-7676 or (616) 965-2229. Or fax at 616-965-4522. Or you can reach me on the Internet at, Website: www.IMASource.com or e-mail: artfettig@voyager.net.

Just maybe, if we all get our ideas together, we can really make this world a better, safer place.

THE
SAFETY
MOTIVATORS
THE
SAFETY
MOTIVATORS

Chapter 3

OW CAN YOU ADD REAL SIZZLE TO your safety meetings? What is the magic key to success in this area? Is there some secret formula known only to a few of the Superstars in the field of Safety? Is there a way to guarantee success for every safety meeting you conduct?

I wish the answer to all of these questions could be a simple yes, but life just isn't that easy for us, is it?

There are a number of things you can do to stack the deck for winning in your favor, however, and we hope to share as many techniques and ideas as we can in the limited boundaries of this book. Let's run through ten of these ideas together.

1. SET A GOAL

Set a goal, a target, for every meeting you conduct. When you know where it is you want to go, then it's a lot easier to get there. Never just hold a safety meeting because it's required. (Perhaps it's true you must hold a meeting; however, don't allow that to be your sole motivation. Go beyond that.)

Pick a specific subject and goal for your meeting. Make it your aim to educate, motivate, involve and inspire.

Some time ago, I discovered an 8 step guide for setting and accomplishing goals. I've used it in a dozen different ways with both business and personal goals and my success rate in this regard is terrific. Try it yourself and learn to apply the system to every meeting you hold.

1. Decide what you want.
2. Write it down; be specific.

3. Set the date of accomplishment.
4. Read your goal three times a day.
5. Think of it often. Imagine yourself enjoying it.
6. Begin to develop a plan of action.
7. Don't discuss it with others.
8. Act as though you are confident and successful and soon you will be!

Many years ago I set a goal to take my family to Europe on a vacation. I checked my cash reserves and found I had about 50 cents that wasn't spent or committed. I took a jar and wrote a note on the jar. "By June 1st., I will have enough money to take my family to Europe." I started on January 1st.

I repeated that goal to myself a dozen or more times each day. I visualized our family boarding that airplane. I went to the travel agent and they gave me a stack of posters and I posted them all over my attic. I could just see myself and my family walking across London Bridge.

I decided to write and submit one new manuscript each day. I wrote up a storm of articles, verses, fillers, short-stories. Every night, I went to my writing room and I didn't come back down until I'd produced something.

I didn't tell anyone but my wife about this idea and if I had it to do all over again, I would tell no one. People simply discourage you.

The checks started to trickle in. Ten dollars for a joke to begin with and then the checks got bigger and bigger and by June 1st, I had enough money in that jar to take my family to Europe. In fact, we made a habit of it and I traveled to Europe nearly every year after that.

Set goals for your safety meetings and your goals will become reality.

2. MAKE IT FUN

Make a safety meeting fun. If a safety meeting is just an excuse to chew your people out for the wrong they have done then don't expect much enthusiasm or cooperation. Approach each meeting with a positive, friendly attitude. As Mary Poppins once said, "In any job that's to be done, there is an element of fun. Find the fun and snap, the job's a breeze."

Remember, the attitude of your attendees is often just a reflection of your attitude. If you feel indifference, then expect indifference from your people. If you have a true sense of commitment and a sincere desire to make things better, then you may expect and demand cooperation.

3. EXPECT THE BEST

Expect the very best. Program your subconscious mind for success.

So often we tell ourselves, "I just know this will be a flop." We actually condition ourselves for failure and then we act surprised when it happens.

Expect good things from your people and from your meeting and you'll find it.

4. GET INVOLVEMENT

Get your critics involved. So often the troublemakers at a meeting are just looking for attention. Steal their thunder right away by getting them involved in the front of the room. Call them up with you and get the group to applaud them for their cooperation.

5. BE PREPARED

Be prepared. This was a great motto for Boy Scouts and it's even better when it comes to safety meetings. In fact, perhaps your motto should read, "Be Over-prepared." Set a time schedule for the material you plan to cover and then add an additional thirty percent. That's right. Add more material than you can possibly handle. That'll demand a certain burst of energy from you that will give your meeting a strong, positive pace.

Most meetings drag along. When you add pace to what you're doing it creates interest and excitement.

When you have long-winded participants, encourage them to keep it short and to the point.

6. STAY ON TIME

Start on time and finish on time. Treat your partici-pants as if their time is really valuable. It is. Don't bore them. Don't preach. Dean Inge once declared that to try to get anything across to a congregation by preaching to it was like trying to fill a number of long-necked bottles by throwing a bucket of water over them. Don't embar-rass the people. Make your meeting move.

7. GIVE PRAISE

Find a way to praise your people, regardless of their performance. Catch them doing something right and praise them for it. Sure, you have to bring out the things that aren't right, too, but don't make a career out of it. If all you do is criticize and complain, they'll soon stop listening. A little praise gives them something to build on.

8. TELL STORIES

Tell stories. Give specific examples. Avoid generalities. Reading a string of safety rules can be mighty dull. Tell a story about a tragedy. Don't be afraid to remind your people that workers are still getting killed and permanently disabled every day because of rule violations.

9. SHOW YOU CARE

Let them know you really care. You've probably heard the expression, "People don't care how much you know, until they know how much you care."

It is so true. Your tremendous knowledge in the field of safety might prove useless unless you can share that knowledge with others and lead them to positive action.

10. KEEP SCORE

Find a way to keep score. If you possibly can, develop a competition between workers, sections, whatever. Seek input. Demand participation. Find a way to provide incentives for improvements, for excellence.

Mary Kay developed a multi-million dollar organization that continues to grow and the real key to her success is a constant parade of meetings. The women who attend these meetings win ribbons for their performance and it's not unusual for some to go home with a dozen ribbons.

Each week, they go out and exceed their own expectations just so they can win a little applause and recognition. Let's face it, some people go a lifetime without winning an award or prize. The ribbons the women receive probably cost about a penny each and yet they make all the difference in the world in their performance.

Your prizes and banners of recognition need not be costly. Just make your people winners at your meeting and they will be winners all the time with their safety performance.

There you have just ten ideas. I'm sure you can think up ten more yourself when you put your mind to it.

Don't fall into the trap of putting off the planning of your safety meeting till the last minute. Work on it every day for a few minutes and get yourself an idea file where you put every positive thought that comes into your mind in this regard.

Like so many other things, great safety meeting ideas are all around us and once we create the climate for growing, the ideas will come and flow for us.

You can conduct great safety meetings that sizzle and succeed. Remember, what you say and do at a safety meeting can make the difference between someone having a serious accident and not having that accident. What you do is really important.

Chapter 4

Y EARS AGO, ON MY SAFETY HOWDY rounds, at the railroad, I used to go up to a yardmaster in a railroad yard and ask him, "Tell me, who's your worst employee?"

It was strange. They always used to have the name of their worst employee on the tip of their tongue.

In Flint, Michigan one time, I asked a yardmaster that question, "Who's your worst employee?"

His response was immediate. "Charlie," he replied. "No doubt about it, Charlie Fenner is the worst." (That wasn't the real name. Charlie Fenner is just a name I use when I want to pin something on somebody. I don't know a real Charlie Fenner and if I ever meet a real one, I guess I'll be in real trouble.)

"What is wrong with Charlie Fenner?" I asked the yardmaster.

"Everything," he said. "He drinks too much. He's absent all the time. He hides out when there is work to be done. He breaks the safety rules. He's an agitator..."

"Tell me something good about him," I suggested.

The yardmaster just shook his head slowly. "I can't," he admitted. "Charlie doesn't have one redeeming quality in his whole being."

I explained to that yardmaster that this was a little experiment the president of our company had suggested I conduct and that I would be back a week later and I wanted him to find one good thing about Charlie Fenner that he could tell me about then.

The yardmaster shook his head again as if it was a hopeless task, but he agreed to try.

A week later I met with him and I asked, "What did you find out about Charlie Fenner that is good?"

He looked rather gloomy and finally replied, "He bowls."

"He what?" I asked.

"He bowls." He replied. "The other night he bowled a 239."

"A 239?" I asked

I don't know a thing about bowling but I asked the yardmaster if he bowled.

"Not really," he replied. "I've bowled some, but not much really."

"What is the best game you ever bowled?" I asked.

"About a 139," he admitted.

"So a 239 is fantastic?" I asked. "Isn't it?"

"Yeah." He admitted. "It's fantastic!"

I went directly out to the yard where, following a long

search, I just happened to run into Charlie Fenner.

"You Charlie Fenner?" I asked.

"Yeah!" He admitted. "What's up?"

"I just wanted to meet you." I said. "The yardmaster was just telling me about you and he said..."

"What did that rotten, no good, son of a ..."

"Hold it!" I said. "He was telling me you bowled a 239 game the other night and he thinks that's fantastic."

Charlie Fenner looked stunned. He just stood there for a minute and then asked, "He said that?"

"Yeah." I assured him. "He said fantastic. He said that you bowled a 239 and the best he ever did in his life is a 139."

Charlie just stood there shaking his head. "He said that?" He kept repeating.

I left him there and walked over to my car and drove home.

I'd messed that Charlie Fenner up so badly. Never again could he be as rotten and mean and useless as he'd been before.

But the fellow I had really changed was that yardmaster. From then on, whenever he'd see Charlie Fenner he'd holler out, "How's the bowling going, Charlie?" And Charlie would stop and tell him and they had a whole new level of communication going between them.

In his book In Search of Excellence, Tom Peters says that great leaders make a practice of catching their people doing things right.

On your next safety inspection, try to look for the good things and comment on them. Praise your people for the good they do and they'll try to do a lot more good for you.

Chapter 5

"WHY ME?" THAT IS A QUESTION I often hear from those who are selected to conduct safety meetings. "I'm not a teacher or a professional speaker. Why did they nail me for this job?"

Who knows the answer to those questions? Probably you displayed some special talent to your boss. Perhaps you showed that extra quality of caring and concern that makes a great safety leader. Or maybe it was your outgoing personality.

Whatever the answer, you still have the challenge of standing up on your feet and facing a group that's often not as inspired or dedicated as you might be.

How do you learn how to instruct so that others will understand? How can you get the group on your side?

I've spent nearly a lifetime gathering answers to those questions and I find that the answers keep changing.

People are people though, and there are a few truths that remain permanent.

First of all, enthusiasm is essential to a good meeting.

Second, enthusiasm is contagious. When a leader is enthusiastic, others soon catch that enthusiasm from the leader. Enthusiasm also feeds on enthusiasm, so that once you get that group enthusiastic, they'll build up your enthusiasm.

What if you don't feel enthusiastic? Then my advice is that you fake it.

Act enthusiastic and you'll soon become enthusiastic.

If you act bored and disgusted and aloof, then your audience will catch that mood from you too.

In my book *How To Hold An Audience In The Hollow Of Your Hand* I say that an audience often reflects the attitude of the presenter.

If you are scared half to death, then your audience will be tense and guarded.

The *Book of Lists* says that the thing people fear the most, more than fear of failure, or the fear of falling from an airplane, or the fear of death itself, is the fear of public speaking.

In other words, people would rather fall from an airplane or die than get up and make a speech.

If you feel a little anxiety, just realize it's a perfectly natural feeling.

Many others who have had that same feeling tell me that the better prepared they are for a meeting, the better they feel.

When they aren't prepared, they find, the anxiety really sets in.

I have developed a simple, seven step formula for opening up a speech or a seminar or any type of program.

(1) If you are introduced to the group, respond to the introduction with humor. You'll find a few of the responses from my book in the humor section of this book. If you're not introduced, start out with a joke about how you were selected to run the meeting. Make it a joke on yourself.

(2) Present a bit of humor that ties in directly with your group and your meeting theme.

(3) Show your concern with the comfort and convenience of the group. (Can you hear me in the back of the room O.K.?)

(4) Get your audience to join with you in applauding something or someone. The sooner you get them involved and participating, the better your meeting will be.

(5) Compliment your audience with sincerity. Find something good that they have done and compliment them right up front.

(6) Ask the audience a question. (Just raise your hands... How many of you ever got a speeding ticket on the expressway? Raise your hands. Good. Well, we won't get any speeding tickets at this meeting but we do hope to keep it moving along quickly.)

(7) Physically invade their territory. That's right. Move right into the audience as you make your presentation. Don't lock yourself behind the lectern. (Some folks actually hang on to the lectern to keep from shaking. Let go and walk among the people. Walk down the aisle.) Attendees will be a lot more attentive and besides, it makes you a moving target.

There's an old joke that says, "A good start is half the bottle." Actually the saying goes, "A good start is half the battle."

That's so true with a meeting too. A good start makes everything easier.

Once you break down that initial resistance and tension that any audience offers, you are well on your way to having a great meeting.

The truth is, this seven step opening also provides you with a formula to build your own confidence too.

Once you get into the swing of things, you will find that opening a meeting gets easier each time. Never, never take your meeting for granted though. The real key to any great meeting is Preparation--Preparation--Preparation.

When I conduct seminars for speakers, I tell them that an audience is a sensitive thing. Somehow, physically, an audience was not meant to sit on a hard chair for hours at a time.

The body needs exercise. When you realize this, you can begin to build a little exercise into everything you do.

I have found that a great laugh every five minutes is a tremendous exerciser.

Watch people when they have a good laugh. Norman Cousins calls laughing "internal jogging".

I've watched hundreds of thousands of people laugh and I discovered that when people laugh they often bend forward.

Have you ever noticed that most chairs are not comfortable and many of them have plastic seats? I don't know about you, but plastic seats make me sweat. I've discovered that when people laugh hard, most of them go through this little ritual. They actually lean forward as they laugh and they lean over to the right and then to the left. I guess you could say they move from cheek to cheek. They let a little air in, they let a little air out; I don't know what they're doing.

I do know they're exercising, though, and somehow it gives me the right to talk for another five minutes or so.

You can't always get great cheek to cheek laughs with an audience though. That's why I use other techniques too. I ask questions. I ask what many might consider dumb questions.

"How many of you ever had a bad day? Get up your hands if you have."

When people raise their hands they shift around in their seats. They stretch their backs. More exercise. More tolerance for more program.

I walk down the aisles to the back of the room while I'm talking. I move from one side of the room to the other.

Your physical presence with those characters who like to hide at the back of the room is both intimidating and invigorating. It keeps them alive.

Since I mentioned the back of the room, let me cover the subject of seating at a meeting.

It is impossible to have an effective meeting when you have 25 people in a room with 100 seats and everyone is sitting at the rear of the hall.

. Let me repeat that. It is impossible to have an effective meeting when you have 25 people in a room with 100 seats and everyone is sitting at the rear of the hall.

Therefore, it's imperative that you have your audience sitting right down front where you are presenting the program.

"Easier said than done," you say and you're right. Difficult but not impossible. And imperative.

The best way I know, if you have control of the seating, is to underseat your meeting. That is, estimate the size of your audience and then set up far fewer chairs. Only when all of the seats are taken do you bring in more chairs. This will not only get people sitting down front, it will also appear that this is a very successful, well-attended meeting.

Another way is to rope off the rear seats and to have people there to see that no one sits in the roped off area.

If people resist, just explain to them that you cannot have an effective meeting with everyone at the back of the room and that you want this to be an effective meeting because it's important to them.

It is ridiculous to start a meeting with your audience huddled together at the rear of the hall near the exit.

At a meeting in Michigan recently, I walked into the room with an audience of 200 in a hall that seated 300. Every rear seat was filled and there were 100 empty seats in the front of the room. I politely asked the audience to come down front. Not one person moved. They folded their arms and glared at me. I asked politely again explaining that it was impossible to have an effective meeting with that kind of set up. They sat there.

I tried a couple of jokes and they glared at me like a bunch of owls. I asked how many of them had to put on meetings and most of them raised their hands. I then told them that I could not put on a good meeting unless they came forward and I asked them once more to move forward.

No one moved.

I waited. And I waited longer.

I then started packing up my notes and my props. I simply stated that I hoped those seated in the last two rows were prepared to conduct the meeting for the next two hours because I was going home.

Since we could not have a good meeting with them seated in the back of the room, I refused to put on a poor meeting.

I was dead serious. I told the chairman he could forget about my fee. I was sorry but I would not go on.

At that point, someone in the last row stood up and came forward. The audience applauded him. Then two others came forward. In fact, the back rows emptied out and came forward--that is, all but two fellows who sat there with their arms folded, looking stubborn.

I felt, what the heck, I'm winning. Maybe I can win them over too. I had a hand mike with a long cord so I went up to the one fellow and said, "What about you?"

He glared at me and said, "If I move, I'm leaving."

I simply said, "Great. I hope you have a good time

today."

I turned to the other guy and asked, "What about you?"

He said, "I saw you at another meeting just a week ago."

And I replied, "Well, no one should have to sit through one of my sessions twice; you're welcome to leave."

Instead, he got up and came forward and the audience applauded.

The other fellow just sat there and I went on with the program.

As I walked back to the stage, I suddenly said to myself, "Art, you are in deep trouble. How are you going to get yourself out of this mess?"

I did a lot of thinking as I walked back to the stage and then it came to me.

"I asked this before, but let me ask it again. How many of you have to put on meetings?"

They all raised their hands.

"Great!" I said. "If you want to have good meetings, then insist your audience sit right down front where they can hear you. I want to thank every one of you for cooperating. Now, with your help we can get on with the job of having a great meeting."

I got a letter later from the program chairperson saying that every evaluation turned in on my program was positive.

Another thing I've learned from over 2,500 presentations is that the smaller the room you use to accommodate your audience, the better the meeting. A little overcrowding is much better than having a dozen people in an arena.

Lighting is another important factor in your meeting. Just because you might be using an overhead projector or slides in your presentation is no reason to conduct your meeting in the dark.

I actually saw a fellow work in darkness for half an hour and he had three overhead exhibits that added nothing to his program. He worked in the dark for half an hour for those three poor exhibits.

Turn up the lights. They say that your body language is a major part of the communications process. Don't expect to really enliven your group in darkness.

The temperature of the room can also affect your meeting. The best rule is to keep it cool. The body temperature of an audience will quickly warm up a room and if you start with a warm room, things will quickly get hot and uncomfortable.

If the audience can't hear you, then don't expect to do an effective job either. Remember, an audience absorbs the sound in a room too, and so when you're checking out a public address system before an audience arrives, make sure it is on the loud side in an empty hall.

If you must allow smoking at your meeting, then make

sure you also provide a "no smoking" section.

So much for the environment. What about the program itself?

The best environment in the world won't help you if you don't have an effective program.

There are as many formats for a safety meeting as there are presenters, but I'd like to offer a few tips that just might help you.

#1. Call on others to make presentations. Bring in experts. Assign them to a specific topic and give them a time limit and let them know that you'll stick to it.

Bring in the experts from your own organization and don't hesitate to bring in interesting speakers and presenters from other organizations.

#2. Use films and videos to enhance your program. There are hundreds of fine products with a safety theme available on the market today. Just reach out and you'll find a source, perhaps as close as your local library. The movie needn't be safety related either to make your point. Look for humor relief when you have a heavy meeting topic. Use your imagination and your creativity and make your meeting sizzle.

See our Products and Services section beginning at the end of the book, for information on the popular videos we have produced for your meetings.

#3. Promote audience involvement. Try to have one period during each meeting where attendees can provide input. Do not, however, allow this time to turn into a negative gripe session. If the meeting starts to go in that direction, just interrupt, take charge and ask the complainer to see you privately after the meeting so you can discuss the complaint.

#4. Make an effort to find at least one positive solution to a safety problem that you can report on during your meeting. Let your people know that your company is listening and is concerned and that positive things are happening.

Great safety meetings call for planning, commitment and dedication. And great safety meetings are worth the

effort. Time and time again, it's been proven that great safety meetings prevent accidents and save lives. Are you up to the job?

Chapter 6

YEARS AGO I DISCOVERED A SIMPLE formula for effective communications. It works if you are writing an article, a speech or planning a meeting. I'm certain that with a little effort you can use it to help plan your next meeting. There are four ingredients to the formula and each of them is easy to apply.

Let me begin by telling you of the four components. First is the hook. You want to grab the other party's interest.

A famous preacher was giving a sermon in the Bible Belt one day and he began his sermon by saying "It is mighty damn hot outside."

The audience was stunned. He had their attention. And then the preacher continued, "That is what I heard a man say right outside this church today."

He then continued with a blazing sermon against profanity.

Sometimes it takes a shock to get an audience interested. If the statistics bear you out, you might begin by saying, "Someone in this room will be killed in an accident. One of us isn't going to make it."

That ought to make the hair stand up on the back of their necks.

Whatever it takes, get their attention. Use a hook.

The second component is the Y O U element.

You've probably often heard the expression, "What's in it for me?"

Well, this is the section of your presentation where you tell them exactly what's in it for them.

Motivation could be described as the reason people do things. It is what makes things important to people. In this second section of your presentation you give them a reason to become interested and involved.

I break these reasons into four basic categories. Money, romance, self preservation and recognition.

Money is a great motivator for most people. Not only are most of us concerned with getting money but there is also a tremendous amount of fear involved regarding the loss of money.

When injuries occur there is always the danger of loss of wages or the ability to earn. It doesn't take much imagination to bring home the point that it's just good sense to avoid injury and death if we hope to keep that flow of money running in our lives.

Romance is our second key to motivation. And with romance we include sex. Certainly certain injuries might make you less attractive to the opposite sex. And certain injuries can badly disrupt your sex life. Just think of any type of injury that would involve a body cast. They can certainly be pretty restrictive.

Self-preservation is what safety is really all about-- avoiding injuries, preventing disease, staying alive and healthy. And so as we start to explore these motivators, we discover that the desire for safety in our lives is a pretty basic thing. We all want safety in our lives. We all want a safe place to live and to work. None of us are interested in risking our lives or getting hurt. But to bring home the point that safety rules and safety equipment and thinking safely are all necessary so we might realize our desire to live safely sometimes takes a real selling job.

The fourth motivator, recognition, is one that gets far too little use. People love recognition. Some thrive on it. No one likes to be pointed out as the village idiot.

"Smart people work safely," might be a slogan that appeals to the desire for recognition.

Safety Awards are another great way to appeal to the need for recognition.

So there you have the four hot buttons to the Y O U element of presentation.

First we had the hook. Then, the Y O U factor. Next, we move on to the Body of the presentation, the guts of it all.

When you make your point, illustrate it with quotes, statistics, anecdotes and, yes, this is a great spot to bring in a film, a video, a demonstration to reinforce your point.

Bring in experts if you can.

This section gives real substance to your program. Pick a specific area of safety that's important to your group and bring home your point in the most effective way you can find.

The final segment of your program is your close.

This is what the meeting is all about. Never, never end a meeting without some call for action.

Ask for cooperation. Ask for dedication. Ask for positive action, for positive results from the group. A meeting without some goal, without some call for action, is just a visit. Make your meeting pay off by asking for the order. Ask and you shall receive. Make your meeting say something important to every attendee.

These are lives we're talking about. The job of safety is to prevent accidents and injuries and death. Isn't that important?

Hook, YOU, Body and Close. Those are the elements and when you put them together effectively, you have the structure of a truly effective meeting.

How do you have better meetings? How do you personally do a better job with your group? Where do you begin?

You start out with a goal, a mission, a desire, a commitment. You work at it every day. You keep your eyes and your ears open for possibilities. You ask for help everywhere you might find it.

Is it all worth it? Yes. Safety is important. It is vital. And believe me, it has been proven again and again. Good safety meetings make a difference.

Chapter 7

ERHAPS YOU'VE HEARD A SPEAKER begin his or her presentation by telling the audience, "My job here today is to speak and your job is to listen. If any of you get done with your job before I get done with mine, I hope you'll let me know."

The problem, of course, is that many members of your audience will let you know just that. Some do it in the first minute of your presentation . Then they fill their time in a number of different ways. Some just get up and leave.

Others take out the newspaper and read it with great

flourishes as they turn the pages. Some just start up a conversation with a friend nearby.

One way to avoid such problems is to get your audience to participate in your presentation. There are a number of techniques you can use and we'll share just a few of them with you. Again, once you open up your mind to searching for such material, it will come to you.

Attend as many presentations by others as you possibly can and when you see something that works, adopt it for your presentations.

One of the major causes of accidents is people's failure to communicate effectively. Let's begin with an example that illustrates this point.

One of my favorites goes as follows.

"Everybody raise your right hand. Get it right up there like this." (Repeat this request several times.) Nod your head. Expect everyone to participate. Just repeat, "Come on, get them up there." And raise your own right arm up high. "Now make a circle like this." Demonstrate, touching the tip of your right index finger to the tip of your thumb, thus making a circle. "Now everybody, bring that circle down to your chin." As you say this, you immediately bring your hand down and have the circle you made touch your right cheek. Just look around and say, "I said chin." Most of them will have their circle on their cheek just like you. You can have a little fun if you point at someone and say this guy cheated. Put your hand on your cheek and, looking very sheepishly, slide it down to your chin and say, "I did it right."

Now say, "Everybody does it wrong. In fact, I did it wrong five times in a row. The whole point is, (*make the circle again and bring it down to your cheek as you say,)* people don't do what you tell them to do; they do what they see you doing."

Now you can make your point on the importance of clear and concise communications.

An easy way to involve your audience is to take a survey. Just ask them, "How many of you... *(whatever)*? Just raise your hands."

Again, not only does this create interest and participation, it also provides a mild bit of physical exercise.

Applause is another easy way to promote audience participation. When you call on a volunteer for anything, most of those you select will resist. But when you physically take their hand and encourage them and get the audience to applaud that volunteer, they usually drop their resistance. Applause is a good way to pay a compliment to some achievement or to someone who deserves credit for some accomplishment. People love to be applauded and it helps bind an audience into a group that's working together.

Of course, laughter is a great way for an audience to participate, provided they're not making fun of someone or badly embarrassing someone. Unless that someone might be you... You might encourage this type of fun and make sure you laugh the loudest and act in a friendly manner.

If you'd like another demonstration on communications, you just might bring home the danger of spreading rumors at the same time. Why not spread a rumor around the meeting room?

First of all, create a rumor that you'd like to use as an

example. People seem to love to be the bearers of bad news so how about a rumor like this one. Write it out carefully on a piece of paper so you can be certain of the exact wording of the rumor as you started it. Something like this might work. "This didn't come from a reliable source, but I heard the company would be sending home twenty five people on December 30th for the rest of the year."

Read that rumor to someone at the front corner of your

room and ask them to pass it on with a whisper. Have the rumor passed right on down the aisle. Ask your audience to imagine that this is a real rumor. Have them do it rapidly and keep it moving. Then, when the rumor arrives at the end of the line, have that party stand up and repeat the rumor they just heard.

Almost always, the final result will be light years from the rumor you originally started. It doesn't take a great number of people to demonstrate this. Ten is plenty so you might do it in a single aisle of your meeting room. If you are seated at a table, you might just pass it around the table and get the desired result.

You can draw your own conclusion for such a demonstration but people generally get a lot better understanding of the danger of passing on rumors without checking them out first.

Seminar leaders throughout the country have learned that attention and retention rates go way up when they have participants fill in the blank words in the work books they provide. You need not have something as elaborate as a work book. You can do this with a single page.

For instance, "One of the major causes of back injuries is the failure to use your knees when lifting."

"If an object is over so many pounds, ask for help." "When in doubt take chances."

You can get the idea from this how you might stress the major points of your program in this manner and as the participants complete the page, it not only reinforces their understanding and retention, it also gives them something that demands they pay continuing attention.

This next one you can do with five volunteers up in the front of the room or you can do it with an entire group.

Give each participant a sheet of plain paper 8 x 11 inches. Each person holds the paper in front of themselves with their eyes tightly closed and follows these instructions:

"Fold the sheet exactly in half. Turn the folded sheet ninety degrees and tear off the upper left-hand corner. Now fold the sheet in half again, reach down the right-hand edge about halfway and tear out a triangle about an inch on each side. Fold the paper once more, turn it ninety degrees, and tear off the upper right-hand corner."
Now have each participant open their eyes and unfold the sheet. Each started with the same kind of sheet and followed the same instructions, but it would be a miracle if any of the sheets were now identical.

Every person listens differently and interprets what he or she hears in their own way. That's why feedback is so essential when giving instructions. Make certain that people understand your exact meaning before proceeding with more instruction.

Here's another quick demonstration on how people fail to listen. Simply ask your audience to clap their hands when you say, "three."

"Ready? O.K. One... two..." (nod your head when the count of three would normally come and say, "and...") then on the beat of four call out "three" and clap your hands.

Nearly everyone will clap their hands when you nod your head.

Another way to promote participation is to have a question and answer session. You'll find a certain little group of attendees will have all of the questions if you allow them to dominate the meeting.

Instead, draw out those who never contribute. Call on

them and ask them to contribute an idea of their own. There are people who never contribute a thing to a meeting, not because they don't have great ideas but because they are filled with low self-esteem or the fear of making a fool of themselves. Draw them into the meeting and try to build up their confidence.

One effective speaker I know has his audience repeat all the key words in his presentation. For instance, he'll say,   "One of the keys to effective communications is *listening*. Would you all say listening. **Listening.** Great!" He might say, "Let's all say that together again, ***listening***. Fine."

"And listening requires that you first shut up. Let's all say shut up. SHUT UP! Terrific! And I promise you I won't take that personally."

An audience has to stay on its toes and listen to what's going on to participate in this manner and the repetition of key words helps to reinforce the major points you're making.

Finally, you can always rely on the great truth that money talks. People love to win money and giving money for great ideas just might fit in with your plan for an exciting meeting.

If you can work it into your budget, give prizes for the safety ideas that participants bring to your meeting.

I once saw a subdued audience catch on fire with enthusiasm at a suggestion session as the host gave away one and five dollar prizes for creative ideas from participants.

Set a time limit on such a session, perhaps 4 or 5 minutes. Pay off only for ideas that make good sense. You might have an Also Ran prize to add a little humor to the occasion. The key to such a session is to make it fast and loaded with high energy.

Any form of participation generally takes a little selling. People are genuinely shy or hesitant to stick their necks out.

Expect the very best with your group and hang in there past their initial resistance to cooperate. Ask them three and four and five times to join in and make it a rewarding meeting.

Once you break the ice, once you get past that initial resistance, you'll find it easier and easier to get people involved.

BRAINSTORMING

Brainstorming is the technique of thinking without judging, thinking with your brakes off.

First you must identify the exact problem you want to brainstorm. Pin that problem down exactly. Write it down in one sentence and limit your brainstorming session to one challenge.

The more ideas your team comes up with, the better chance you have of finding the right solution.

Brainstorming is a technique where a number of people hold a meeting with a single purpose in mind--to think up, together, as many ideas as possible in order to solve one, well-defined problem.

Between 5 and 10 participants seem to be the best size for such a gathering.

It's a good idea to let each participant know in advance of the session the problem to be worked on.

When the group meets, make sure each has a pen and

pad to capture ideas that might get away before they have a chance to share them with the group.

Have someone present to take notes to record every idea produced. Then later, have the notes transcribed and sent to all participants so they might further improve and combine such ideas.

Always have a leader but keep the sessions as informal as possible.

Encourage everyone to speak out.

Before starting, it's helpful to run through the four rules for brainstorming:

1. Only positive thinking allowed! The wilder the ideas, the better.

2. Suspend judgement. Judgement can come later.

3. You want the largest possible number of ideas.

4. Combination and improvement of ideas is what you're after. Hitchhiking on others' ideas is encouraged.

Let the storming begin. Attack the problem from all sides without let up.

You'll find the ideas start flowing like a chain reaction, something like a string of firecrackers. Often a group of 10 brainstormers will come up with 100 ideas in a half hour, so expect results.

The friendly rivalry and personal interaction produces results but perhaps even more important, the teamwork such sessions create often helps later when you go to implement these ideas.

Chapter 8

SEVERAL YEARS AGO, I HAD THE HONOR of attending a seminar for professional speakers conducted by Cavett Robert, one of America's finest professional speakers. There were twenty attendees and each of us had paid slightly more than $500 for this day-and-a-half program.

This was back in the days when video taping was just becoming popular as a training tool. One of the major features of the seminar was the fact that each attendee would be video taped doing their best ten minutes of speech material.

Nearly every attendee was (or else aspired to become) a full-time professional speaker, and we were most eager to see and hear ourselves on videotape; but more than this even was our desire to have a personal critique on our performance by Cavett Robert himself.

The first morning was mostly filled with a lecture by Cavett Robert and then we spent nearly the entire afternoon making the videotapes.

That night, most of us didn't sleep very soundly because we were excited about the videotaping and eager to hear the personal words of wisdom from Cavett Robert.

The next morning, bright and early, they wheeled the TV and videotape recorder into our meeting room.

Cavett smiled and turned on the switch. Immediately, a picture of one of the speakers appeared on the screen.

Cavett reached over and turned up the sound and there was silence in the room. A couple of the other speakers turned up the sound on the TV and still nothing happened. Next, they checked the connections and finally they called in a serviceman from the company that had rented the videotaping equipment to Cavett.

After a half hour delay, the technician announced, "There's no sound. Somehow you recorded this whole tape without sound."

We all groaned out loud.

Cavett Robert sort of tugged at his French cuffs, smiled, and said excitedly, "Good, Good, Good!"

The only thing I could think right then was, "Bad, Bad, Bad!"

Twenty attendees at more than five hundred dollars each--over ten thousand dollars in fees! If those other speakers felt like I felt right then, we would all be asking for our money back. There just wasn't time to do the videotaping over and there stood Cavett Robert saying, "Good, Good, Good." Now, I'd seen Cavett Robert in all sorts of challenging situations that professional speakers seem to get into and in other disasters I had heard Cavett say, "Good, Good, Good." I never understood it before but this time I was to learn just what the expression really meant.

Slowly Cavett looked at the silent video picture and then he looked at us and he asked, "How many of you already have audio tapes of yourselves giving speeches?" What a question! I have hundreds of audio tapes of my speeches. I tape nearly every speech I give and the same was true of every other speaker in that room. We all raised our hands.

Cavett smiled once again and repeated, "Good, Good, Good." This time he laughed, "Then you wouldn't get very much out of hearing yourself on tape." He nodded at us and continued, "We have discovered that, in communications, the words we say have very little to do with what people hear. My partner, Merlyn Cundiff is an expert on body language, and together, we are going to critique you on what people see when you speak."

That seminar was really a turning point for every speaker in that room. Each of us learned that we must really feel what we say in our hearts or else it will not really get through to an audience.

"Good, Good, Good." That is the attitude that Cavett Robert brings to every situation he faces and every person he meets. He looks for the good in everyone and every situation.

I went home from that seminar with an even greater respect for Cavett Robert and his "Good, Good, Good" philosophy.

Recently, I've discovered that I'm not alone in my addiction for used books. I often haunt Salvation Army and Goodwill retail stores and I can seldom resist a garage sale when there's a hint that used books will be for sale. Of course, I don't read all the books I buy. One of my hobbies is the matching up of friends with old books I've found that I believe will interest them.

Just a day before my trip to Chicago to attend that speaker's seminar, I had purchased a tall stack of used books and I had put them on an antique vanity chest in our front entryway. The first book I picked up on my return home was a book by Dr. Norman Vincent Peale. I cannot recall the title but the subject was "Blessings." The book suggested that no matter how distasteful people might be to us, we should develop the habit of blessing them. Actually, chapter after chapter was dedicated to the concept that we should bless everything: people, things, events, you name it and then bless it.

For instance, think of the most disgusting person you've ever met. You know the type, the kind of person who brightens up the whole room just by leaving. Well, according to this book, we should look at this type of person and say to ourselves, "I bless you for the goodness that's in you." I've tried this again and again. Sometimes, I secretly add, "You sure are keeping it covered up, but still, I bless you for the goodness that's in you."

I was amazed. This was the same philosophy I learned from Cavett Robert. "Good, Good, Good."

Once I tuned in to this concept, I began to see that it was nothing really new. In fact, there's an old fable about the Three Princes of Serendipity. The princes gained wide

fame in Horace Walpole's book written in 1754, because of their rare ability to see good in everything, every event, and every person they met. From this fable comes the word, "serendipity," which means the ability to see good in everything.

My friend, Joe Batten, has a wonderful film titled, *Keep Reaching--The Power of High Expectations.* While the film deals with the ten keys to motivation, its prevailing message is that we get just about what we expect from people and from life. If we expect the best, we generally get it.

There is a law of balance in this universe that says for every negative happening there's an equal force for a positive result. Quite often, if we simply meet a setback with a positive outlook, we will see the seed for a triumph.

Take, for instance, the worker who pressed wallboard with far too much pressure in the factory where he worked one day. The attitude of serendipity ruled that day and instead of a useless scrap, a wonderful new product was discovered called "masonite." Instead of screaming, "You idiot, you messed up that wallboard," somebody looked at the result with a positive outlook.

There is a story about a worker who went out to lunch and left a vat of soap boiling. When he returned, he discovered the overcooked soap was floating on top of the boiling water. He is reported to have said, "That stuff is 99 and 44/100 percent pure." Thus, *Ivory* soap was first produced.

What happened when an apple fell on the head of Sir Isaac Newton? Did he double up his fist and yell out, "You rotten apple!" Of course not. Instead he smiled the smile of discovery and called out excitedly, "Gravity!"

Just where was Christopher Columbus headed? He was going to India, but did he curse and stomp his feet when he didn't find India? No--he was content and happy when he discovered America.

Coca Cola was originally made with tap water.

A fountain clerk in a local drug store made the mistake one day of pouring soda water onto the coca cola syrup and the customer liked it even better.

Corn Flakes were a mistake. Hand tissues were the result of a faulty batch of toilet paper.

In fact, if many of you who read this book will check with your parents, I'm certain at least a few of you will discover you're not the direct result of planned parenthood.   What happened? Well, I guess your folks, like mine, just shrugged their shoulders and said, "Well, we've got this kid; we just might as well make the best of it."

Fred Smith, the dynamic founder of Federal Express, while a student at Yale University, presented his concept for an overnight freight service. His teacher gave him a "C" grade for the paper and told him it would never work.

Now, over 300,000 pieces of freight flow in and out of Memphis every night with revenues of over $4 million each night. "Good, Good, Good." Fred Smith had an attitude of serendipity.

"Good, Good, Good." Do you get the idea now? Life is what we make of it.

Some people look at a glass of water and tell you it's half gone. Others see it as half full.

I know people who consider each and every setback in their life as a stepping stone to even greater achievement.

Why not start today to make "Good, Good, Good" the password in your life? Make it the guiding principle in your outlook toward the people you work with. Catch them working safely.

Look for the good in everything they do. Encourage others to keep on trying just a little harder. Remember to remind them there is truly greatness in them, that they have special talents, and that you know they will do great things in their lifetime. Tell them again and again. Implant this one message deeply in their subconscious minds so that in times of doubt or temptation, they will realize they are unique and special and valuable.

There is greatness in you. Remember that fact yourselves--there is truly greatness in you too.

Chapter 9

WHAT IF YOU COULD HOLD ONE safety meeting and save a child's life? What if there was something you might say to a group of children that would help them say no to drugs and to a lot of harmful things in their lifetime?

What if, like me, you'd had the opportunity to make a presentation to a group of over 40 young girls, ages 14 and 15? The girls all had one thing in common. They were all pregnant. Oh yes, another thing they all had in common. Their boyfriends were no longer their boyfriends. What if you could have made a presentation that might have helped these girls avoid the situation they were in?

What if? What if? That's a question that's been burning in my mind for a dozen years. I asked that question as I spoke at a success rally in Kalamazoo many years ago. We had 7,500 people crammed into Wings Stadium that day and the program read like a *Who's Who* in motivation.

Dr. Wayne W. Dyer, noted psychologist and author of *Your Erroneous Zones*; Dr. Robert Schuller, world famous "Possibility Thinker" and pastor of the celebrated Crystal Cathedral; Earl Nightingale, Dean of Personal Motivation;   Joe Girard, the world's greatest salesman; Marilyn Vanderbur, top female speaker and former Miss America; and Denis Waitley, noted author of *The Psychology of Winning.*

I was a bit intimidated both by the size of the audience and the fame of the other speakers. In fact, I kept doing research all day trying to get a handle on why these people were there that day. I asked most of the other speakers that question and came up with a variety of reasons but most agreed that people who attend success rallies are looking for a boost in their lives. They are seeking answers, inspiration and hope. Many are recovering alcoholics, people who have had drug problems, men and women who have just survived horrible divorces, people with financial troubles, some who have just gone through bankruptcy.

In other words, just ordinary people like you and me.

It was a fantastic day in my life with a wonderful audience response to my message. A standing ovation. It was so exciting and that night as I drove home on Interstate Highway 94 it suddenly dawned on me that most of what was being done in the field of positive motivation was in the way of rehabilitation.

Most people had to fail in their lives before they became really interested in success and in winning. The burning question came to my mind, "Why can't we teach our young children the keys to success? Why can't we build high self esteem and a sense of true values so they might avoid all of the pain and unhappiness that most of us have experienced?

That night I dedicated my life to bringing positive living concepts to children. My first effort was a book titled *The Three Robots*.

In the book, Pos is the happy, successful girl robot. Semi-Pos hopes to be happy some day, not now, but tomorrow. And Neg is the negative robot.

One day our Three Robots are playing in the park and Pos says to Semi-Pos, "What is that clasp on the back of your head?"

"I can't see the back of my head," Semi-Pos explains.

"Let me turn the clasp." Pos asks.

"It will hurt." Semi-Pos objects.

"If it hurts, I'll stop." Pos promised, as she turns the clasp.

A panel flops down and there is a TV screen on the back of   Semi-Pos' head. Words like "Not now! Tomorrow! Forget it,   Charlie! Someday!" flow past on the screen.

They look at Neg's screen and it's filled with negative messages like, "Don't, can't, shouldn't, frown, lose."

On Pos' screen they found words like, "Win, smile, happy."

Semi-Pos and Neg turned the dials on their fronts to try to change the words on their screens, but the words wouldn't erase. Some people try drugs, alcohol, a lot of dumb things to erase the things on their screens too but you cannot erase those words. But the Three Robots learn that we can overwhelm the negative thoughts in our minds by the process of using positive affirmations. Our robots would meet in the park every day for a Positive Affirmation Meeting and they'd sing this song:

> *I'm happy, I'm Healthy, I'm Somebody*
> *Not a sad nobody, I'm Somebody*
> *And I wear a smile*
> *just to let the whole world know,*
> *That this Somebody's happy inside.*

Over the years, we've created a total of 8 children's books.

Perhaps, like me, you have become concerned with the epidemic of drug abuse in America. Millions and millions of dollars have been spent and yet the problem seems to be getting worse each year. My special concern is with our children.

I watched as the *Just Say No* program swept America. It seemed all wrong to me because of its negative approach.

Certainly children must be taught to say "no" to drugs, but I didn't feel that was nearly enough.

We must teach our children some positive values upon which to build a happy successful life and somehow, we were no longer doing this in many of our schools.

Our Three Robots went to work on the problem and Pos, our happy, successful robot, came up with a program that seems to be working in a number of homes and schools today. She suggests that our children be taught to say Yes and her plan is contained in her *Just Say Yes*

© Art Fettig 1987

Just Say, "Yes"
To believing you're special.
Just Say, "Yes"
To being kind.
Just Say, "Yes"
To caring for others.
Just Say, "Yes"
To improving your mind.
Just Say, "Yes"
To trying harder.
Just Say, "Yes"
To banging in.

Just Say, "Yes"
To growing daily.
Just Say, "Yes"
To learning to win.
Just Say, "Hey there—
I'm somebody
And you are, too.
Let's do our best."
Stand up! Listen,
To what is right
Respect youself
And just say, "Yes!"

verse as follows:

This verse, a *Just Say No* verse by Neg and a *Somebody* verse by Semi-Pos are contained in the book *The Three Robots Learn About Drugs*.

If you'll examine the *Just Say Yes* verse, you'll note each line contains a value that'll help our children grow into strong, positive thinking citizens. We prepared a *new Just Say Yes* activity book that helps teachers and parents conduct an ongoing program to teach these values.

To give substance to the program, we produced "I'm A Pos" stickers and pins and activity sheets. The program really teaches each value to children. For instance, begin with the first three lines of the verse, "Just say yes to believing you're special." An entire week can be spent exploring the ways each of us is special.

"Just say yes to being kind." One class started a kindness crusade in their school.

I wish I had more space in this book to elaborate on this concept but if you want further information, just call or write me.

I often go into schools and do assembly programs for students and then follow up with classroom visits. Then, I conduct in-service programs for teachers and exciting parent programs in the evening.

And back to the "what if" that started this chapter. I truly believe that if we can reach our children in the early grades with a firm set of positive values, if we can raise their self-esteem and help them believe they're worthwhile and wonderful, then we can stop this horrible cancer of drug abuse that's threatening the very future of our great country.

Won't you join me in conducting the most important safety meeting you might ever conduct in your lifetime?

Reach out to the school in your community. Help me teach our children to Just Say Yes to a positive, healthy, drug-free future.

Call me or write me, Art Fettig, at Growth Unlimited Inc.,
31 East Ave. S., Battle Creek, Michigan 49017
Phone: 1-800-441-7676 or (616) 965-2229
On the Web: www.IMASource.com
e-mail: artfettig@voyager.net

Together we can change the world.

Chapter 10

I WANT TO ASK YOU A QUESTION. HAVE you ever been to an Amway meeting? Be honest, nearly everybody has. Sure... and no doubt you can remember the wild enthusiasm shown at that meeting.

Well, this isn't an Amway meeting but I want you to simulate that same kind of excitement, if you will. I want you to really join in with me on this.

Before we go on with this, let me do a little more research. Have you ever taken arithmetic? Certainly you have. Great!

Right now, I want you to combine your enthusiasm and your mathematical expertise for a little experiment in simple addition. Let's go. I will give you the problem and you just say the number out loud with as much gusto as you can produce. Ready? Great!

Just call out the answer... Take one thousand and add forty. What's your answer?

ONE THOUSAND FORTY!

Right. Now we add a thousand. What did you get?
TWO THOUSAND FORTY.
Fantastic! Now add thirty. What did you get?
TWO THOUSAND SEVENTY.
Unbelievable... Let's add a thousand.
THREE THOUSAND SEVENTY!
Great! Now add twenty. The answer?
THREE THOUSAND NINETY!
Wonderful. Now add a thousand. The answer?
FOUR THOUSAND NINETY!
Now add ten. What do you get?
FIVE THOUSAND!
How much?
FIVE THOUSAND?
One more time.
FIVE THOUSAND?
Wrong! The answer is forty-one hundred. We had four thousand ninety and we added ten. That is forty-one hundred.

Let's look at it:

1,000		+	40	=	1,040
1,040 +	1,000	=	2,040		
2,040 +	30	=	2,070		
2,070 +	1,000	=	3,070		
3,070 +	20	=	3,090		
3,090 +	1,000	=	4,090		
4,090 +	10	=	4,100		

Forty-one hundred is the correct answer. Now let me show you how modern education works.

We have been running our system on something called

"majority rule." The majority of people give the answer as five thousand. Now here's what we do. We change the questions so the answer will be right. After all, if everybody fails, then the teacher is stupid. I asked you the wrong questions. What I should have asked was this: "What is one thousand plus four hundred, not forty?" Plus a thousand and three hundred? Plus a thousand a two hundred? Plus a thousand a one hundred? Then the answer would be five thousand. Everyone passes and everybody is happy. Then we go marching out of the classroom into this bright, big beautiful world. Everything is fine. Everybody is O.K.

That's what we've been doing in too many classrooms in America recently. That's why Johnny can't read and Mary can't spell, and why we're in big trouble in our educational system today.

The same applies to safety. Some people think we bend the rules and we discover when we do we come up with the wrong results. When we ignore safety rules people get hurt.   So let's play it straight.   Let's add up a string of accident-free days that we can all be proud of.

Chapter 11

IF YOU HAVE THE LUXURY OF BEING introduced at a meeting, have the introducer do the best job possible of stating your special qualifications to conduct the meeting. Let the other person build you up and then you pop the balloon with your opening lines. Someone said that people don't laugh because they're happy. People are happy because they laugh. Laughter is cathartic. It relieves tension, stress, anxiety. It helps people relax so they might be more open to your message. Open your meeting with a bit of laughter and I guarantee you'll have a better meeting.

* *Has anyone else here got a nervous stomach?*

* *For all my accomplishments, I'm sure you were expecting a much younger person.*

* *They say that if you're nervous before you speak, then you will be good. I should be positively great!*

* I'm glad to be here this evening looking into your faces... (Pause and look at the group) ...and golly knows there are some faces here that need looking into.

* The one nice thing about being a really poor speaker is that you never have to worry about having an off night.

* Someone once introduced me as an "Expert". You know "x" stands for an unknown quantity and "spurt" is a drip under pressure. I guess, come to think of it, I am an expert!

* This is one of the high points in my life, so you can just imagine what it's been like up to now.

* Originally we had a different speaker scheduled, but three days ago (he or she) was called to the great eternal resting place. (He or She) went to work for the federal government.

* If you help a person who's in trouble, he or she will never forget you -- especially the next time they're in trouble. Now you know why I'm here tonight.

* I never realized how little I had on my mind until I stood up here just now.

* When I came in here this evening I said to my wife, "Did you see that pretty woman smile at me?" She said, "That's nothing, the first time I saw you I laughed right out loud." I want you folks to feel free to laugh right out loud here this evening.

* Our city band had finished a vigorous and not overly harmonious selection, and as the perspiring musicians sank to their seats after acknowledging the applause, the trombonist asked, "What's the next number?" The leader replied, "The Stars and Stripes Forever." "Oh no," gasped the trombonist, "I just played that." I hope I don't

have the wrong number set out in my speech here this evening.

* *They said that they wanted someone who was responsible to take the speaking assignment here this evening and I felt well qualified. Everywhere I ever worked, when anything went wrong, I was always responsible.*

* *The hardest thing about prize fighting is picking up your teeth with your boxing gloves on. The worst thing about an after-dinner speech is that it comes after dinner.*

* *In Indianapolis the other night the M.C. said, "Many of you don't know this, but our speaker used to write advertising. In fact, she wrote that famous slogan, 'Good to the last drop.' Unfortunately, she was working for Otis Elevator at the time.*

* *Einstein explained his theory this way. "Sit with a pretty woman for an hour and it seems like a minute; sit on a hot stove for a minute and it seems like an hour -- that's relativity!" I'm going to speak only a few minutes, and I certainly hope it doesn't seem like a few hours.*

* *Everyone has some useful purpose in life, even if it's only to serve as a horrible example.*

* *The only time a fisherman tells the truth is when he calls another fisherman a liar. I've got no more fish stories to tell, and so I'm going to stick pretty close to the truth.*

* *Thoreau once said, "If I know that a man is coming to my house with the conscious design of doing me good, I should run for my life." I don't want any running. I promise that I won't do you a bit of good here this evening.*

* *Some speakers who don't know what to do with their hands would do well to try clamping them over their mouths.*

* *Sitting and listening to a speaker is a little like sitting on jury duty. The only frustrating part is that you aren't*

afforded the opportunity to seal the fate of the speaker.

** Standing here I feel a little like a mosquito who just landed in a nudist colony. I hardly know where to begin.*

** It's unfortunate that a mere ninety-nine percent of the speakers in this country give the other one percent a bad name.*

** Mark Twain said, "It isn't so astonishing, the number of things I can remember, and the number of things I can remember that aren't so." Our memories are similar and mine might be showing this evening.*

** Fred Allen once remarked, "I have trouble remember-ing three things: Faces, names and... (Pause) I can't remember what the third thing is."*

Chapter 12

IF YOU'RE LIKE ME, YOU CAN BUY A NEW joke book and read through the whole thing without finding a single joke that looks good to you.

Most of the jokes I use and like, I hear from someone else and when they get a great laugh, then I feel the joke just might be right for me.

Over the years, you get a group of favorites that work for you. I've included just a few of my favorites here. My book *How To Hold An Audience In The Hollow Of Your Hand* has nearly 700 jokes and the following are just a sampling of them. Cassette tapes of my live performances are loaded with jokes that work.

Remember, don't expect to tell a joke if you haven't

practiced it a number of times. And the best way to practice is on your friends.

Most professional speakers will try a joke out a dozen times before they will try it on a real audience. I hope you find a few here that are to your liking and that you can use at your meetings.

Accidents

* Traffic cop: "Sir, your wife fell out of your car about two blocks back."
Husband: "Great!" I thought I'd gone stone deaf!"
* The reason there were fewer accidents in the horse and buggy days is that drivers didn't have to rely on their own intelligence.
* Out on a lonely highway one night, a speeding car crashed through a guard rail, leapt over a retaining wall, rolled down an embankment, and came to rest on its back in a creek. A state policeman, arriving on the scene almost immediately, said to the driver, "What's the matter -- are you drunk or something?"
"Of course I'm drunk," said the driver. "What do you think I am -- a stunt driver?"
* Driver showing well-dented car to garage man: "The fender's been acting up again."
* A man was applying for a job as a switchman for the railroad.
"Tell me," said the yardmaster, "what would you do if you saw two trains coming at each other on the same track?"
"I'd switch one of them right off and onto another track."
"And what if the lever was stuck?"

"I'd run right out with a red flag and wave one of them down."
"And what if the engineer didn't see you?"
"I'd call my mother."
"Call your mother! What could she do?"
"Nothing, but she loves to see train wrecks."
 *   The top salesman was given a rare old bottle of Kentucky sippin' whiskey as a gift at the office Christmas party. On his way home, he tripped over a sled that had been left on the sidewalk. He tumbled tail over teakettle, smacked against a patch of ice, and ended up sprawled against a tree. Suddenly he felt something warm trickling down his leg.
"Oh!" he moaned, "I hope that's blood."
 *   It had been a long, drawn out lawsuit in a small country courthouse on the hottest day of the year and finally the railroad's defense lawyer called upon the train's engineer to explain what happened and to do it as briefly as possible. "Well, first I saw the cow come out of the grass," he said, "and then I saw the grass come out of the cow."
 * A farmer was suing the railroad for a crossing accident where his horse had been killed and he had been severely injured. The defense lawyer said to the farmer, "Isn't it true, that immediately following the accident the conductor of the train asked you directly if you were injured and you said, "No?" The farmer admitted it was true but there were unusual circumstances. The defense lawyer forged on. "And will you tell this jury what circumstances could lead you to lie to this conductor?"
"Well, you see, first the conductor went up to my horse and he saw that his leg was broken and he shot him. He

hand and he says to me, "What about you? Are you hurt?" And I told him no. What would you do, your honor?"

* Is it true that more people are caused by accidents than accidents are caused by people?

* Irate driver: "Why didn't you look out for me? You are the third person I've hit today!"

Airlines

* I don't know how you feel about flying, but with me, "Up, Up and Away" refers to my lunch.

* What a cheerful place an airport is! You pull into the airport and there's a big sign that says "TERMINAL". First thing you see inside the airport is a bunch of people selling life insurance. Then some clown comes on over the loud speaker and says, "Flight 291 is now ready for its final departure."

* Last night the flight attendant brought me my dinner and I said, "You've got your thumb in my steak." And (he or she) said, "Oh, I didn't want to drop it on the floor -- again."

* Someone called the airline in Kalamazoo and asked, "How long does it take to fly to New York?" The clerk said, "Just a moment." And the caller said, "Thank you," and hung up.

* Just think, it took Lindbergh thirty-three and one-half hours to fly the Atlantic and he was the last person to have his baggage arrive at the same time he did.

* I flew here on a 747. That's a big airplane! They have 400 passengers and three restrooms. That's what you call a holding pattern!

Children

* I want to tell you about my neighbor's son, Roger. That kid is for sale.

* In the game of school, Roger does not play with a full deck. He came home from school the other day and said, "Here's my report card, Dad. And I'm sick of watching television anyway." The next time he comes up and says, "Here's my report card, Dad, and one of yours I found in the attic."

* Roger is a light eater. It gets light and he starts eating.

* He brought home a note from school. He flunked recess.

* The other night, I told Roger to turn on the radio. He walked over, hugged the thing and said, "I love you, radio."

* I think someday Roger will be an astronaut. Right now, he's home taking up space.

* Last night his dad argued two hours with Roger about running away from home. He just won't go!

Definitions

* Arthritis -- twinges in the hinges.

* Necessary Evil: One we like so much we refuse to do away with it.

* Reckless driver -- someone who passes you when you're speeding.

* Amateur athlete: An athlete who's paid in cash, not by check.

* Sports mechanic -- a guy who fixes races, football games and fights.

* Slob -- he orders three eggs for breakfast, two to eat and one for his shirt.

Golf

* I don't want to complain about my partner today, but let's just say that with (him or her) around, the birdie and the eagle will never become an endangered species.

* (He or she) asked me, "Do you think I can hit the green with a six-iron?" I said, "Sure, if you hit it often enough."

* (He or she) lost fourteen balls today -- eight of them in the ball washer.

* I won't play ball with Max. The other day he hit a hole in one and wrote down a zero.

* I guess playing golf is a lot like raising kids. You keep thinking you'll do better the next time.

* When I'm playing golf, I always address the ball twice -- before and after each swing.

* My friend is trying to play like Lee Trevino. He keeps playing in rainstorms, hoping lightning will strike.

* Charlie there had a miserable day and on the eighteenth hole he took out some of his frustration on his caddy. He looked at his caddy and he said, "You know, you must be the worst caddy in the whole world." And the caddy just shook his head and said, "Oh no, Sir, that would be too much of a coincidence."

* (His or her) doctor told (him or her) to quit playing golf. The way (he or she) looks (he or she) shouldn't chance getting so close to a hole in the ground.

* I shoot golf in the low 70's. When it gets any colder I quit.

Hotels

* Isn't this a great hotel? Suave. It's so suave I called room service and ordered a deck of cards and the bellhop brought them to me one at a time. Good thing I'm a great tipper.

* Room service has an unlisted number.

* This place has grown famous as a last resort.

* They didn't have twin beds but they offered me the next best thing. A double bed with a white line down the middle.

* My room has indirect lighting -- across the street there's this big neon sign.

* They said my room was air conditioned and they were right. I never smelled air in such condition in my life.

* That hotel had these fantastic huge bath towels. Five feet long. That wide. That thick. Why, I had everything I could do to get my suitcase closed.

Overheard Conversation

* One nice thing about having an unlisted telephone number -- when you get an obscene telephone call, at least you know it's from a friend.

* I asked them how they felt about ignorance and apathy and they said, "We don't know and we don't care."

* Harry has a new solution for his baldness. He soaks his head in Preparation H. It doesn't grow hair but it shrinks his head to fit the hair he's got.

* Do you know who the biggest liars in the world are? The second biggest liar is the person from a government

agency who walks into the manager's office and says, "I've come to help you." And the biggest liar in the world is the manager who smiles and says, "I'm glad to see you."

* I've got a sign in my car that says, "I'm a Catholic. In case of an accident, call a priest." And our priest has a sign in his car that says, "I'm a Catholic priest. In case of an accident, call an ambulance."

* This surgeon was scrubbing up after an operation and somebody asked her, "How did the appendectomy go, doctor?" And the doctor says, "Appendectomy? I thought it was an autopsy."

* I just love to get away from it all, but every time I try, I run into a gang of people who are trying to get it all away from me.

* "Senator, what are your views on pornography?" "Twenty-twenty"

* "Senator, what do you think we should do about the abortion bill?" "I think we ought to pay for it."

* "How do you feel about the Nicaraguan position?" "Frankly, I've never tried it."

* This fellow says, "I got me a new job and it's really easy. They gave me this thing called a hod. All I do is fill it with bricks and carry it up the ladder sixteen flights. There's a guy up there who does all the work."

Put Downs

* He just sort of brightens up a room by leaving it.
* Her get up and go just seems to have got up and went.

* He keeps waiting for his ship to come in and he forgets that he never sent one out.

* I'd say she has a mental B.O.

* If he heard opportunity knock, he'd complain about the noise.

* She's like a blister. She never shows up until the work is done.

* When he was four, his mother tried to give him away as a bridge prize.

* They used to wrap her lunch in road maps.

* His father kept looking for a loophole in his birth certificate.

* Her parents used to play blackjack with her and they used real blackjacks.

* He thinks that automobiles and airplanes are just a plot to drive down the cost of horses.

* If he's a self-made man, then I wish he'd get on with the job.

* She went to the psychiatrist and she said to him, "Doctor, nobody listens to me." And the psychiatrist said, "Next."

* Her varicose veins are the only thing that keeps her from being completely colorless.

* He is absolutely underwhelming.

* She figures that bad breath is better than none at all.

* This guy smells flowers and he starts looking for a funeral.

* You tell her that life begins at forty and she'll say, "So does rheumatism."

* Somebody told him he should be a doctor, just so he would put a mask over his face.

* She's the only woman I know suffering from terminal

dandruff.

* And Charlie, don't worry about having kleptomania. You can always take something for it!

* He's the kind of guy that would vote a town dry and then move.

Restaurants

* Fellow went into this restaurant and there was a big sign that said, "Giant Lobster Tails - 50c". He gave this waiter half a dollar and he smiled and said, "Once upon a time, there was this Giant lobster..."

* What a restaurant. I called the waitress over and asked her, "What's this fly doing in my ice cream?" And she says, "How should I know? Maybe he likes winter sports."

* I called the waitress over and I said, "This meat tastes funny." She says, "So go ahead and laugh."

* That restaurant we visited last night had only one restroom so they pinned a sign to the door that said, "Please knock. This is an equal opportunity restroom."

* And did you hear about that rotten band in that restaurant? During their intermission, one of the waiters dropped a tray full of dishes and six couples got up and started dancing.

* Talk about impatience. A guy runs into a restaurant and yells, "Hey, waiter! Hey, waiter!" And the waiter finally says, "O.K., but we'll have to send out for it."

* Finally the guy orders a corned beef sandwich and he says to the waiter, "And make it lean." And the waiter looks at him and asks, "Which way?"

Safety

* While driving at night, when approaching an oncoming auto, dim your headlights... if you don't have any headlights, turn up your radio real loud.

* And now for our safety tip of the week: While out driving, beware of reckless, irresponsible, road hog speeders -- especially if it's you!

* Nothing brings the traffic regulations to mind quite like spotting a police car in the rear view mirror.

* A safety belt is the best way to keep from leaving the scene of an accident.

* One car hit the other on the highway and the one driver yells to the other, "What's the matter with you? Are you blind?" "Blind?", yells the other driver. "Whatta' ya mean? I hit you, didn't I?"

* In Chicago they have just two seasons -- winter and construction.

* Traffic was so thick on the expressway this morning that I drove 10 miles in neutral.

* Sign on the rear of a tractor-trailer: "This vehicle has had six accidents and it hasn't lost one yet."

* Poor Charlie was run over by a steam roller. He's in the hospital now in rooms 17 to 22.

* This tourist nearly falls off a cliff, so he says to a native of the area, "That is a very dangerous cliff. Why don't you put up a danger sign?" "We had one," the native responds, "But nobody ever fell over so we took it down."

Skiing

* We've been skiing for hours on end. Maybe it's time we took lessons.

* By the time I learned to stand up, I couldn't sit down.

* I never tried skiing. I figured I'm already going downhill fast enough.

Some People

* Some people get credit for having a nice personality when they're just proud of their teeth.

* Some people are funny. They spend money they don't have on things they don't want to impress people they don't like.

* Some people want the front of the bus, the back of the church and the middle of the road.

* Some people are like tea bags. They don't know their own strength until they get in hot water.

* Some people are wise and some are otherwise.

* Some people aren't as anxious to get where they're going as they are to get away from where they've been.

* Some people can't tell a lie and others can't tell the truth. And others can't tell the difference.

* Some people who lose weight always seem to find it.

* Some people get lost in thought because it's unfamiliar territory to them.

* Some people itch for success when they should be scratching for it.

* Some people know a lot more when you tell them something than when they ask you something.

* Some people never get interested in anything unless it's none of their business.

* Some people spend half of their life telling what they're going to do and the other half explaining why they didn't do it.

* Some people think they're busy when they're only confused.

* Some people who jump at conclusions often lose sight of the hurdle.

* Some people will believe anything if they overhear it.

Taxis

* We took a taxi from the airport. What a ride! That driver will probably expire before his license does.

* I told him, "Driver, you're too drunk to drive." He said, "I sure can't walk."

Spouses

* "We still hold hands. If we didn't, we'd kill each other."

* My wife has a sobering effect on me. She hides the bottles.

* Our marriage wasn't a gamble. In gambling, you have a chance.

* I heard this one lady yelling at her husband out in the hall. Somehow he had had a few too many and she was

yelling, "Stop telling me that I remind you of your first wife. I AM your first wife!"

*   I'll never forget the night I proposed. The moon was full and I was a little loaded myself.

*   What is the worst thing a woman can get on her 25th wedding anniversary? Morning sickness.

*   She says, "Whatta' ya mean you have nothing to live for? What about the house mortgage, the credit union, what about the savings and loan?"

*   I didn't know what real happiness was until I got married. And then it was too late.

*   I married her for her looks. But not the kind she's been giving me lately.

*   Do you know what I did before I got married? Anything I wanted to...

*   Comedian Foster Brooks tells his audience, "Many of you don't realize it, but my current wife is my third wife. My first two wives died a violent death. The first one died from eating poison mushrooms. The second one died of a fractured skull. She just wouldn't eat her mushrooms."

*   "For over twenty-five years, my wife and I were fantastically happy."
"What happened?"
"We met."

*   This newlywed fellow arrives home from work and his bride is crying. "We've had a horrible accident," she says. "I baked a pie for dinner and the dog ate it." "Don't you cry, honey," he says. "I'll buy you a new dog."

Tennis

* This place is so tough, even the tennis court has a dog leg.

* Somebody explained it to me yesterday on the court; the three most important things to develop in your tennis game are a strong serve, a good backhand and a convincing limp to explain why you lost the game.

* Life is a lot like tennis. The one who can serve the best seldom loses.

* This morning Charlie drove the ball two hundred yards right down the line. Unfortunately, he was playing tennis at the time.

Weather

* It was so cold, I went to take the garbage out and it wouldn't go.

* When I opened my bedroom door, the light went on.

* Just yesterday a snow plow operator was knocked senseless by a piece of flying ice. He spit into the wind.

Hospitality Suites

* What a party last night! I'm afraid a few of you overdid it. At 2 AM I saw two of you draped over each other in our hallway and the one fellow said to the other, "Say, when you drink, does your tongue burn?" And the other one says, "Gee, I don't know. I never got drunk enough to light it."

* I overheard one of you say to the bartender, "Give me another Grasshopper, and this time put a little hop into it."

*   This one lady was drinking Sloe Gin and it really speeded her up.

*   Somebody was drinking a Colonel Sanders Cocktail -- two of them and you start using foul language.

*   Some guy was going around for the city taking a poll last night and he discovered that boxcar loadings are down twenty-three percent and alcohol consumption is up thirty-two percent, which means that more people are getting loaded than boxcars.

*   We were supposed to have an elaborate Hospitality Suite but the boss had to cut the budget. Instead, (he or she) threw a big free beer party and bolted the bathroom door.

Doctors

*   He was the most honest doctor I ever met. When he signed the death certificate, where it said, "Cause of death?" He signed his name.

*   Doc didn't believe in unnecessary surgery. If he didn't need the money, he didn't operate.

*   A guy goes in to see this doctor and he asks, "How do I stand, doctor?" And the doctor says, "That's what I can't understand. Why, if you were a building, you'd be condemned."

*   The doctor says to the patient, "Go over to the window there and stick out your tongue." The patient asks, "Doc, what good will that do?" And the Doc says, "I just don't like that guy across the way."

*   The Doc says to the patient, "Cough. Now cough again. Now cough again. How long have you had that

cough?"
 * The Doc says to the patient, "I've got good news and bad news: The bad news is, I took out the wrong kidney. The good news is that it wasn't malignant."

Chapter 13

SEVERAL TIMES OVER THE PAST YEARS, I've arrived at conventions on the last day as the closing speaker and the meeting planner met me at the door with a deeply troubled look. "This whole convention has been a disaster," they reported. "The food was bad. The accommodations were horrible. The other programs have all failed in one way or another. We're counting on you, Art, to work a miracle and to salvage this whole thing."

That is quite a load to carry, but somehow I've been lucky, and often they wrote me later to say that I had come through and that they had received a number of favorable comments on the entire convention.

Probably, in truth, things had not been nearly as bad as they had viewed them; but still, a great close can salvage a number of things, including your safety meeting. Sometimes it's a single verse that will stick in an attendee's mind and make a difference. Perhaps it's a quote that someone repeated.

Who knows what will do the job? Maybe if you send each attendee home from the meeting with a copy of a verse it will help.

This section contains a few of my favorite things. Some are my verses and some are by others. If you like, you have my permission to make copies of my verses for your attendees. I truly hope these help you and that you send your people home from your meetings with a new dedication to the safety movement.

I've never seen any studies on the subject; however, it has come to my attention that many people who suffer injuries and who have accidents are victims of low self-esteem. My verses, Somebody and Self-Esteem Credo have brought me thousands of letters from people saying that they helped them build up their self-esteem. Perhaps they'll work with someone you know.

I'm not the right height,
And my face is a mess
I'm not any good at sports,
And I'll never play chess.
My grades aren't the highest,
And it's easy to see,
But I'm happy to tell you
I'm glad to be me.
I'm somebody special,
Just one of a kind,
I'm unique, with a greatness,
I'm seeking to find.
I'm happy, I'm healthy,
I'm somebody, true
And I'm sure glad to say,
That you're somebody, too

Art Fettig
Copyright 1998

A RAILROAD TRAGEDY

Years ago I wrote this verse when one of our locomotive firemen was killed because he was hit in the head with a beer bottle thrown by someone along the right-of-way in Chicago. Eventually they caught the kid who had thrown the bottle and, sure enough, he said he was just trying to hit the headlight.

Somebody threw a bottle

Kenny was a hogger
On the Grand Trunk Western line
Kenny made it all through 'Nam
And now things were goin' fine.
Had him a growin' son.
Had him a lovin' wife,
Then somebody threw a bottle,
And ended Kenny's life.
'Cause somebody threw a bottle,
Raisin' a little hell'
Breakin' the engine headlight.
Hopin' to ring that bell...oh yes.
Somebody threw a bottle.
Just havin' a little fun,
But don't try to tell that story,
To Kenny's wife and son.
All his life he watched the trains,
Loved them, yes he did.
Wanted to be an engineer,
Ever since he was a kid.
Finally got his chance, and yes he
Hired out right away,
And somebody threw a bottle,
And he won't be back today.

'Cause somebody threw a bottle,
Raisin' a little hell,
Breakin' that engine headlight,
Hopin' to ring that bell... oh yes.
Somebody threw that bottle,
Just havin' a little fun,
But don't try to tell that story,
To Kenny's wife and son.
Throwin' things at passing trains,
Is a crazy thing to do.
'Cause trains are run by people,
Just like me and you.
Trains keep the nation rolling,
Hummin' right along.
Think of Kenny and his family,
Whenever you sing this song.
'Cause somebody threw a bottle,
Raisin' a little hell.
Breakin' the engine headlight,
Hopin' to ring that bell...oh yes.
Somebody threw that bottle,
Just havin' a little fun,
But don't try to tell that story,
To Kenny's wife and son.

(c) Art Fettig 1998

A TRIBUTE TO VIET NAM VETS

I was twelve years older than my brother, Joe. When I was a combat rifleman in Korea, I used to send my medals home to my brother. He figured I was a hero and decided that was what he wanted to be.

At eighteen, he joined the Army and became a Green Beret, a Ranger Scout, a Master Jumper. And then he went to Viet Nam twice. He won all the medals. He was wounded several times. And when he came home from two tours in Viet Nam, people treated him badly, as they did many Viet Nam veterans. My brother drank to forget his problems and finally alcohol killed him.

Some 52,000 Americans gave their lives in Viet Nam and I've heard that over 100,000 American Viet Nam vets have taken their own lives since then. God alone knows how many more have died from alcoholism and drug addictions.

I believe the reception veterans received when they came home played not just a little part in the problem.

So if you run into an American Veteran of the Viet Nam war, will you give them a big hug for me and another for yourself and thank them for serving their country and fighting in the toughest war Americans have ever fought in and then coming home to fight a second war of public opinion?

Welcome home, American Veterans of Viet Nam, where ever you are.

A SAFETY CHALLENGE

In 1978, I spoke at the National Safety Congress for thousands of safety leaders at the Early Morning Sessions. I recited a verse titled, *My Brother's Keeper* and it caught on and was rather popular in the safety field. Times have changed since then, so has my thinking. I have rewritten the verse so now it's titled:

My Sister's and My Brother's Keeper

I am my Sister's and My Brother's keeper,
Their safety lies within my hands,
And mine in theirs,
For safety demands a team effort
We must protect ourselves, of course,
And work with constant vigilance,
And yet, that's not enough,
We need each other as Sister and Brother,
Showing loving concern,
For the good of everyone.
I am my Sister's and my Brother's keeper,
Dedicated to making this a better,
Safer world, for all humankind.

(c) Art Fettig 1998

ONE OF MY FAVORITES

Over the years, I've used the following poems in my presentations. They make a wonderful close for any session.

The Builder

I watched them tearing a building down—
A gang of men in a busy town,
With ho-heave-ho and a lusty yell,
They swung a beam and a side wall fell;
I asked the foreman, "Are these men skilled
and the men you'd hire if you had to build?"
He gave a laugh and said, No, indeed,
Just common labor is all I need;
I can easily wreck in a day or two
what builders have taken a year to do!"
And I thought to myself as I went away
"Which of these roles have I tried to play?"
Am I a builder who works with care, measuring
by the rule and square?
Am I shaping my deed to a well made plan,
Patiently doing the best that I can?
Or am I a wrecker, who walks the town,
Content with the labor of tearing down?

by Jess Kenner

GROWING UP

When I was an executive with the Grand Trunk Western Railroad, I used to practice my speeches out loud, with gestures, as I walked up and down our passenger train platforms.

There are a lot of people in New York City who do that today, and they call them weird.

Then, when I decided to learn to speak to children, I practiced juggling three balls as I walked around the executive offices.

The other executives thought I was really an oddball and often they would walk up to me and ask, "Art, what are you going to be when you grow up?"

I would reply that Peter Pan had answered that question for me. Peter Pan said, "I don't ever want to grow up, because then you lose the magic."

Mary Poppins answered the same question, saying "I don't want to grow up because when you're grown up you can no longer talk to the animals."

We've got this wonderful Dalmatian dog, named Babe and every morning Babe leaps up on my bed and we talk. She says, "I have to go outside. Now!"

And we go outside together and have a great little conversation.

I tried to sum up my feelings on growing up in my little verse titled: *Growth*.

Growth

I don't ever want to be what I want to be
There is always something out there yet for me.
I get a kick from living in the here and now.
Yet, I never want to feel I've learned the best way how.
There is always one hill higher with a better view.
Something waiting to be learned that I never knew.
'Til my life is over never fully fill my cup.
Let me go on growing.
UP!
UP!
UP!

Art Fettig
Copyright 1998

MORE FAVORITES

Here are some favorite things of mine you may find

interesting. The Roman philosopher and statesman, Cicero, said this some 2,000 years ago and it's still true......

The Six Mistakes of Man

1.   The delusion that personal gain is made by crushing others.

2.   The tendency to worry about things that cannot be changed or corrected.

3.   Insisting that a thing is impossible because we can not accomplish it.

4.   Refusing to set aside trivial preferences.

5.   Neglecting development and refinement of the mind, and not acquiring the habit of reading and study.

6.   Attempting to compel others to believe and live as we do.

Serenity

Grant me the serenity, to accept the things I cannot change
Courage to change the things I can
And the wisdom to know the difference.

Desiderata

You are a child of the universe, no less than the trees and the stars; You have a right to be here. And whether or not it is clear to you, no doubt the universe is unfolding as it should.

Remember

The bus was travelin'
On I-71
Bringing kids home
From a day of fun.
Saturday night,
It was good and dark,
A comin' home
From the amusement park.
And what a day it was,
You bet!
A playin' and a yellin'
And gettin' wet.
And then the crash,
Head-on they say,

The bus and a pick-up
Goin' the wrong way.
And flames and smoke,
And screams and fright,
And twenty-seven
Died that night.
And what's the message,
Loud and clear,
That everyone
Of us should hear?
As long as we,
Are still alive
Don't ever, ever,
Drink and drive.

Art Fettig
Copyright 1998

The Challenge

Chapter 14

So THERE YOU HAVE IT: The World's Greatest Safety Meeting Idea Book. Our goal was to create a book that will help you to have the world's greatest safety meetings. Of course, only you can make that happen.

I sincerely hope that in some way this book has sparked an idea or two in your mind and that you will do an even better job than you've done before at your safety meetings.

I want this book to present a real challenge to you too.

If I live to be a hundred years old, I know I'll never forget the feeling I felt when the telephone would ring in the middle of the night.

It meant just one thing to me. Another accident. More people were dead or badly injured. Families would be torn apart. The world was filled with a bit more pain and suffering and grief.

I can remember very well when the safety director's job was to keep score. He kept a careful count on the number of employees and others who had been killed or injured each month and then he sent in his reports to the various state and federal agencies.

There was very little in the way of safety equipment, very little training and somehow, the railroad seemed to operate on the premise that people were expendable.

If you were a switchman or a road brakeman then it was just about the norm for you to be missing a couple of fingers because of unsafe coupling devices on the box-cars.

Safety helmets, safety glasses -- these were items that were seldom found around the railroad industry.

When children were killed by a train, we sometimes paid the funeral expenses and that was the extent of our liability, regardless of the way the accident occurred.

How far we've come since that day in early 1948 when I first walked into the main office of the Grand Trunk Western Railroad Company in Detroit and began my career in the General Claims Department!

At that time it was not unusual for a train to kill motorists and their whole families at unprotected railroad crossings.

As I progressed up the ladder of jobs, it wasn't long until I was sent to the hospitals and to the homes of the injured and the survivors of those killed to conduct an investigation of the accidents.

I was a claim agent for nearly 25 years working in

Detroit and Chicago and throughout Michigan, Indiana and Illinois, and I'd say I investigated several hundred fatal accidents. I went into the homes and visited the wives of those killed. I sat with the surviving kids. I went into the hospitals and attended the vigils as we waited for a merciful death of men who had been rendered as vegetables from accidents.

I saw it all -- the pain, the hurt, the suffering, the agony.

Then, finally, I had the opportunity for ten years to do something about this. I worked to prevent accidents and injuries. I produced audio-visual shows and wrote speeches and prepared posters and did a hundred other things and conditions changed. They got better. There was less red ink going into our day books.

If you've never had to make a personal call at the home of one of your employees who had just been killed, then maybe safety is not really a personal thing with you. If you haven't visited the hospital room of a man who had just suffered a triple amputation, then maybe you don't really realize what safety is all about.

Safety is a calling. Safety is a commitment. Safety is something that should so inspire you that you will suffer the flack and the heartache that can come from working your heart out and putting up with people who come to safety meetings and act as if you're just a clown sent out there to laugh at.

Let me tell you, from the bottom of my heart. I've been there and safety is important. It is critical. It is worthwhile and safety meetings do make a difference.

I only hope that our paths will cross some day and you'll share with me some breakthrough you produced at a great safety meeting.

If you tell me that, then I'll feel that my efforts might have been worthwhile.

BOOK *Two*

MORE GREAT SAFETY MEETING IDEAS

The response to our book modestly titled: *The World's Greatest Safety Meeting Idea Book*, was overwhelming, to say the least.

First, let us establish that Growth Unlimited, Inc., is not one of the nation's major publishing firms. Growth Unlimited is really just me, Art Fettig, plus some great freelance people, like artist, Bill Tatroe, and book designer and typographers, Robbie & Robyn Fortner.

Once in awhile I splurge and have a secretary for a while. Once, I actually had two full-time employees; however, it was just during a transition period when the one was training the other before her retirement.

So it really doesn't take a lot to overwhelm. Nevertheless, the response had our UPS driver making several trips out to his truck every day just handling our orders.

And the feedback from readers was marvelous. Most of them said about the same thing, "I read it. I tried the ideas and we just had the best safety meeting we've ever had here."

So when readers started calling me with new jokes and meeting ideas, I took out one of those manila folders and wrote on it, *Second World's Greatest Meeting Idea Book.* Then, *Son of World's Greatest Meeting Idea Book,* and finally, *More Great Safety Meeting Ideas.*

The file was filled daily with a new joke or a new meeting idea, and now we've gone to press.

I hope you enjoy this book, but more important, I hope it works as well as the first book. I hope you read it; I hope you try the ideas; and I certainly hope that your safety meetings get better and better.

If they do, please write me. If you get an idea that we haven't used, send it along. If we use it, we will certainly send you a complimentary copy of the next book.

Remember though, ideas without action are useless. You can memorize this book., and if you don't go out into the real world and try these ideas yourself then they aren't worth the paper they're written on.

Good luck, I hope that together we save some lives.

Art Fettig

Safety People don't get standing ovations much.

No cheering or shouting, when they get in touch.

Sometimes groans and moans and nasty cracks.

It's a heavy load safety people carry on their backs.

No, safety people don't ever get a lot of praise.

And perhaps, they have to fight a wee bit harder for a raise.

And safety is a job that is never done.

It's an uphill fight that's never won.

Mostly, it's a thankless job and yet:

Are we proud to be in safety work? YOU BET!

For with all the hours of thankless toil and strife,

Deep down, we know, we just might save one life.

Art Fettig
Copyright 1998

Chapter 1

UNLESS YOU HAVE PERSONALLY EXPERI-
enced it yourself, it is impossible to realize the
vast scope of the safety field.

For some years, safety to me meant surviving child-
hood, learning to walk, to ride a bicycle and then to drive
a car safely.

Then for the next 25 years safety meant investigating
and negotiating claims for accidents at the railroad and
making extensive reports on accident investigations.

Oh, there was a 21 month interruption in there when
safety meant surviving basic training, a pass to Juarez,
Mexico, a typhoon in the Pacific and then months of
combat where a Purple Heart ribbon testified to my
imperfections.

Then safety meant surviving a homecoming where no one seemed aware that we had a full-blown war going on in Korea.

Next, safety meant investigating more railroad crossing accidents, a horrible passenger train tragedy and employee fatalities and amputations.

Next, safety meant learning to speak at State Safety Meetings and then at National meetings and invitations came from a myriad of industries. Now, safety meant meetings with strip miners and auto workers, Federal Express and postal workers, with coal miners and oil riggers and truck drivers and construction workers.

Safety meant speaking for chemical workers, dynamiters, hospital employees and government workers too.

And safety meant capturing all of the experience and expertise which I encountered everywhere from everyone I met and it meant bringing it all back to the railroad to try to change their losing safety record into a winner's.

Safety was producing dozens of audio visual shows on safety rules and hazardous materials, and safety was reaching millions of students with a message on railroad crossing safety.

And today, safety is everywhere in this world for me. Safety is Chattanooga, Tennessee, and it is Peoria, Illinois. Safety is Honolulu, Hawaii, and St. Johns, Newfoundland, Anchorage, Alaska, and it is Hong Kong, too.

Safety is friendly, totally-committed people from all over the world who call and write to say, "We want you to talk with our people, Art."

And safety is a parade of letters, too; from supervisors and managers who say they've read The *World's Greatest Safety Meeting Idea Book* and they've tried a few of the ideas in the book and they worked.

Safety is speeches and books and articles and video tapes and posters, and whatever it takes to get the message out there every day and every hour and every moment.

Safety is a way of life; safety is a lifetime; and I just hope I can go on being *Mr. Safety* for the rest of my time on this earth.

Chapter 2

ERHAPS THERE ARE AS MANY DEFINI-tions of the term "Safety Meeting" as there are definitions to the word "party".

A safety meeting might be an elaborate affair at a fine hotel, complete with decorations and awards and spouses, or it might be as simple as a fellow standing on the back of a pick-up truck talking with a dozen employees.

In fact, a safety meeting can be simply a one-to-one encounter between two people.

Different strokes for different folks. Different approaches are right for different situations.

A safety meeting might be a simple reminder or it might be a full blown production.

Years ago I used to make "Howdy rounds" at least

once a week. Whenever I was visiting a location I would allow a few extra hours just to walk around and say, "Howdy" to people.

It wasn't unusual at all for someone to bring a hazardous condition to my attention. Quite often, they had already complained about the condition with no results.

Later, when I would mention this condition to the foreman or supervisor or manager, or whomever I felt could correct the situation, they would almost always act surprised that the condition existed and grateful that I had called it to their attention. As the saying goes, "Their Mama didn't raise no fool."

A short time later, I would always check back to see that corrective action had been taken.

So, sometimes, a safety meeting can be as simple as making yourself visible and available to others.

A safety meeting can be a celebration, an occasion for praising.

I can recall attending safety meetings at our railroad's locomotive shops. The superintendent evidently had a serious low self-esteem problem. His idea of a safety meeting was to call all of his foremen and workers together and spend a good hour screaming at them and chewing them out. It was a humiliating experience for the entire group.

When workers brought up safety problems, they were berated by the boss.

When an environmentally conscious worker complained about the heavy fumes from a cleaning vat, he was instructed to grow up and act like a man and take it without complaint like the other men did.

Nearly every safety meeting would end with a room full of disgusted workers. Often, Union grievances would be the outcome.

Morale, whatever morale existed, was badly damaged. The entire process was demoralizing and disgusting and the men dreaded the announcement of yet another safety meeting. To be honest, the meeting did absolutely nothing to prevent injuries. In fact, the poor attitudes that these meetings produced could well have been the underlying cause of some injuries.

Now contrast this with what a safety meeting might be.

A safety meeting can be an educational session where employees learn how to avoid accidents and injuries.

It can be a team meeting where the spirit of competition and caring is encouraged.

A safety meeting can be fun with active participation by all attendees.

It can be a creative experience where attendees discover that their collective experience can produce answers that create a safer, more productive environment.

Attendees might leave a safety meeting in many different frames of mind.

How would you like your attendees to feel following your next meeting?

Do you want them angry? Disgusted? Frustrated? Bored? Seeking revenge? Or would you like them to feel that the company and the management really care about them? Would you like them to believe that their input is really important?

A number of firms I have worked for have an Annual Safety Meeting with trophies and praise and challenges in good measure for all.

Quite often, the top brass of the firm participates to make certain that everyone understands that safety is really an important part of their organization.

Such a program or meeting should be relaxed and fun for everyone.

Speeches are short and pertinent. Awards are presented with dignity and praise.

And then I put on a fun program loaded with good humor and a challenge.

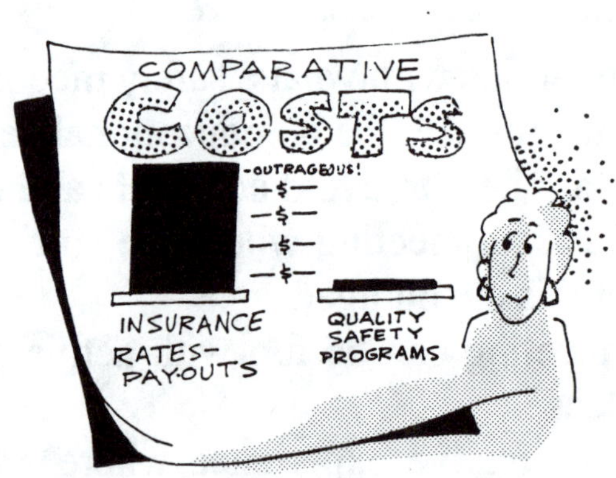

I'm always amazed at some organizations who say they simply cannot afford such safety programs. Many pay horrendous insurance rates because of their high accident experience and yet they fail to pay the price for safety and prevention.

Those who insist on safety say this: "We can't afford to do it any other way. Safety pays."

If there was one word that I would select to be the key to a truly great safety meeting, regardless of its size or location, it would be the word *empathy.*

Climb into the shoes of the attendees for a while before you plan your meeting.

What do they need? What do they want? How do they feel? How can you get them to want to think and act in a safe manner?

Enlist the help of a few attendees. Ask for input before the meeting. What would they like to see and hear at that meeting? What do they think that the really important problems and challenges are?

So often I have seen managers destroy a meeting by harping on some trivial point of record keeping when really serious challenges go unresolved.

What is a safety meeting? It is a meeting to promote safety in some manner. Remember that as you plan your meeting and examine every aspect of your meeting under the light. Ask yourself, will this help to make the world a safer place? Will it make this a safer place to work? If your answer is yes, then go to it with all your energy.

Safety meetings can and will make a difference if you care enough.

Chapter 3

OUR BOOKS AND VIDEO PROGRAMS HAVE caused a minor revolution at many organizations when it comes to safety meetings.

No more dull, unimaginative sessions where attendees sign in and then proceed to either go to sleep or else asked to be excused so they can hide in a rest room until the meeting ends.

As people started using our meeting videos we started getting calls from attendees for copies of our different verses that are often presented in our videos.

From my own experience I realized how much attendees like to take home handouts from a meeting and so we started playing with ideas for special meeting handouts and also creative safety items that could be sent to employees homes or else stuffed into their paycheck envelopes.

Our creative team, consisting of my personal friends, a group of safety leaders, two freelance artists, two typesetters and myself, are forever coming up with new ideas and products to help produce better safety campaigns, meetings and high impact items that keep safety on the tip of everyone's minds.

We've made arrangements to produce customized or generic handouts to add sparkle and lasting power to your monthly meetings.

We are currently developing a dozen different hand out items so you can have a fresh monthly approach for a whole year.

At the time I write this, we have a dozen such items developed and the number seems to be growing weekly.

Now we are developing a system so that a meeting planner has the option of using such items as handouts for meetings or using them as monthly safety mailers that go directly to the employees' home, thus involving the entire family in the safety effort.

One card handout carried a dozen safety pins and the statement, "We pin our hopes on one another as brother's and sister's keepers. Use Positive Interaction."

On another we glued a one inch screw with the statement, "You've got to have a screw loose to break a safety rule. Don't forget to use Positive Interaction."

We went outside on one fall day and grabbed a handful of oak leaves and glued one to each handout card with the statement, "Leaves must fall...but people shouldn't. Be careful, be watchful and be safety-full! Be a sister's and brother's keeper! Use positive interaction!

On one card we glued on one of those little Christmas bells with the question, "Will you be there to answer when the jingle bells ring? Work and play safely during the holiday season....and throughout the year."

At craft and hardware stores we picked up eyeballs, nuts, golf tees and many other items. All it takes is a cooperative artist and a lot of imagination but once you start this the momentum builds and people come to safety meetings with high expectations and a lot of curiosity. What will the handout be this time?

When you go into a safety meeting with a theme, with handouts, with follow ups, then you practically guarantee the success of your meeting.

Just last Friday I received a call from a successful safety manager of a major electric company. "Art," he said, "I want to have my safety leaders leave our meeting with one idea burned into their subconscious. That is the idea that a safety meeting is not a gripe session. A safety meeting is a positive experience for attendees where they leave the meeting with some new knowledge and with a greater determination to do the job safely.

That is a great goal for any safety meeting and we believe that handouts and follow up material can greatly increase the impact of your meeting.

SO OFTEN WE READ ABOUT PEOPLE WHO have struggled along without success as individuals, but when they finally teamed up with the right partners their results were phenomenal. Whenever the results of two or more joined together far exceed the results that the parties might achieve individually we have what we call a synergism.

Often when people get together for a common objective, they bring out the very best in one another. I'm sure you've had jobs or attended meetings in the past where you often amazed even yourself with your results.

Why have safety meetings? Because, in addition to the

power of enthusiasm, a meeting might produce that magic
ingredient called synergism and the results can be amaz-
ing.

I am certain you will agree with me that safety meetings have the potential to save lives. Realizing this we
should get on with the business of making our safety
meetings great.

Just for a minute, think about some of the great teams
in history. Abbott and Costello. Rogers and Hammer-
stein. Sears and Roebuck. We may have never heard of
these individuals if they had gone it alone.

Get together with others and expect great things to
happen at your meetings.

Patience is another great virtue to practice at your
meetings. Often the party with the best solution to your
safety challenge is a bit shy and needs to be encouraged

to join in. Make certain that you give that party every opportunity to participate.

Thomas Edison is considered to be the greatest inventor of all time and yet, the truth is that he surrounded himself with other great minds at his Menlow Park Laboratories. He inspired greatness in those he worked with. The process of synergy was at work constantly.

Open up the door to creativity with those you come in contact with each day.

At one plant I visited they have a worry wall. It is a bulletin board type area where managers and supervisors tack up notices and challenges regarding their special problems. They challenge the entire staff to come up with solutions.

Many progressive managers have come to terms with the old outdated management concept that since they are managers they are the logical ones to come up with great solutions. They realize that people with their actual hands on the equipment on a daily basis often have great ideas and solutions to problems that they have never mentioned because they were just never asked.

Make your safety meeting a place where the power of Synergy can play its important role.

Open up the doors to creativity.

One plus one can add up to a great deal more than just two. With enthusiasm and openness and synergy it can often add up to an idea that will save lives and prevent injuries.

SEE IF YOU CAN COMPLETE THESE POPU-
lar sayings...

"Anything worth doing is worth doing..."

"Practice makes..."

"A little chicken fat is good for the..."

How did you do with our quiz? Did you get all three right? How do you feel about that? Does it give you a feeling of belonging?

Let's go over this quiz from the top. First, "Anything worth doing is worth doing..." What was your answer? "Right?" WRONG... Try this instead. "Anything worth doing is worth doing wrong."

I don't do new things right. Not right away. Most of the time I do things wrong. And then I try again and again and again and with one heck of a lot of searching and practice and luck... then, and only then, do I do things right. And so I like to think that anything worth doing is worth doing wrong and, if need be, failing a few times in order to get it right. Remember when you first tried to walk? Well, in case you forgot, just watch a youngster who is just learning. They get back up off the floor a number of times before they do it correctly.

Recently in Texas I spoke for safety leaders in the Chemical Industry. My talk was on the importance of "employee orientation." The question was, "Is Employee Orientation Necessary?" I suggested that we look at the option, that is, employee disorientation.

I suggested that employees should be oriented not for one day but for at least one year. Every time they are asked to do something new they should be instructed how to perform that task safely.

It is OK to try new things but deep inside us we must be guided by a value, something we hold dear, and that value must be that every job must be done safely.

Now let's try the second question. "Practice makes..." What was your answer? Now level with me. I'm sure by now that you expect me to tell you that "Perfect" is perfectly WRONG. You're right. Practice does not make perfect. Not unless you are practicing the right things. Take golf for instance. If you are a lousy putter and you practice lousy putting for sixteen hours a day for seven days a week forever, you will continue to be a lousy putter. That is why it is so essential that we get an outside evaluation of what we are doing now and then just to make sure we are on the right track with our practicing.

Now the third one. "A little CHICKEN FAT is good for the..." Did you get that one? What was your answer? "Broth." "Soup." "Chicken." I don't know about you but I never ever heard that expression before. I just made it up.

Maybe somewhere, sometime, somehow, someone's Jewish grandmother has that in her collection of famous sayings but for me it is something new. And I didn't include it just to mess up your perfect score either. I put it there as a challenge. I want to challenge you to take all of the sayings, all of the quotes, all of the old wive's tales that you have been living with all these years and I want you to examine them.

When is the last time you fluffed off a new idea or a suggestion with these old bromides... "That won't work in our department." "We tried that before." "If it was any good we'd already be doing it." "It's not in the budget." "Too radical." "Let's assign it to a committee." "We've never done that before." The list of idea killers is endless.

And don't think for a moment that I am saying that all new ideas are good ideas.

When we listen to fresh ideas something often happens in our minds. Somehow the chains of conformity loosen and although a new idea might not be feasible, it might trigger an idea that will work.

Try the process of hitchhiking. Take the idea you don't like and jump on board for a free ride. Let your imagination soar.

How can you change that idea? Magnify it. Magnify it. Turn it around and yes, turn it upside down. Try the exact opposite of the idea. Turn hot to cold. Big to small. Right to wrong.

In other words, keep your mind open to other possibilities.

So many wonderful things have been discovered and improved by accident. Yes, by accident and by someone with an open and inquiring mind.

Keep your mind and your eyes open for possibilities. And for real personal growth give yourself the freedom to fail. Anything that is worth doing is worth doing wrong. Practice makes permanent so try to evaluate just what it is you are practicing. A little CHICKEN FAT is good for the imagination. Let your imagination take a healthy stretch every day and take a lesson from those three Princes of Serendip. Look for new possibilities and allow your mind the freedom to think differently.

Exciting safety meetings are often the result of just asking the question,
"What if?"

Chapter 6

SHARON LYNN CAMPBELL, A GOOD FRIEND and a wonderful writer, has given us a great idea for a safety meeting.

Have your participants try doing things that will give them a small taste of a permanent disability. Let them taste of what it sounds like hearing with a noise-induced hearing loss.

Blindfold attendees and let them try going from the meeting room to the bathroom and back. Be sure to assign a trusted partner to keep the blinded employee out of serious trouble.

Strap down a dominant arm and let them try writing a note with the other hand.

Borrow a wheelchair and send some attendees on the

same type of trip that those blindfolded took.

Later, let them report on their experiences.

For more ideas on how to do this exercise safely, she recommends that you speak with an occupational therapist and with organizations that serve people with various disabilities.

The benefits of such an exercise are two-fold. Not only will your participants become more aware of the reason behind safety rules, but it may even make them all a bit more helpful when they encounter people with physical challenges.

Every now and then someone creates a gem like this one and it finds its way to a copy machine or onto the Internet. I just couldn't resist including this one for you.

Stove, pipe, installation, etc..	$458.00
Chainsaw	$149.95
Care and Maintenance for chainsaw	$44.60
4-wheel drive pick-up, stripped	$8,379.04
4-wheel drive pick-up, maintenance	$438.00
Replace rear window of pick-up, (twice)	$310.00
Fine, cutting unmarked state trees	$500.00
Fourteen cases of Michelob	$126.00
Littering Fine	$50.00
Towing charge-truck from creek	$50.00
Doctor's fee, splinter from eye	$50.00
Safety Glasses	$29.95
Emergency room(broken toes-dropped logs)	$125.00
Safety shoes	$49.95
New living room carpet	$800.00
Paint living room wall and ceiling	$110.00
Log splitter	$150.00
Fifteen acre wooded lot	$9000.00
Tax on wood lot	$310.00
Replace coffee table (burnt while drunk)	$75.00
Divorce settlement	$33,678.92
Savings in conventional fuel, first year	$72.33
Net cost of first year's wood burning	**$54,805.95**

Chapter 7

RECENTLY AT A TELECOMMUNICATIONS safety meeting in Toronto, Ontario, one of the presenters gave a short introduction to a video presentation and fifteen minutes later he was a hero with that audience.

At the end of the video presentation he passed out information on how the attendees might obtain a copy of the tape and he concluded to a wonderful round of applause.

How long did it take him to prepare for that presentation? Well, since he was deeply involved in the production of that particular video tape, I presume he spent many hours of dedicated effort plus it involved the cooperation of dozens of other highly trained people. Of course, he did not prepare the video tape just for that particular audience. It was prepared for all employees of the corporation where he was employed as its safety director. Because of the importance of the topic and the excellence of the production, that tape will no doubt reach thousands of the employees of the firms which the attendees represented.

Those safety directors who obtain that particular tape and present it properly to their employees will also be heroes. The message here is that it is not always necessary to reinvent the wheel. Quite often there are wonderful video productions already in existence if you simply make the effort to discover them and obtain them for your meetings.

Here at Growth Unlimited, Inc., we have discovered that there is a tremendous need in the safety field for short, entertaining, informative, inspiring video tapes for use at employee safety meetings. These tapes must deal with employee attitudes and positive motivation.
We have created a new series of 24 Safety Meeting Sizzler Tapes to help fill that need.

With each tape we have developed a short, easy to use, suggestion sheet that deals with that particular tape.

These are not tapes on specific safety problems. There are already thousands of wonderful productions available on technical problems and solutions.

Our Safety Meeting Sizzlers were created to add fun, excitement and enthusiasm to your Safety Meetings. Do you believe that sometimes your safety meetings lack those ingredients?

The major firms who have purchased our tapes tell us that when they use them with their meetings they get positive results.

One warning. Do not turn on a tape and then escape from your meeting. Stay involved. Challenge your audience. Keep them involved too.

You can learn more about our Safety Sizzler Video Series at the end of the book. If you have questions, just call us at 1-800-441-7676. After all, we share a mutual goal and that is to make your safety meetings produce the results you desire.

Chapter 8

AS EXHIBITORS AT MAJOR SAFETY CON-ferences we had a wonderful opportunity to ob-serve people at their very best and at their very worst.

So many people walk down the center line between exhibits as if they were Zombies. They seem hell bent on not getting involved with anything or anybody.

I make a point to leave my own exhibit and visit the other exhibits. I am always amazed at the friendliness and helpfulness of the other exhibitors.

For instance, a fellow at one of the safety glasses exhibits turned out to have ten years on-line experience as a safety director. In fact, he'd won national awards for his innovative safety programs.

He took time to lay out a complete program to improve the safety performance of one of my client's plants.

In fact, he suggested a back training program and a computer program to help track the causes of injuries. He went so far as to leave his own exhibit and take me around and introduce me to three other exhibitors who might help me with services and information.

At an exhibit such as the National Safety Congress there are literally thousands of top professionals gathered together to be friendly and helpful and believe me, that Zombie who walks down the center line ignoring everybody and everything with closed eyes and a closed mind is missing out on one of the most rewarding experiences available to those who work in the safety field.

I made this suggestion in my talk at the Congress and dozens of attendees came to our booth and remarked that walking through the exhibit area took on a whole new meaning for them and it was truly an educational experience.

Want some great safety meeting ideas? Next time you attend a safety conference ask the exhibitors for safety meeting ideas. They really want to help you. In fact, they just might volunteer to do a safety program for you on their particular field of expertise.

If you are afraid that you will be harassed by overly aggressive salespeople when you show any sign of interest in a product, forget it. With thousands of prospects all around, no sales person will really bother you unless you want the attention. Remember, the people at the exhibits are there to provide service and answers. They want to share their particular expertise with you and they want to inform you about their products or services.

The more you learn about what is available, the better qualified you are to make correct, productive decisions.

Next time you go to a safety product-service exhibit, get involved. Ask questions. Keep an open mind. Set a goal to learn just one new thing at every booth. And be sure and pick up the free samples. That is what an exhibit is all about and it can be a fun, learning experience if you care to make it so.

I T ISN'T ALWAYS NECESSARY TO BRING AT-tendees to a safety meeting. With a bit of creative imagination you can bring the meeting to them.

At many of the major plants I have visited I've heard wonderful stories of how truly creative teams have dreamed up ways to get an important safety message to their people.

One such firm used the Minute Men. These were enthusiastic employees who dressed up in rented costumes. Like the Minutemen of the Revolutionary War, they marched from one location of the plant to another and they delivered an entertaining, well rehearsed one minute safety message to small groups of employees.

Some firms use clowns. Others wrap a victim up in bandages.

Personally, many years ago I played the role of a loser named Joe No No in a number of safety AUDIO VISUAL presentations and then, whenever the spirit moved me, I would dress up for the role and make a personal appearance in one of the yard offices or locomotive shops.

The important thing is that you have a real message and that you are totally involved in whatever role you are playing.

Keep the message short and clear. At Holiday Season, one plant I know of sends a fellow out dressed like a wino. He talks about the joy of getting bombed and passing out at family parties. He reminds workers about their families and their responsibilities at just the right time of the year.

Occasionally the visitors offer inexpensive hand outs just to increase the interest.

Where do you find such volunteers? Just ask around. Every community is crammed full of aspiring actors, clowns, entertainers and many of them are already on your organization's payroll.

Make it fun and it will work successfully.

A good Minute Man or a Dolly Madison can promote your safety message in just a minute and that minute just might save a life.

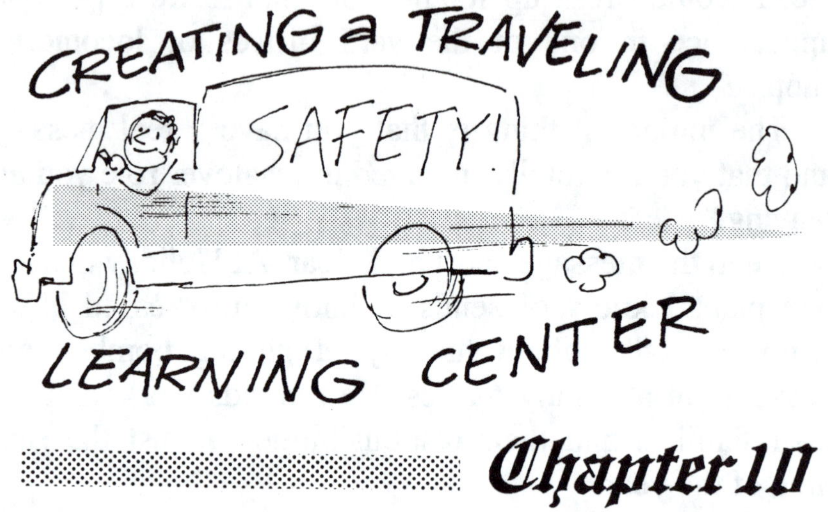

Chapter 10

THE OTHER DAY I HAD TO DRIVE OVER TO Southfield, Michigan, to record a message for a client.

It took me about two hours and ten minutes to drive there and about the same time to come back home.

I managed to get in four hours of learning on that trip. Since I was scheduled to do a two hour session on public speaking next week, I listened to a four tape album of cassettes of a fellow speaker whom I admire, plus a couple of tapes of my own on the subject recorded at previous sessions.

Twice I pulled off the road at rest stops to write down some ideas that came to me as I traveled along the highway.

Sometimes I carry along a portable tape recorder and just record my ideas on tape without stopping.

I learned about the powerful process called "spaced repetition" many years ago. When you listen to cassette tapes it is easy to believe that just one listening is enough. That can be a fatal mistake if you really wish to learn and grow.

I try hard to listen to every tape that interests me at least five times.

Every listening is a different experience.

Did you ever stop to think about the fact that often a tape represents a lifetime of research and learning by the person who creates that tape?

A great tape program, recorded at a live presentation before an audience often flashes new material at your mind at a rapid pace. Far too fast for you to totally absorb, understand or to think about. That is the beauty of spaced repetition.

I have often observed my own experiences listening to tapes and I find that the first time through I generally just enjoy the tape. Sometimes I will try to steal the best jokes. The second time through, the real meaning begins to soak in. I really learn a lot more the second time through.

Third time through is generally an "Aha!" experience. My mind starts to combine the ideas that are being presented with ideas that are already in my subconscious and I often come up with original ideas. Most new ideas come from the combination of two or more other ideas and so the greater the input I provide, the greater the creativity.

The fourth time I listen to a tape, I begin to feel comfortable with the ideas and the fifth time something in that presentation sticks to my mind and it is mine. Later in my talks or in something I am writing, I find myself repeating that concept in my own words.

Most of the great ideas that I have managed to cram into my head have found their way there through the process of "spaced repetition."

Yes, we have a series of audio tapes available. Just call me at 1-800-441-7676 for a current catalog.

Why am I talking about audio cassettes and learning in your car in a book about safety meetings? Because audio tapes are the most important process that I have as yet discovered for learning. What I learned with tapes doubled and then tripled my income and took me from a job that I despised to one that I truly love.

They changed my life and they will change yours if you simply turn your auto into a travelling learning center. Set a goal to learn something new and important every time you turn on the ignition of your auto.

Chapter 11

C. K. PRAHALAD, PROFESSOR OF CORPO-rate Strategy at the University of Michigan School of Business Administration delivered a speech at the Carnegie Council on Ethics and International World Affairs, World View Breakfast in New York City on December 6, 1989.

He discussed the shift in world leadership and went on to say that one of the underlying issues that permeate most of the dramatic changes in competitive positions is that those companies which have effectively challenged a global leadership over the last ten years seem to have, what we call, a strategic intent. And what he meant by a strategic intent he explained, "is not a strategy plan, but rather, an obsession with winning that permeates the total organization and is nurtured and sustained for a long period of time."

As I read the content of his speech, I kept going back to that one description. "An obsession with winning that permeates the total organization and is nurtured and sustained for a long period of time."

It stuck to my mind. And as it rolled around in my subconscious I became more and more convinced that this statement had an important role in defining the key to winning the safety battle against accidents and injuries.

Then I tried to define my own role with regard to the safety movement. As a professional speaker I am called upon to speak to all types and sizes of audiences. Sometimes it is a national or international convention involving thousands of people. Sometimes it is a dozen or less blue collar workers at a plant site. Always the goal is the same. To promote safety and reduce and eliminate the number of incidents, accidents and injuries.

As I repeated that strategic intent in my mind, I began to define my goals, my role in safety. To help create this obsession for winning the battle against accidents within a firm or organization. To help permeate this obsession throughout the organization so that it involves every employee, every member. Then to help nurture this obsession. To feed it. To help it grow. And finally to help to sustain it within that organization over a long period of time.

When I spoke for several hundred managers, including their plant managers for Milliken and Company in South Carolina recently I discussed this strategic intent. I tried to impress upon them that what they were experiencing was not simply a safety drive. Not just a one time promotion. It was their intent to make it a value within their organization. Something they truly hold dear.

Every now and then I am exposed to a new idea, a new concept, a new technique. Generally I wrestle with that new idea for a long time. I might be a slow learner, I'm not sure just how to describe it, but it takes a while for something to sink in. And then I explore it and test it and try the concept on others.

I truly believe that Professor C. K. Prahalad has isolated a truly significant factor in winning. First, the obsession. Next, the fact that the obsession must permeate the entire organization. And that it must be nurtured. Finally, for a long period of time.

As I look around at the winners and losers in world competition I find this strategic intent at work. And as I travel from one organization to another throughout the United States and find the winners in the battle against accidents and injuries I find a similar strategic intent at work.

Safety doesn't just happen. Safety is the result of an all out war against accidents and injuries. I hope that the sharing of this Professor's concepts help you focus in on what is required for a victory.

Safety meetings offer the opportunity to create this obsession for winning the battle against accidents and injuries. Safety meetings provide the opportunity to nurture that obsession, to feed it and keep it alive.

Safety meetings enable us to keep that obsession current and active. It allows us to permeate that obsession so that it reaches every employee every day of their lives.

a Meeting for COMMITMENT

Chapter 12

WHEN I FIRST RECEIVED A CALL FROM a representative of the Alabama Power Company, he explained that they were kicking off a "Total Commitment For Safety" program and they'd like me to come in and do an hour speech for their supervisors and managers.

They were arranging for about one third of their first line supervisors to attend a three day meeting in Birmingham. If the program proved to be a success then they would bring a third of their supervisors each year for a three year cycle.

I asked them about the troops. "What are you doing for the linemen?" I asked. "The guys who put their hands on the live wires?"

He explained that they have safety meetings for all of their employees but that they were not planning anything special at this time.

I explained to him that when I worked for an organization that my goal was always to reach every employee with a positive message on safety. Of course, I understood when he explained that their employees, some 10,000 of them, were spread out all over the state and that it would be impossible to get all of them together for a safety meeting.

I asked if they might get a couple of hundred workers for a meeting and he agreed it could be possible.

"So let's make a video tape of my talk and then you can show it to some of the other employees at Birmingham," I suggested.

Alabama Power Company has a wonderful group of professionals and they have a video crew that really knows what they're doing. We arranged to video tape both the presentation to the linemen and also the program for the supervisors and managers.

At a number of my presentations I had been experimenting with the signing of a document we have created now called *The Declaration of Inter-Dependence*. It reads as follows:

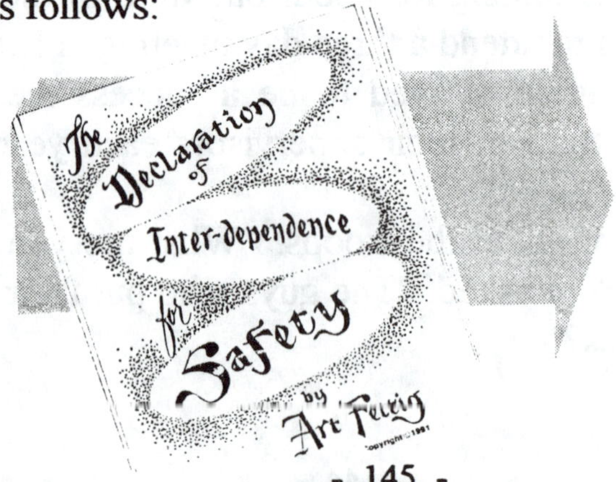

In Session

Declaration of Inter-dependence
(c) Art Fettig, 1998

When in the course of human events it becomes necessary for an organization and its members to make a total uncompromising commitment to Safety for its future growth and for the good of all employees.

And whereas, we do hereby resolve that we will do all in our power, every moment of every day, to make a safety value which we hold dear and integrate into our planning and in the fulfillment of our goals and activities.

Therefore, we do hereby declare and acknowledge our dependence upon one another. For the practice of safety is both a personal and mutual obligation.

We state our commitment in this verse titled: "Our Sister's and Our Brother's Keepers."

We are our Sister's and our brother's keepers.
For Safety calls for our uncompromising commitment
to one another, and to safety, too.
I promise I will positively inter-act
when I find you performing in an unsafe manner.
And I expect positive inter-action
from you on my behalf when I go wrong.
We are human you and I and accidents and injuries occur
when we forget or just react, wrongly not doing what's right
and reasonable for our own safety.
We are our sister's and our brother's keepers.
Trusting in one another, for a safer world.

And for support of this declaration, we mutually pledge to each other our lives, our futures and our sacred honor.

For information & permission to use this declaration contact:
Art Fettig (800)441-7676

We have discovered that when employees make a signed commitment to safety and to one another, then great things can happen. We arranged to have the Declaration blown up to about three foot by four foot and mounted on a board.

At the presentation to the linemen we had the Vice President of their Birmingham Division come up at the appropriate moment and sign our Declaration, much like John Hancock first signed the Declaration of Independence.

At the conclusion of my presentation, I invited other members of the audience to come up and sign it and I was thrilled to watch every attendee come forward and sign the Declaration.

One of the linemen made an issue of signing right above that signature of their Vice President. I asked him why and he explained, "A few months ago I pulled my dead buddy out of a bucket. We'd bent and broken quite a few safety rules that day," he explained. "And I signed on top of that Vice President's signature because I want to make a greater commitment to safety than anyone else here today. I don't want to see anyone get killed or hurt on the job ever again in my lifetime."

At the second program that day, the one for some 500 supervisors and managers, the president of Alabama Power, Elmer Harris, came up and signed the Declaration and when I finished my talk it was thrilling to receive their standing ovation and their praise, but it was even more thrilling to watch that long line of attendees as they waited to personally sign their own commitment to safety and to the welfare of one another.

We gave a personal copy of that Declaration to every attendee at both meetings and shortly after that meeting the Safety Department received requests for over a thousand more copies of the Declaration.

Then the Safety Committee got together and some representatives of the Union suggested that they name the month of September their *Declaration for Safety* month and that the video of my talk for the linemen be shown to every employee on their Birmingham Division and that their employees all be given the opportunity to sign the Declaration.

Well, the idea spread and I understand that the program was shown to every employee of Alabama Power and 10,000 employees made a signed, personal commitment to safety.

One of their managers called me and reported on how the safety movement was growing. "They are holding special meetings to discover ways they can implement the safety program for greater results," he said.

Then he laughed and told me that the different employees throughout their system had requested blown up, mounted copies of the Declaration personally signed by the Corporate President so that they could sign the declaration, too, and proudly hang it in their work area for all to see. The reason he laughed was because he was the one assigned to the task of persuading the president to sign over 60 such mounted documents.

Most organizations stamp "Human Error" as the cause of 60-80% of all of their accidents.

When people make a written commitment to one another and to safety things get better.

Attitude plays an important part in the success of any venture and I believe that as the attitude of employees improves that the safety record must improve.

Since that first safety meeting for linemen at Alabama Power Co. I've had the honor of introducing our Declaration of Inter-dependence Program to organizations all over the United States and Canada.

Hundreds of thousands of workers have signed their own personal commitment to safety and to positive inter-action.

I'll tell you more about this declaration program later in our book.

In Canada we changed our declaration to a pledge for safety as follows:

A Personal Pledge To Safety And To Positive Inter-action

Acknowledging the need for a total, uncompromising commitment to safety, recognizing the truth that we are human, we acknowledge our dependence on one another for safety demands that we truly become our sister's and brother's keepers and the practice of safety is both a personal and a mutual obligation.

There-fore, I promise to let my co-workers know that I value and appreciate their safe actions. When I observe them doing something unsafely, I will positively inter-act in a caring, tactful, respectful and honest manner.

In return, I do hereby give my permission and request that all of my co-workers and managers inter-act in that same positive manner with me. I promise to accept that

*Let us draw our inspiration from the words of the
great Canadian, Terry Fox, who said, "Somewhere the
hurting must stop. I'm determined to take myself to limit
for this cause."*

Of course we also customized our entire presentation
and we've won a total signed commitment from Canadian
groups, too.

To supplement our presentation we have created customized booklets and many of our clients now send their
booklets to employees' homes thanking them for making
their own personal signed commitment to safety.

The booklets contain several of my most popular
verses and the reader of the booklet is invited to share the
positive interaction concept with their families along with
our verses.

With this booklet you can benefit from another individual safety meeting, right in the workers home at a very
minimal cost. (At home is where most accidents occur,
too.)

We've created customized video programs including
the declaration presentation for many corporate clients
and for the U.S. Air Force and U.S. Navy.

Now we offer a total safety package including Declaration presentations plus two dozen safety meeting sizzlers.

The sizzlers were created just to help you make your
safety meetings sizzle.

You will find a complete list of our products at the
back of this book.

If you want more information just call me at Growth Unlimited Inc. 1-800-441-7676 or our fax number is (616)965-4522. Or website www.IMASource.com

I keep thinking about that fellow who signed his name above the signature of the vice president. I wonder if he had had the opportunity to make such a total commitment a year ago, whether his buddy might still be alive today.

Last week a friend of mine called me and I was away from the office. He left a message on my answering machine that will stick in my mind. He said, "Art, a lot of men will be sitting down to dinner with their families tonight, alive and in one piece, just because of your continued efforts in safety."

That is enough to keep me going and I hope it is enough to help you try a little harder to create a great safety meeting that will make a difference.

We believe that the follow-up is essential to any safety program and we are becoming convinced that powerful, entertaining, customized video tapes can do a lot to keep safety commitment alive and growing all year long.

Chapter 13

TEDDY ROOSEVELT SAID IT PRETTY WELL when he said, "One man in the arena is worth ten, a hundred, a thousand carping critics."

It often amazes and amuses me when a sweet old man will come up following one of my speeches where I had given that audience every ounce of energy and effort and expertise I could find, and the audience had responded with love and understanding and a roaring ovation, and all that nice old man could say was that he didn't like the way I moved my left arm during my talk.

He didn't like the way I moved my left arm. Really. Or maybe a sweet young thing will come up and say that although I had used the word "salesperson" a dozen times, still... I had used the term "salesman" and she found it offensive.

In the year 400 B.C., Zeuxis wrote, "Criticism comes easier than craftsmanship." And some time later, Elbert Hubbard wrote, "To escape criticism, do nothing, say nothing, be nothing."

One speaker friend of mine sums up his reaction to critics this way. "I always try to include something offensive for the nitpickers. I hate to have them go home disappointed."

After a talk in Indiana one lady came up to me and said, "Mr. Fettig, I always come to these meetings, but I always walk out on the speaker because they say such awful things. I want you to know that I stayed for your entire talk." She made me feel like I had somehow let her down.

The wonderful Groucho Marx had this to say about being a critic. "I was so long writing my review that I never got around to reading the book." I'd bet a steak dinner in the finest restaurant that the local reviewer who panned my first book never read it.

It is not at all unusual to read local newspaper reviews of theatre events and seriously wonder if the critic attended the same play that you witnessed. Members of that cheering, foot stomping happy audience can open their newspaper only to learn that the play was a flop. The actors and actresses didn't measure up. The direction was faulty, the lighting was poor. It sometimes makes you believe what noted critic William Archet wrote. "One of the first and most important things for a critic to learn is how to sleep undetected at the theatre."

And what has all this talk about critics got to do with the development of your safety meeting skills? Just this. You can never--Let me repeat that--You can never, ever, please all of the people.

Whatever greatly pleases a number of people will always displease others. What is funny to some is sick or distasteful to others. And then there is the matter of misunderstanding. Whatever you say will somehow be distorted or misquoted. It is said that people only hear 25% of what you say and retain only half of that. So, if you really want to find yourself confused, frustrated and hurt, just try to be everything to everybody. "To thine own self be true." That is a pretty good creed if you plan to teach or lecture or lead. Decide how you stand on an issue and just what you would stand up and fight for. And when the flak flies, face it.

Harry S. Truman once responded to a newspaper critic's review of his daughter's singing as follows. "I have read your lousy review of Margaret's concert. I've come to the conclusion that you are an eight ulcer man on a four ulcer pay... Some day I hope to meet you. When that happens, you'll need a new nose, a lot of beefsteak for black eyes, and perhaps a supporter below."

Yes, I must admit that I have spent sleepless nights and felt deep hurt inside because of critics. And I have examined and reexamined my work and I have tried very hard to see things from the other person's point of view. After much reflection, I must admit that I would rather be there in the arena where the real action in life takes place than to be sidelined in a critic's chair.

Perhaps the saying has been overdone, but I cannot keep it out of my mind. There are three kinds of people. Those who watch things happen. Those who do not even know anything that is going on. And those who make things happen. And if perhaps, I get some unpleasant feedback from those who are watching or who do not really know what is happening, then that is part of the price.

I believe Teddy Roosevelt was right on target with, "One man in the arena is worth ten, a hundred, a thousand harping critics." And I hope to be there in the arena of life for a long time to come. Will you join me?

Chapter 14

WHEN WAS THE LAST TIME YOU HAD your attitude adjusted? Your mind bent? Your head put back on straight?

At a recent convention I attended, I noticed that that ritual we used to call a "cocktail party" was now being referred to as the "attitude adjustment hour." My first reaction was to think, "What was wrong with these peoples' attitudes in the first place and why?"

I believe the reasoning behind that program designation was to take their members from the busy workaday world and relax them for an evening of friendly sociability. I observed this ritual and believe me, there is very little fine tuning being done at these "adjustment hours." Most of those in attendance made no adjustment at all and some made too great a change.

As a professional speaker I am often asked, "Aren't you nervous?" And too many would be speakers confide in me the fact that they have a few good belts before they have the courage to face an audience. These same people will admit to having a few good belts before an important conference or before just about anything important in their lives. Somehow they feel that alcohol is needed to adjust their attitudes to winning ways.

As a sometimes outsider to the human race, my continuing study of people leads me to believe that the reason they need "adjustments" is because their heads aren't screwed on right in the first place. They have continuing malfunctions in their daily attitudes. When we learn to take personal control of our attitudes it is like a breath of fresh air to our lives. We make one painless personality and behavioral adjustment and from then on life just ain't never gonna be the same. Instead of setting aside hours for drinking to attain a temporary adjustment to try to bring some semblance of positiveness into our way of life, we learn to make whatever adjustment is necessary in our thinking as we wake up and face each day.

Some time ago, I wrote a short verse for a children's magazine and it has been republished a number of times. It says simply,

Not for me, L.S.D.
I will pass that liquor glass,
I don't want marijuana,
Life is too great--straight.

When my mind is in gear and my being is tuned in I can easily walk on water and leap over tall buildings and soar with the eagles. It doesn't require a mind boggling drug to accomplish that feat because I am already there on the norm. Life is exciting and great feats are possible. There is a new adventure out there for every one of us every day when we get our attitude screwed on properly.

William James of Harvard said the greatest discovery of his generation was that "Human beings can alter their lives by altering their attitudes of mind."

Listen to the losers of this world and they will say, "I don't go for all of that positive thinking jazz."

Or if you want, just hear them as they explain, "But I'm different. It wouldn't work for me."

Then there are those who insist that they do not need any outside help. That somehow they have been gifted with super intelligence and that outside input would just mess things up. And they plod through life unhappy with their negative attitudes providing the stumbling block to deter every positive effort they make in life.

Attitude adjustments--the attitude adjustments that lead to growth and success and happiness are not served in little sparkling glasses. Attitude adjustments that lead to a life of adventure and attainment come from the careful care and feeding of the mind. When we learn to focus our truly positive attitude toward making it a safer world, then great things will happen.

Chapter 15

A WHILE BACK I HAD THE HONOR OF keynoting the Telecommunications Safety Conference in Toronto, Ontario and I had a friend with me.

We were lucky enough to get two tickets to the great musical *Phantom of the Opera*.

We had aisle seats and the instant that final curtain came down, the couple seated next to us stood up and we let them pass us to leave.

For an instant, I had the urge to leave with them. I do not like crowds and shoving but I resisted the temptation and I'm so glad that I did. What happened next reinforced a belief I hold dearly. I hope you share that belief at your next safety meeting.

The curtain rose and the dancers came on stage and bowed as the audience applauded and then came the parade of the other members of the cast. The chorus, those with small singing roles, then the featured players and then the applause turned to cheers as the star came on stage and the audience, as a whole, rose to its feet with giant waves of applause.

As the cheering continued the star walked to the front of the stage and directed the incoming applause to the various sections of the orchestra.

And then the entire cast took their final bows and the curtain descended.

What's the point?

The point is that the couple sitting next to us cheated the performers out of their just due. The entire process of theatre was somehow incomplete for them and they did not even realize what they'd missed. They missed something very special. Something precious. A special moment that would stick to their minds. That special communion between performers and the audience that is possible at the end of a great performance.

Applause! Applause! That very special way of paying tribute and yet, unfortunately, some folks travel from the womb to the tomb without receiving a single standing ovation.

Start planning this moment to applaud some special achievement at your next meeting. Perhaps you can announce a special award for excellence in safety.

You might find a little resistance at first, but let your own enthusiasm shine. At times it calls for the talents of a

cheerleader to conduct a great safety meeting but go for
it! Lead that applause and watch your people grow.

Benefits

Chapter 16

HOW MUCH IS A GREAT MEETING WORTH to you? Is it worth a bit more than a poor meeting?

I'm forever amazed when meeting planners tell me, "I'm sorry, Art, but the committee decided to go with a free speaker. We just can't afford your fee."

Often, a free speaker is the costliest investment you ever made.

When you put a value on the time of the members of your audience, add to it the cost of the meeting place, the meal, and then add a generous tip to that total for the wonderful results that didn't happen because of your meeting--then you might understand what I'm saying.

What are the benefits of going with a pro? Well, first of all, you get some fresh input into your organization-- new excitement, new ideas, new energy. And new commitments to your goals that can often be realized too.

Another benefit a pro brings you is this: A pro makes a hero out of the program planner(s). When your audience cheers that speaker, they are also cheering your judgment.

Just what does Art Fettig do for an audience? One of the best answers that we have come up with is this--"Art Fettig helps people feel better about themselves, their job, their organization and their future. He helps them do a better job."

He also wins a signed, personal commitment to safety and to positive interaction from your people at all levels.

Now, that just might not sound like much to you but the way people feel about themselves, their jobs, their organization and their future makes a tremendous differ-ence in their performance.

People who feel good about themselves are better workers, better lovers, better parents. People who feel good about themselves are safer; they have fewer alcohol and drug problems. Their productivity is generally higher. The quality of their work is better.

Feelings create attitudes and attitudes make a major difference in an organization.

About that signed personal commitment, it often provides the missing element in your safety program. Commitment is that missing link to make your whole safety program work.

When you make your decision for your speaker, make certain you consider all of the factors involved.

For an entertaining, productive, inspiring, exciting, result-producing meeting that will send the audience home feeling better about themselves, their jobs, their organization and their futures, call me today at 1-800-441-7676.

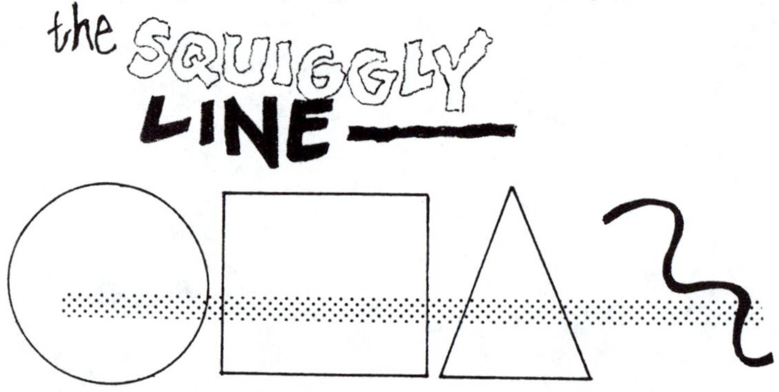

Chapter 17

WITH AN AUDIENCE OF OVER A THOU-sand people, it is easy to know how you are doing when they all take out their pens and paper and write down what you've just done. It is obvious that they plan to steal your material for use at their next safety meeting.

Such a thing happened at my Early Morning Session at the National Safety Congress recently. I'll try to give you the material, just as I did it for that audience.

Ladies and gentlemen, I am going to give you four symbols and I want you all to look them over and decide which one you personally prefer. Just pretend that these symbols are friends and you get to take one home with you. Here they are. First, a circle. Next a square. Now a triangle. And finally, a squiggly line.

Look them over. O.K. Now we have a circle, a square, a triangle and a squiggly line. Ladies and gentlemen, if you could choose just one, how many of you would choose the circle? Fine. And how many of you like the square? Not very many squares here today. What about the triangle?   How many of you like the triangle; just raise your hands.   And finally, how many of you like the squiggly line?   Would those of you who like that squiggly line please stand up. Get right up. Great.

Alright. Now this test has been psychologically tested again and again and it is supposed to be very accurate. By determining which symbol you choose, we can find out what your hot button is. We will know what motivates you.   What turns you on?

Again, how many of you chose the circle? You people are motivated by money.

Now the square. Just a few squares. Squares are motivated by security. You like to play it safe. You should get a government job.

Now triangles. How many of you chose the triangle? Great! You folks are turned on by recognition. You like to climb the social ladder. You like to take home plaques and awards.

Now, where are the squiggly lines? Raise your hands. Get them way up there. Terrific! You people are motivated by sex. (Aside--"Did you get their names like I asked you to?")

Now... how many of you would like to change your symbols right now?

Let me tell you what happened. The other night I spoke in Kansas City and I had my girlfriend with me. After the program, this little blonde thing came wiggling up to me and she said softly, "Mr. Fettig, I was one of those squiggly lines."

My girlfriend heard her. Man, did she straighten out her line in a hurry.

Ladies and gentlemen, how many of you were not really turned on by any of those signs? Sure. I'd like to say that I think that people who work in the field of safety should have their own special sign.

Let's look at these signs. First of all, how many of you will agree that there is not a terrific amount of money to be made in the safety field? Oh, some folks make out well, but generally speaking, unfortunately, it is not one of the highest paid fields you can get into. Do you agree?

O.K., let's move on to the second symbol. What about security? If you are the safety director or the safety manager and you have a string of bad luck and your injuries go soaring, how many of you will agree that your security just might be in jeopardy? So the security isn't all that great.

Now about recognition or prestige. Have any of you noticed that people do not actually genuflect or bow low when you tell them you are in safety? It doesn't happen very often. Perhaps there is not all that much glory in the safety field.

Now the squiggly line. With the long hours a lot of safety people work, I understand that their sex life suffers. Is that true?

So, just maybe none of those symbols fit.

Ladies and gentlemen, I submit that the safety profession is truly a loving profession. I think your sign should be a heart.

Most of the great safety leaders I have met over the past 40 or more years are truly loving people. They care about others, care for their needs.   They learn to know people and to understand them. And so, I believe that we have a room full of great lovers here today.

Safety is a loving profession, and I congratulate you for being in one of the most important jobs in the world-- that of saving lives and preventing injuries.

Chapter 18

Meeting Openers

I was rather apprehensive about speaking at this meeting, but then I read a research report from Harvard University on Meetings and Audiences that gave me comfort. It reports that at the average meeting, some 23% of the audience is busy thinking about personal problems and they do not listen to a speaker. Just 10% of the audience listens. The other 67% are having sexual fantasies. I feel better knowing that no matter what I say, two thirds of the audience will enjoy it.

Truth in Advertising

ingle ells,
ingle ells.
The holidays aren't the same without J&B.

This is a commercial I found for J&B scotch in an issue of *Newsweek*, and all I could think is "That's for sure. Thank Goodness."

Christmas just isn't the same without alcohol. Nor is Easter, or Thanksgiving, or the Fourth of July or life itself. Thank Goodness.

It is not the same without the blacking out, the making a fool of myself, the getting sick, the awful mornings after. Life is not the same without alcohol, and I pray each night that I will never forget it.

Thank you, J&B, for reminding me with your Christmas message.

 * Is your girlfriend pretty or ugly? Both, pretty ugly.
 * He took the guard off the grinder and now he's doing everything single-handed.

* If you think finding a worm in your apple is bad, then try finding half a worm.

* He's an intellectual. When his son fell down a manhole, he went and bought a book on raising children.

* My dentist recently became a brain surgeon. His drill slipped.

* She won't leave the living room. She's afraid of dying.

* Some people came by collecting for the Old Folks' Home, so we gave them Grandmother.

* If Batman is so smart, why doesn't he put his underwear on underneath his trousers.

* New sign in the cafeteria: "Don't complain about the coffee. You'll be old and weak yourself someday."

* When Adam met Eve, he turned over a new leaf.

* He thinks baldness is a great cure for dandruff.

* "Doctor, Doctor, I feel like a yo-yo."
"Sit down. Sit down. Sit down."

* Two World War I veterans met at a reunion and the one says to the other, "Charlie, do you remember that saltpeter they used to put into our mashed potatoes?"

* "Yes, I do," Charlie replies.
And his buddy replies, "Well, I think it is beginning to work."

* Man in lobby, "Lady, do you mind if I smoke?"
Lady, "Not if you don't mind my getting sick on you."

* I just heard about a new drink they call the Kentucky Colonel Cocktail. You drink two of them and you start using fowl language.

* Foreman in manager's office, "I didn't come here to be insulted."
Manager, "Oh, no, where do you usually go?"

* Out at the farm the milking machine froze up and there was udder chaos.

* A man broke his false teeth and a friend discovered his plight. "Not to worry," the friend said. "I'll take these pieces and my brother will have a replacement for you in the morning." Sure enough, the friend arrived with the teeth; they fit perfectly. "Your brother is a wonderful dentist," the man said. "Oh, no," the friend replied. "He's an undertaker."

* Quiz: What has a bottom at the top? A leg.

* Note on a shop wall: Firings will continue until morale improves.

* Doctor, Doctor, I'm boiling!"
"Just simmer down, Sir."

* Boy: "Your sister's spoiled, isn't she?"
Other boy: "No, that's just the perfume she wears."

* I have three little reasons why I go to work each day: Visa, Master Charge and American Express.

* Some members of Congress are finally doing something about the high crime rate. They are resigning.

* I just gave my wife plastic surgery. I cut up her credit cards.

* Congress has been considering setting new ethics standards for themselves, but a committee decided it would be a conflict of interests.

* In Washington's war on drugs, they are cutting down their Happy Hours to just a Fairly Amusing Fifteen Minutes. It's a start.

* As a protest, Congress recently staged a three-week slowdown, and nobody knew.

* My girlfriend's name is Pearl Horowitz. Every Decem-

ber 7th she attacks herself.

* I went to the library and here is this line of high school kids checking out classical video tapes for their book reports.

* What an antsy audience. You all look like aerobic listeners.

* The reasons for this safety meeting are endless. I just hope the meeting doesn't turn out that way too.

* Over half of the money taken in on federal taxes goes for interest on the national debt. Sounds like my credit card.

* The sword swallower next door just swallowed an umbrella. He wanted to put something away for a rainy day. And that's where I should have put that joke.

* "Mommy, Mommy, they say I look like a werewolf!" "Shut up and comb your face!"

* He left his job because of illness and exhaustion. His boss got sick and tired of him.

* As the boy octopus said to the girl octopus, "I want to hold your hand, hand, hand, hand."

* A motorist runs into a store and asks the owner, "Do you own a large black and white cat?"
The shop owner says, "No."
"Oh, man," the driver says, "I must have backed over a nun."

* I got a puppy for my wife."
"Fantastic," says the friend. "I wish I could make a trade like that."

* Sign on a school gate: Wet Paint. Note, this is a warning, not an instruction.

* Warden: "Do you have any requests before we execute you?"

Prisoner: "I'd like to sing a song."

Warden: "Go ahead."

Prisoner: "500,000 bottles of beer on the wall; 500,000 bottles of beer."

* Congress seems confused. Instead of upholding the Constitution, they seem to be holding up their constituents.

* Flash: Thieves recently broke into our local police department and stole all of the toilet fixtures. So far, officers have nothing to go on.

* He does the work of two men: Laurel and Hardy.

* He asked his boss for a raise but so far, he doesn't know what the answer is. Security won't let him back in the building.

* I didn't get any sleep last night when I was planning this safety meeting. I hope that none of you get any sleep while we are having it.

* A great criminal lawyer recently received a phone call from a client who reported, "I'm in prison. They've shaved my head and transferred me to death row. They've cut a slit in my trousers. What should I do?"

* And the lawyer answered, "Don't sit down."

* The doctor told me to stop playing golf. He says the way I look, I shouldn't take a chance getting that close to a hole in the ground.

* A Safety Engineer is a person who can tell you to go to Hell so tactfully that you look forward to the trip.

* That lawyer works on a contingency basis. That's an old gold mining term, meaning--he gets the gold after you get the shaft.

* He'd make a great blueprint if you wanted to build an

idiot.

* This fellow runs a stop sign and a cop pulls him over and asks, "What's wrong? Don't you believe in stop signs?"
And the guy replies, "Sure, I believe in them, but I'm not fanatic about them."

* Ten Hell's Angels storm into a restaurant and start insulting one of the customers horribly. The customer ignores them and then leaves the restaurant. When he'd gone, one of the Hell's Angels says to the Manager, "He wasn't much of a man, was he?"
The Manager looks out the window and says, "No, and he wasn't much of a driver either. He just backed his semi over ten motorcycles."

* He's so efficient. He feels he's failed when he misses one slot in a revolving door.

* Knowledge is knowing the fact that fire will burn. Wisdom is remembering the blister.

* If work is virtue, he's living in sin.

* A motorist brushed against a youth who was standing in the street. The youth fell to the ground in great pain. "Whatsa matter, mister, didn't you see me?
"See you--sure I saw you! I hit you didn't I?"

* I just bought a cheap suit and the label says 100% wool. That's the label. I don't know what the suit is.

* A good measure of intelligence is the length of time it takes to get to your wit's end.

* The doctor told me I was stupid. I said I'd like a second opinion. He said I was ugly too.

* Any safety campaign that does not throttle booze overlooks the main cause of accidents and crime.

* He's got a heart of gold--like a hardboiled egg!

Las Vegas

* The first time I went there was for fun, the second time for revenge. Now I'm going back to visit my money.
* A friend of mine got married in Las Vegas. He figured that as long as he was on a losing streak he might as well go all the way.
* I lost everything but my cold.
* I figure gambling is a disease. I deducted my losses as a medical expense.
* The best way to get out of a poker game with a small fortune is to start out with a big fortune.
* Shooting craps is a shaky business.
* The late Sammy Davis was driving 90 miles an hour in Vegas. They locked him up for speeding and the judge said, "Are you crazy? 90 miles an hour!?"
Sammy said, "What do you want? I've only got one eye. Do you want me to keep my eye on the road or on the speedometer?"

A Safety Classic

Here's a classic piece of safety humor that has been circulating in the Safety Field for many years. I have not been able to determine its original author. I've heard it read many times at safety meetings and other meetings, and it has been fantastic and it has bombed, too. If you plan to use it, rehearse it and put some real life into the reading.

Dear Sir:

I am writing in response to your request for additional information. In block number 3 of the accident reporting form, I put "Trying to do the job alone," as the cause of my accident. You said in your letter that I should explain more fully, and I trust that the following details will be sufficient.

I am a bricklayer by trade. On the day of the accident, I was working alone on the roof of a new six-story building. When I completed my work, I discovered that I had about 500 pounds of bricks left over. Rather than carry the bricks down by hand, I decided to lower them in a barrel by using a pulley which, fortunately, was attached to the side of the building, at the sixth floor.

Securing the rope at ground level, I went up to the roof, swung the barrel out, and loaded the bricks into it. Then I went back to the ground and untied the rope, holding it tightly to insure a slow descent of the 500 pounds of brick. You will note in block 11 of the accident reporting form that I weigh 135 pounds.

Due to my surprise at being jerked off the ground so

suddenly, I lost my presence of mind and forgot to let go of the rope. Needless to say, I proceeded at a rather rapid rate up the side of the building.

In the vicinity of the third floor, I met the barrel coming down. This explains the fractured skull and broken collar-bone.

Slowed only slightly, I continued my rapid ascent, not stopping until the fingers of my right hand were two knuckles deep into the pulley.

Fortunately, by this time, I had regained my presence of mind and was able to hold tightly to the rope in spite of my pain.

At approximately the same time, however, the barrel of bricks hit the ground--and the bottom fell out of the barrel. Devoid of the weight of the bricks, the barrel now weighed approximately 50 pounds.

I refer you again to my weight in block number 11. As you might imagine, I began a rapid descent down the side of the building.

In the vicinity of the third floor, I met the barrel coming up. This accounts for the two fractured ankles and the lacerations of my legs and lower body.

The encounter with the barrel slowed me enough to lessen my injuries when I fell onto the pile of bricks and, fortunately, only three vertebras were cracked.

I am sorry to report, however, that as I lay there on the bricks, in pain, unable to stand, and watching the empty barrel six stories above me--I again lost my presence of mind--*I let go of the rope*--the empty barrel weighed more than the rope, so it came down on me and broke both my legs. I hope I have furnished the information you require as to how the accident occurred.

A Few of My Favorite Things

Chapter 19

IN THIS CHAPTER YOU'LL FIND MANY OF MY favorite poems, verses and quotations. I've found many of these to be ideal "meeting closers".

Courage and Leadership

The credit belongs to the man who is actually in the arena; whose fate is marred by dust and sweat and blood; who errs and comes short again, who knows the great enthusiasms; the great devotions, and spends himself in a worthy cause; who at best knows in the end the triumph of high achievement; and who at the worst, if he fails, at least fails while daring greatly; so that his place shall never be with those cold and timid souls who know neither victory nor defeat.

Theodore Roosevelt

We Need Men and Women

... who cannot be bought... whose word is their bond.

... who put character above wealth... who possess opinions and a will.

... who are larger than their vocations.

... who do not hesitate to take chances.

... who will make no compromise with wrong.

... who will not lose their individuality in a crowd.

... who will be as honest in small things as in great things.

... who will not say they do it "because everybody else does it."

... whose ambitions are not confined to their own selfish desires.

... who give thirty-six inches to the yard and thirty-two quarts to the bushel.

... who will not have one brand of honesty for business purposes and another for private life.

... who are true to their friends through good report and evil report, in adversity as well as in prosperity.

... who do not believe that shrewdness, sharpness, cunning and long-headedness are the best qualities for winning success.

... who are not ashamed or afraid to stand for the truth when it is unpopular, who can say "no" with emphasis, although all the rest of the world says "yes."

California Free Enterprise Association

If you can keep your head when all about you
Are losing theirs and blaming it on you;
If you can trust yourself when all men doubt you,
But make allowance for their doubting too;
If you can wait and not be tired by waiting,
Or, being lied about, don't deal in lies,
Or being hated, don't give way to hating,
And yet don't look too good, nor talk too wise;

If you can dream -- and not make dreams your master;
If you can think -- and not make thoughts your aim;
If you can meet with Triumph and Disaster
And treat those two impostors just the same;
If you can bear to hear the truth you've spoken
Twisted by knaves to make a trap for fools,
Or watch the things you gave your life to, broken,
And stoop and build 'em up with worn-out tools;

If you can make one heap of all your winnings
And risk it on one turn of pitch-and-toss,
And lose, and start again at your beginnings,
And never breathe a word about your loss;
If you can force your heart and nerve and sinew
To serve your turn long after they are gone,
And so hold on when there is nothing in you
Except the Will which says to them: "Hold on!"

If you can talk with crowds and keep your virtue,
Or walk with Kings -- nor lose the common touch,
If neither foes nor loving friends can hurt you,
If all men count with you, but none too much;

If you can fill the unforgiving minute
With sixty seconds' worth of distance run,
Yours is the Earth and everything that's in it,
And -- which is more -- you'll be a Man, my son!

Rudyard Kipling

It Couldn't Be Done

Somebody said that it couldn't be done,
But he with a chuckle replied
That "maybe it couldn't," but he would be one
Who wouldn't say so till he'd tried.
So he buckled right in with the trace of a grin
On his face. If he worried he hid it.
He started to sing as he tackled the thing
That couldn't be done, and he did it.
Somebody scoffed: "Oh, you'll never do that;
At least no one ever has done it";
But he took off his coat and he took off his hat,
And the first thing we knew he'd begun it.
With a lift of his chin and a bit of a grin,
Without any doubting or quiddit,
He started to sing as he tackled the thing
That couldn't be done, and he did it.
There are thousands to tell you it cannot be done,
There are thousands to prophesy failure;
There are thousands to point out to you, one by one,
The danger that waits to assail you.
But just buckle in with a bit of a grin,

Just take off your coat and go to it;
Just start to sing as you tackle the thing
That "cannot be done," and you'll do it.

Edgar A. Guest

Mail Call

"MAIL CALL!" The most beautiful
words in the world, when you're overseas,
and lonely and longing for home.
"MAIL CALL!" It follows you through life,
and mail means a million different things
to a million different people.
MAIL CALL means a check, or a bill,
or a love letter or a "Dear John."
It was "Greetings" for inductees.
It's a dreaded letter from the I.R.S.
Or, perhaps, the good news that you passed
that test, or won that award,
or qualified for that life changing experience.
"MAIL CALL!" "Yes, you got the job."
"Yes, I will marry you."
"Yes, the operation was successful,
and your Mom's O.K."
MAIL CALL is news from the family back home.
It's a note from your kids at college,
or a postcard from summer camp.
MAIL CALL is Christmas cards from
long forgotten friends.

For businesses, it is ads and orders.
It's checks and reasons to go on trying.
And yet, we take it all for granted.
I give thanks for MAIL CALL
and for those who make it happen.

(c) 1998 Art Fettig

Just for Today

Just for today, I will live through the next 12 hours and not tackle my whole life problem at once.

Just for today, I will improve my mind. I will learn something useful. I will read something that requires effort, thought and concentration.

Just for today, I will not find fault with a friend, relative or colleague. I will not try to change or improve anyone but myself.

Just for today, I will have a program. I might not follow it exactly, but I will have it. I will save myself from two enemies -- hurry and indecision.

Just for today, I will exercise my characters three ways. I will do a good turn and keep it a secret. If anyone finds out, it won't count.

Just for today, I will do two things I don't want to do, just for the exercise.

Just for today, I will be unafraid. Especially will I be unafraid to enjoy what is beautiful and believe that as I give to the world, the world will give to me.

Ann Landers
Nationally Syndicated Column

The Ten Rules of Human Relations

1.Speak to people. There's nothing as nice as a cheerful greeting.

2.Smile at people. It takes 72 muscles to frown and only 14 to smile.

3.Call people by their names. The sweetest music to the ears is one's own name.

4.Be friendly and helpful. If you would have friends, be friendly.

5.Be cordial. Speak and act as if everything you did were a pleasure.

6.Be genuinely interested in people.

7.Be generous with praise, cautious with criticism.

8.Be considerate with the feelings of others; it will be appreciated.

9.Be thoughtful of others' opinions. There are three sides to every controversy -- yours, the other's -- and the right one.

10.Be alert to give service. What counts a great deal in life is what we do for others.

"A Man Who Makes A Mistake And Does Not Correct It Is Committing Another"

Confucius

"Unless You Try To Do Something Beyond What You Have Already Done And Mastered, You Will Never Grow."

Author Unknown

The Volunteer

(c) Art Fettig, 1991

Give a cheer, give a cheer
For the Volunteer.
While others say
They'll see to it--

Give a cheer, give a cheer
For the Volunteer,
They simply go out
And they do it.

Give a cheer, give a cheer
For the Volunteer.
They are brave and
Ready for scrappin'.

Give a cheer, give a cheer
For the Volunteer.
They're the people who make
Good things happen.

Give a cheer, give a cheer
For the Volunteer.
I think they are sent down
From above.

Give a cheer, give a cheer
For the Volunteer.
Yes, they fill this whole world
Full of love.

The Wisdom of Benjamin Franklin

Benjamin Franklin is credited with having made more Americans millionaires than any other one person, including Andrew Carnegie, Henry Ford, or General Motors. He did it by setting down these twelve rules for business success:

TEMPERANCE: Eat not to dullness; drink not to elevation.

SILENCE: Speak not but what may benefit others or yourself; avoid trifling conversation.

ORDER: Let all your things have their places; let each part of your business have its time.

RESOLUTION: Resolve to perform what you ought; perform without fail what you resolve.

FRUGALITY: Make no expense but to do good to others or yourself; i.e. waste nothing.

INDUSTRY: Lose no time; be always employed in something useful; cut off all unnecessary action.

SINCERITY: Use no hurtful deceit; think innocently and justly, and if you speak, speak accurately.

JUSTICE: Wrong none by doing injuries, or omitting the benefits that are your rightful duty.

MODERATION: Avoid extremes; forbear resenting injuries so much as you think they deserve.

CLEANLINESS: Tolerate no uncleanliness in body, clothes or habitation.

TRANQUILITY: Be not disturbed at trifles, or at accidents common or uncommon or unavoidable.

IMITATE JESUS AND SOCRATES.

Check yourself against the twelve points of Franklin as part of your planning.

Abraham Lincoln was reported to have said:

1. You cannot bring about prosperity by discouraging thrift.
2. You cannot strengthen the weak by weakening the strong.
3. You cannot help strong men by tearing down big men.
4. You cannot help the wage earner by pulling down the wage payer.
5. You cannot further the brotherhood of man by encouraging class hatred.
6. You cannot help the poor by destroying the rich.
7. You cannot establish sound security on borrowed money.
8. You cannot keep out of trouble by spending more than you earn.
9. You cannot build character and courage by taking away man's initiative and independence.
10. You cannot help men permanently by doing for them what they could and should do for themselves.

Press On

Nothing in the world can take the place of persistence.

Talent will not; nothing is more common than unsuccessful men with talent.

Genius will not; unrewarded genius is almost a

proverb.

Education will not; the world is full of educated derelicts.

Persistence and determination alone are omnipotent.

Nine Ways to Change People
Without Giving Offense or Arousing Resentment
(Author Unknown)

1. Begin with praise and honest appreciation.
2. Call attention to people's mistakes indirectly.
3. Talk about your own mistakes before criticizing the other person.
4. Ask questions instead of giving orders.
5. Let the other man save his face.
6. Praise the slightest improvement and praise every improvement. Be hearty in your appreciation and lavish in your praise.
7. Give the other person a fine reputation to live up to.
8. Use encouragement. Make the fault seem easy to correct.
9. Make the other person happy about doing the thing you suggest.

Why Worry?

There are only two things to worry about: either you

are well or you are sick. If you are well, then there is nothing to worry about. But if you are sick, there are two things to worry about: either you will get well, or you will die. If you get well, there is nothing to worry about. If you die, there are only two things to worry about: either you will go to Heaven or Hell. If you go to Heaven, there is nothing to worry about. But if you go to Hell, you'll be so busy shaking hands with friends you won't have to worry.

Can't

CAN'T is the worst word that's written or spoken;
Doing more harm here than slander and lies;
On it is many a strong spirit broken
And with it many a good purpose dies.
It springs from the lips of the thoughtless each morning
And robs us of courage we need through the day.
It rings in our ears like a timely-sent warning
And laughs when we falter and fall by the way.
CAN'T is the father of feeble endeavor,
The parent of terror and half-hearted work;
It weakens the efforts of artisans clever,
And makes of the toiler an indolent shirk.
It poisons the soul of the man with a vision;
It stifles in infancy many a plan;
It greets honest toiling with open derision
And mocks at the hopes and the dreams of a man.
CAN'T is a word none should speak without blushing;
To utter it should be a symbol of shame;
Ambition and courage it daily is crushing;
It blights a man's purpose and shortens his aim.

Despise it with all of your hatred of error;
Refuse it the lodgement it seeks in your brain;
Arm against it as a creature of terror,
And all that you dream of you some day shall gain.
CAN'T is the word that is foe to ambition,
An enemy ambushed to shatter your will;
Its prey is forever the man with a mission.
And bows but to courage and patience and skill.
Hate it, with hatred that's deep and undying,
For once it is welcomed 'twill break any man;
Whatever the goal you are seeking, keep trying
And answer this demon by saying, "I CAN"

Edgar A. Guest

Anytime You Feel Like Quitting

Throughout your career, perhaps you'll remember this
story of one of our people:
He failed in business in '32
He ran as a state legislator and lost in '32.
He tried business again and failed in '33.
His sweetheart died in '35.
He had a nervous breakdown in '36.
He ran for state elector in '40 after he regained his health.
He was defeated for Congress in '43,
defeated again for Congress in '48,
defeated when he ran for Senate in '55, and
defeated for Vice President of the United States in '56.
He ran for the Senate again in '58 and lost.
This man never quit.

He kept trying 'til the last.

In 1860, this man, Abraham Lincoln, was elected President of the United States of America.

I cannot give you a formula for success, but I can give the formula for failure — which is: Try to please everybody.

Herbert Bayard Swope

The Indispensable Man

Sometime when you're feeling important, sometime when your ego's in bloom. Sometime when you take it for granted you're the best qualified in the room. Sometime when you feel your going would leave an unfillable hole, just follow this simple instruction and see how it humbles your soul.

Take a bucket and fill it with water, put your hand in up to your wrist, take it out -- and the hole that's remaining is a measure of how you'll be missed. You can splash all you please as you enter, you can stir up the water galore, but stop, and you'll see in a minute that it looks quite the same as before.

There's a moral in this quaint expression, just do the best that you can. Be proud of yourself, but remember there is no indispensable man.

(Author Unknown)

The Truly Wise

The man who knows not that he knows not aught --
He is a fool; no light can ever reach him.

Who knows he knows not and would fain be taught --
He is but simple; take thou him and teach him.

And whoso, knowing, knows not that he knows --
He is asleep; go thou to him and wake him.

The truly wise both knows and knows he knows --
Cleave thou to him and nevermore forsake him.

Arabian Proverb

When things go wrong, as they sometimes will, when
the road you're trudging seems all uphill, when the funds
are low and the debts are high, and you want to smile but
you have to sigh, when care is pressing you down a bit --
rest if you must, but don't you quit.

Life is queer with its twists and turns. As everyone of
us sometimes learns. And many a fellow turns about,
when he might have won had he stuck it out. Don't give
up though the pace seems slow -- you may succeed with

another blow.

Often the goal is nearer than it seems to a faint and faltering man; often the struggler has given up when he might have captured the victor's cup; and he learned too late when the night came down, how close he was to the golden crown.

Success is failure turned inside out -- the silver tint of the clouds of doubt, and when you never can tell how close you are, it may be near with it seems afar; so stick to the fight when you're hardest hit -- it's when things seem worst, you mustn't quit.

Author Unknown

Every great improvement has come after repeated failures. Virtually nothing comes out right the first time. Failures, repeated failures, are fingerposts on the road to achievement.

Charles F. Kettering

It is not because things are difficult that we do not dare; it is because we do not dare that they are difficult.

Seneca

I Shall Not Pass This Way Again

I Shall Not Pass This Way Again
Through this toilsome world, alas!
Once and only once I pass;
If a kindness I may show,
If a good deed I may do
To a suffering fellow man,
Let me do it while I can.
No delay, for it is plain
I shall not pass this way again.

Author Unknown

A Bag Of Tools

A Bag of Tools
That princes and kings,
And clowns that caper
In sawdust rings,
And common people
Like you and me
Are builders for eternity?
Each is given a bag of tools,
A shapeless mass,
A book of rules;
And each must make --
Ere life is flown --
A stumbling block
Or a steppingstone.

R. L. Sharpe

Do It Now

If with pleasure you are viewing any work a man is doing,

If you like him or you love him, tell him now.

Don't withhold your approbation till the parson makes oration

And he lies with snowy lilies on his brow;

No matter how you shout it he won't really care about it;

He won't know how many teardrops you have shed;

If you think some praise is due him now's the time to slip it to him,

For he cannot read his tombstone when he's dead.

More than fame and more than money is the comment kind and sunny

And the hearty, warm approval of a friend.
For it gives to life a savor, and it makes you stronger, braver,

And it gives you heart and spirit to the end;

If he earns your praise -- bestow it; if you like him let him know it;

Let the words of true encouragement be said;

Do not wait till life is over and he's underneath the clover,

For he cannot read his tombstone when he's dead.

Berton Braley

"Macho... Does Not Prove Mucho."

My Wage

I bargained with Life for a penny
And Life would pay no more,
However I begged at evening
When I counted my scanty store;
For Life is a just employer,
He gives you what you ask,
But once you have set the wages,
Why, you must bear the task.
I worked for a menial's hire,
Only to learn, dismayed,
That any wage I had asked of Life,
Life would have paid.

Jessie B. Rittenhouse

Breathes There The Man

Breathes there the man with soul so dead
Who never to himself hath said,
This is my own, my native land!
Who heart hath ne-er within him burned
From wandering on a foreign strand?
If such there breathe, go, mark him well;
For him no minstrel raptures swell;
High though his titles, proud his name,
Boundless his wealth as wish can claim,
Despite those titles, power, and pelf,
The wretch, concentred all in self,
Living, shall forfeit fair renown,
And, doubly dying, shall go down
To the vile dust from whence he sprung,
Unwept, unhonored, and unsung.

Sir Walter Scott

Along The Road

I walked a mile with Pleasure,
She chattered all the way,
But left me none the wiser
For all she had to say.
I walked a mile with Sorrow
And ne'er a word said she;
But oh, the thing I learned from her
When Sorrow walked with me!

Robert Browning Hamilton

Code of Conduct

Written in 1858 for the four employees of Carson, Pirie & Company, now Carson, Pirie, Scott & Company, Chicago.

"Store must be open from 6 A.M. to 9 P.M. the year round. Store must be swept; counter base and showcases dusted, lamps trimmed, filled and chimneys cleaned; pens made; doors and windows opened; a pail of water, also a bucket of coal brought in before breakfast (if there is time to do so and attend to customers who call.)"

"Store must not be opened on the Sabbath, unless necessary to do, and then only for a few minutes."

"The employee who is in the habit of smoking Spanish cigars, being shaved at the barber shop, going to dances and other places of amusement, will surely give his employer reason to be suspicious of his integrity and honesty."

"Each employee must pay not less than $5 per year to the church and must attend Sunday school regularly."

"Men employees are given one evening a week for courting and two if they go to prayer meeting."

"After fourteen hours of work in the store, the leisure hours should be spent mostly in reading."

Some of these rules may seem a bit humorous now, but there are lessons in this code for all of us.

Chapter 20

WHAT DO YOU WANT TO BE WHEN YOU grow up, Art?" I was asking myself that question again this morning when it suddenly dawned on me that I am just a few weeks away from yet another birthday. And I realized that I seem to be no closer to that answer than I was as I walked down the aisle of the auditorium with my high school diploma in my hand.

I guess the real answer is that I don't want to grow up. Ever.

Peter Pan explained it to the children when he said, "When you grow up, you lose the magic!"

And Mary Poppins explained it to the Banks twins when she told them that like it or not, they will forget how to talk to the animals as they grow up.

"Up" is too far for me. I just want to grow and to keep on growing as a human being. I want to climb mountains and I'm willing to fall into the depressions time and again and to keep on climbing. I want to write books and to give speeches and I want to try to say everything in a few lines of verse that will touch someone's life.

I want to create songs and musical comedies and to imagine things and write them down on paper and some day I'd like to see some of those imaginings in movies.

"What do you want to be when you grow up, Art?" That is too final for me because if somehow I "lucked out" and became whatever that something was, then there would be no place else to go. Too many become what they set out to become and it is only a fraction of what they might have been.

I see people retiring from what they set out to be and then discover that there is no longer a reason for living.

I want to take a picture some day that will become a classic. It will be on a card that people give to one another. People will hang it on their wall. Something I alone captured with my lens.

I want to write a jingle for a radio and TV commercial that in just 15 seconds will convey a vital message.

Tonight before I go to bed I want to touch just one life. To make living better for just one individual and if I can do that for the next 365 days and then do it for year after year I will have possibly touched the surface of my human potential.

I study happiness and joy. And it occurs to me that it is the journey that provides life's greatest moments and not the arrival. It is the struggle itself that makes you happy and when the struggle is over and the victory won there is but little joy in just reflecting.

And so the key is to give it your best shot every day. And to live every moment with expectation, yes, but to live every moment with awareness of what is going on and savoring moments.

I've met too many people who are an hour or a day or a month ahead of themselves and they are not really doing what they are doing at the time. They are mentally working on the next thing and they miss all the joy of life.

Instead of savoring the applause they are already getting on the next plane to fly to the next engagement. Instead of enjoying the company and friendship of people they meet they are mentally rushing to the next experience. And nothing really happens in their life no matter how successful they become because they are always somewhere else. There is no today for them. Only tomorrow and some new battle ahead, some new foe to conquer, some new peak to climb.

Some time ago I heard a lecture on the total person. And the thought was advanced that man is made up of mind, body and consciousness. And this constitutes a trinity. And the true measure of success is the development of all of these. And if you failed in any of these then you could not be truly successful and happy.

I think of Howard Hughes and no doubt he was brilliant in many ways and by some measures he was the most successful man in America. If wealth is the measure then he excelled. But think of the trinity of Mind, Body and Consciousness.

How did Howard Hughes measure up by this standard? And how did he thrive in the happiness department?

I think of some of the really wonderful and interesting people I've met. Those whom you'd like to spend a whole week with instead of a lunch hour and nearly all of them seem to have worked a total development.

And what do I want to be when I grow up? I want to be eleven feet tall and the only way I can reach that goal is to really help my fellow man. When I do that I feel twelve feet tall.

I want to leap over tall buildings without effort. And I accomplish that feat when I find someone with doubt and with true talent and with my words of hope I lead them to the use of their rare talents. When I see those talents working I can leap tall buildings with the greatest ease.

I want to sing like The Great Caruso and Al Jolson combined. And I sing that way when my words march out in proper order on a sheet of paper and a publisher accepts them and shares them with a reader.

And when I die you can write on my gravestone... "He never grew up. But he never gave up either."

I will try hard to keep on growing. Will you join me?

MR.
UP

"Nothing Happens Until Some-body Sells Something!"

Red Motley,
Parade Magazine

Preface

My telephone still rings with wonderful invitations to speak at special safety meetings. Often it is an invite from a major corporation to do several programs. These are generally sessions for all of their scheduled or hourly employees and then they often share with me special sessions of management people.

Some calls are for meetings with corporate safety teams. And I get invites for Governor's Safety Conferences and state associations for keynote assignments.

Then there are the various safety banquets held by associations or corporations for members and employees.

Over the years I have been invited to 50 states and have been able to accept invitations in all of them.

I've spoken in Nassau, Bermuda, The Virgin Islands, Hong Kong, Malaysia, and the invitations from Europe keep coming in on a regular basis.

And what is it that nearly every planner says to me? It's this: "Art, we want you to bring your special brand of magic to our meeting. Make safety interesting and exciting for our people and renew their enthusiasm and commitment to safety."

What I hear them saying regardless of their words, is this. "Sell them on the importance of safety."

Sometimes the calls are for consulting work. "We'd like to just pick your brain for a day, Art." they say and I am truly flattered.

About once a week I get a phone call from someone who wants to be a professional speaker, just like me, and make a million dollars a year just having fun.

I'd like to figure that one out myself but after a couple of decades of professional speaking I've learned that giving speeches is just the tip of a giant iceberg.

Getting the speeches and preparing the material and pushing your way through crowded airports with over-booked flights is the real challenge in this business.

So I am saying that selling yourself and taking care of the details is the real key to success. And that is exactly what this book says about safety. Selling yourself and selling ideas on safety and taking care of the details is the real key to your success in the safety field.

I truly hope that this book will provide a breakthrough for you in your career. I hope it will serve as a key to a happier, healthier, wealthier future for you and those you love.

If the ideas work for you, then, will you be good enough to write me and tell me about your success? The letters and phone calls I've received from my previous books have provided me with the inspiration to carry on with my writing.

If you try my ideas and they fail you, let me know that, too. Maybe I can give you some direction to make them work for you.

If there is any way that I might be of service to you then just call me at (800) 441-7676. I'm in the people business and if I can help, I'll try.

Art

Chapter 1

SELLING SAFETY TO THE MOST IMPORTANT PERSON

THERE IS AN OLD CARTOON IN MY FILE that shows a railroad section boss meeting with his crew of track laborers and the boss is saying, "Any man who ain't got a hernia just ain't carrying his share of the load."

My background in safety is in the railroad industry and that old cartoon is not as ridiculous as it might seem. Injuries and deaths were a way of life and the cost of a human life was very low as late as the 1940's when I began working in the General Claims Department of the Grand Trunk Western Railroad Company in Detroit.

At that time the railroad had extra gangs out working on the tracks and the "gandis" as they were called--that is, the extra gang laborers--were recruited at a hiring office located on the skid rows of Detroit and Chicago. These men were housed in extra gang camps consisting of a string of outfitted boxcars and they were fed there, too. The contracting company that provided these laborers took about half of their pay for food and a bunk and when they were paid, most of the men would disappear until their money was spent. This was often just the matter of a couple of days.

The men were often mistreated and abused by the track supervisors and foremen. It was not unusual for the body of a dead extra gang laborer to be found near the camp shortly after payday. Generally, the man had been drunk and had fallen asleep on a live track, or in some cases there had been a fight or a murder.

Our personnel director at that time was the son of a former general manager of the railroad and his chief function was to try to get a birth certificate to definitely establish the date of birth of an employee for railroad retirement law purposes. Other than that he simply kept a card on each employee showing the date hired and each successive change of job status.

There were little or no physical exams and no training program. How things changed!

Safety Director -- A Record Keeper

In the later forties we had a safety director too. His primary function was to complete forms on injuries for the Interstate Commerce Commission and for the various State Commissions. He counted the dead and injured.

He made out a report on each injury that resulted in a disability of 72 hours or more. He had no staff. He typed the reports himself. And the mere reporting of the injuries promptly to the various commissions took up just about all of his time. The rest of each day he spent in the hallways complaining about the fact that he had no help.

Now and then our safety director would attend a meeting with other safety people or else read a particularly inspiring article and he would go in to a meeting with his boss and request some help so that perhaps a secretary could make out the reports and he might go into the field and try to do something about the fact that we invariably showed up at the very bottom or second from the bottom of the standings among railroads with regard to accidents.

Sometimes he made requests for safety equipment such as safety glasses, helmets and such, but most of the time he was told that money was not available for such luxuries and within a few weeks he was back to normal, spending his time and efforts in making out the reports to the agencies on time. After all, there was a fine for late reporting. And after all was said and done, the principal job of the Supervisor of Safety was to report accidents. His real title should have been Supervisor of Reporting Accidents.

He had no authority. He had no budget. He had no training. He had no incentive. And he had absolutely no impact on the organization.

Red Motley -- A Selling Legend

Once upon a time a truly great salesperson named Red Motley said this, "Nothing happens until somebody sells something." That idea is vital to what we will be talking about for the remainder of this book. Let me repeat it for you, "Nothing happens until somebody sells something."

Red Motley was responsible for the success of *Parade Magazine.* You've probably seen *Parade Magazine.* It comes along with your Sunday newspaper in most cities. It has a circulation of several million copies each week and Red Motley went out and sold the publication to one newspaper after another until it was a national weekly household item.

Nothing happens until somebody sells something. How true. No idea, no product, no venture ever succeeds until somebody first sells it. And so when we look at the concept of safety, should it seem so strange to us to think that safety must be sold, just like everything else?

In today's business there is a major effort in the United States to sell workers on the importance of quality. With growing foreign competition in so many of our industries, we are also learning of the importance of productivity. Without better quality and increased productivity, America will have a very tough time competing .

Bit by bit, the American worker is being sold on these concepts. It just doesn't make any sense to send your sales force out into the field to tell prospects and customers that your organization is totally committed to excellence and service and performance if they cannot deliver these things to the customer. The minute the customer orders, he learns that the salesperson was only dreaming.

So it is with safety. Just having your corporate president or chief executive officer issue a proclamation that "Safety is of the First Importance," doesn't mean a thing. You and I have seen one organization after another issue such an edict and nothing changed. So let us begin with the acceptance that "nothing happens until somebody sells something." And let us take it a step further and agree that today, Safety most definitely must be sold.

Where Do We Begin?

Now we come to the question, "Where do we begin?"

Who is the most important person in your organization to sell if you expect to have any chance for success at all? Who is the most important person in your organization when it comes to safety?

Take a deep breath. Now walk over to a mirror and take a good look. You are it! The most important person in the world that you can and must sell on safety is yourself.

There is a well known maxim in the sales profession. "You cannot sell anything until you, yourself, are sold."

Even a con man who is selling lies must first convince himself on the truth of those lies before he can sell them. A con man believes. Not that you must become a con man or woman to succeed in the safety profession, but you must become a super salesperson. And the first sale you must make must be on yourself.

You might fail in this mission and if you do, I suggest that you run, not walk, to the person who hired you and tell him/her that you are not suited for a job that requires selling.

Unless you can totally, absolutely sell yourself on the importance of safety, then you will fail. If you can't work yourself into a white hot heat over preventing accidents and saving lives, then forget it. Give the job to somebody else who can make that commitment. Really. Give it up.

THE MOST IMPORTANT PERSON
ME

Go find something that you can dedicate your life to because safety is a tough field. It is a demanding master. You have to be the only gladiator out there on the battle field many times. You will have setbacks, and defeats and before you finish one battle, you will often find you have two more facing you.

You will learn that the monetary returns are not what they should be in many cases too. And if you do your job properly, the glory will most likely go to others. The other people will get the plaques and the awards. The credit, most of the time, must go to others because that is the nature of the job.

If you are one of those people who charge out the door the minute the clock strikes quitting time, then most likely this job is not for you.

I've heard it said that with true professionals, first you get the job and then the job gets you.

I do some of my best work as I lie awake in the early hours of the morning with creative ideas rushing through my mind. I love every minute of it and often I go into the bathroom and turn the light on so that I might capture some of these ideas on paper.

Safety: Not A 40 Hour Job

Safety is really not something you work at for 40 hours and then shut off. Safety people get telephone calls in the middle of the night. Accidents happen on holidays and on birthdays and on wedding anniversaries.

I know. I've been there.

So before you go out to sell anybody else on the importance of safety, first sell yourself. And just selling yourself is not enough. This is something that needs reinforcing every single day of your life.

It is easy for me now, after more than 48 years of involvement with safety. I just have to think back on the visits I've made to hospitals as our employees fought a losing battle for their lives following an accident. I think of the widows and the kids whose husband/father wouldn't be there for them when they needed them. I think of the amputees, of the gruesome scenes I'd visited year after year without end.

Am I sold on safety? With every living bit of my existence.

Are you sold on safety? If not, work on it. Go sit in the emergency room on Friday night in a major city hospital and watch them bring in the victims. That is, if you have the stomach for it.

Ben Franklin's Wisdom

Try the Ben Franklin method of closing as you endeavor to sell yourself on safety. Take two sheets of paper. On one, list all of the reasons why you want to dedicate your life to saving lives and preventing injuries and accidents. On the other sheet list the reasons why not. Unless you can really fill out that sheet in favor so that it absolutely overwhelms the why-not sheet, then look for another job immediately.

Sound tough? Not really. Either sell yourself or get out because unless you sell yourself on safety, then you will be in for a miserable experience. You will fail and anything you attempt in the safety field will fail. And people will die and people will get injured and accidents will happen because you did not go out there, completely sold yourself and make a miracle happen.

Unless you yourself are sold you will soon be just a person who fills out reports and complains in the hallway that you don't have the help or the money or the authority to do a thing.

The world needs people who are passionate about a cause, because when you are, you will succeed and you will make a difference.

Talking about being passionate about the cause of safety, I think about my friend Charlie Simpson who was the manager of safety over at Huntington, West Virginia, with Inco Alloys International, Inc.

You didn't expect Charlie to answer his telephone when you'd call him. You'll nearly always get his answering machine because Charlie is constantly making the rounds at his massive plant. I made the rounds with Charlie one day and discovered that he is one of the most loved men I've ever met. He called everyone we met by their first name and asked about their spouses and kids by name. Charlie lives safety. It oozes out of his pores. And I honestly believe that if you could somehow track it down, you would discover that over the years Charlie has saved a number of lives and prevented hundreds of accidents by his constant efforts on his people's behalf.

I don't believe Charlie is a dying breed. Charlie is retired now, but as I travel around America I find great hope in the young people I meet in the safety field. More and more I am discovering that safety is a very special calling and it is exciting to find young men and women who are hearing that call and dedicating their lives to the safety movement.

Nothing happens until somebody sells something. Nobody sells anything until they are first sold. Are you sold on safety? If so, let's get on with it.

Chapter 2

FIRST COMES THE DREAM

PHILIP B. CROSBY IS KNOWN WORLD-WIDE as one of the top authorities on quality management.

He is best known for "Zero Defects," a quality program used in many organizations. Crosby was corporate vice president and director of quality at ITT for fourteen years.

During the formative years, most of ITT's actions were directed toward dispelling the erroneous beliefs that workers didn't really care about quality.

The concept that they sold was that when managers believe that workers do not care then workers do not care.

Working on group by group, unit by unit, his quality team plowed its way through the entire corporation with

"...FIRST COMES THE DREAM..."
AF
AF
AF
SS CRUISES

its quality philosophy.

Note--they didn't have the chief executive officer issue an edict that quality was of first importance at ITT. They went out and sold the concept unit to unit, team to team, person to person. They helped people understand and believe that it was better and easier and more cost effective to learn to do things right the first time rather than figure a way to fix things after they'd gone wrong.

When they won converts, they enlisted the support of those converts to win others to their cause.

When Quality finally became a way of life at ITT, new managers joining the firm were made to feel that participation in the quality program was routine and expected.

Earlier this week I had a phone call from a secretary of a safety man at a major corporation. She explained that she had seen a copy of my book titled *World's Greatest Safety Meeting Idea Book* and that they had been having terrible safety meetings. "In fact," she explained, "they are a disaster." She went on to say that their safety record was bad and getting worse.

"My boss has to put on the meetings and he hates to put on meetings. People make excuses for not attending. They walk out on him. They sleep and complain and it is really awful."

I asked her more about their safety record and she explained, "I think a lot of it is that the workers want time off and so they get injured." And when I asked her if her boss felt that way too, she said, "He sure does. In fact, when the workers get a little something in their eyes, they want a couple of days off right away just so they can lay around the house."

When I asked her more about their safety meetings she told me that the top safety guy came into their meetings sometimes and talked, but he was boring and arrogant. "He feels that people are lazy and that they get hurt on purpose too."

It just happened that I had been rereading Philip B. Crosby's great book *Quality is Free, The Art of Making Quality Certain,* and his statement was still ringing in my ears. "If management thinks people don't care, then people won't care."

Incidentally, the quality book was a gift from Bill Robinson, a good friend who was a great safety director for Milliken and Company at Spartanburg, South Carolina. Bill did wonderful things there and he is applying many of the principles which produce great quality to the field of safety with outstanding results.

So often we can take concepts that work in one field and adapt them to our safety work with success.

What Kind Of People?

There is an old story that I often use in my speeches. I might have used it in one of my other books, in fact, but I think it applies right here.

There was a man who was moving from one community to another and as he traveled along the road, he stopped at a farm house and he talked with the farmer for a while. He explained that he was moving from the one community to the other and wanted to know what kind of people he might expect to find in the new community.

The old farmer thought for a moment and then he asked the man, "Just what kind of people did you find in your old community?" And the man said they were kind and caring and responsible and that they'd do most anything for you. And then the old farmer thought again for a moment and he said, "Well, I think you will find that the people in the next town are pretty much the same."

And the story goes on to tell that another fellow was travelling along the same road, moving from the one community to the other and he too stopped and asked that farmer the same question. "What kind of people might I find in this next town?" And again the old farmer asked the fellow, "What kind of folks did you find in your last town?" The man explained that the people were hateful and mean and that they went out of their way to make things miserable for him. And the farmer reflected on this for a moment and then he said, "Well sir, I think you will find the folks in this town to be pretty much the same."

Do the people you work with want to work safely and avoid accidents? Are they looking for time off and lazy? Is it really possible to sell a safety program?

Who do you sell first? First you sell yourself on safety. And next you sell yourself the idea that people really will buy into a safety program. You buy the concept that safety can really and truly be of first importance in your organization.

Visualize Your Goals!

Many years ago I learned the process of visualization. Seeing something in my mind's eye. It is a process of imagination. First comes the dream, the spark of an idea. Something flashes into my mind. Perhaps it is the idea for a book or a poem or an article. It is like an electric flash going off in my mind. And if I allow it to, it will go away and be forgotten.

But often, I write the idea down and I work on it. I nurture it. I do some research on it. And often I then let it ripen in my imagination.

First comes the idea. First comes the dream. And then, quite frequently I set a goal.

For instance, when I first began writing I set a goal to become a successful author. At the time I was not sure what the word successful meant but in my mind I felt that if I could have one book published it would truly prove to the world that I had existed.

I often visualize myself as a successful author and I could just see that book on the shelf.

Today, I have a whole shelf full of my books published in various editions, a different language. A total of 43 different books and booklets are represented.

I once visualized creating an album of cassette tapes of my speeches. And today there are a dozen different albums on various topics.

Then I visualized the creation of a video of one of my live presentations. Now we have over fifty videos for sale.

Recently I dreamed of becoming a song writer and already we've produced a CD of my songs.

Every one of these achievements was only a dream to begin with. Just the spark of an idea and we fanned that spark and I visualized the success of that idea in my mind's eye.

Certainly, I worked on each project, and often I had the help and expertise of others.

To achieve the accomplishment of my goals in the field

of videos I had to find the right video producer, a man named Terry Porchert, who shared my dreams.

Fortunately, my dreams coincided with his own dreams and when we created these video series, we each accomplished our own dreams in our own way.

Right now, working on this book, I have a dream. I can just see this new book in my mind's eye. I know its size, I know that it is 6"x9" and it will run approximately 450 pages.

I can see how the four books we are combining will each fit into the overall product and I can visualize readers enjoying the convenience of this new format.

Until I can first see this book in my mind I cannot hope to complete it. First comes the vision.

First comes the dream.

Do you want safety to be of #1 importance at your place? Do you want to save lives? Do you want to reduce the number of accidents and injuries? Do you believe that your people really care about themselves and about each other?

What kind of people did you work with at the last place you worked? Were they lazy and really hoping to get injured so that they could get some time off with pay?

Once while doing some research for a speech that I was giving for the Texas Chemical Council's Safety Seminar in Galveston, I had a few moments to visit with George F. Golden, then Site Safety Coordinator at the Exxon Chemical Americas' plant at Baytown, Texas, where I was conducting a series of safety meetings for all of their employees. I saw a sign in his office that read, "Asking me to overlook a simple safety violation would be asking me to compromise my entire attitude toward the value of your life."

The talk I was planning was on employee orientation and George said something that stuck to my mind. He said that safety was not a priority, it was a value to live by. Priorities change quite frequently. For instance, one client I worked for in North Carolina was rather proud of the fact that they had moved safety up to the #2 priority spot in their organization. Customer service was #1. I asked their CEO if he believed it would be OK to get hurt in the cause of providing great customer service. Of course, he said no.

What George Golden was telling me was that safety does not have a priority number, it is just there above all else as a value you live by.

A pretty exciting concept and no doubt a powerful factor that helped George's plant to set such an outstanding safety record. Yes, they are among the safety superstars I have worked with recently.

I'm sitting here with a smile on my face and a chuckle. Am I overdoing this? Did you get the point? Is it inside your gut? OK. Maybe now you are ready for the visualization process.

Close your eyes and visualize things as they could be. Picture your place just the way you want it to be. Go on an inspection in your mind. See it happening. See the vision of safety reflected in the eyes of your managers and your supervisors and your workers.

Visualize the harmony and the commitment.

Enhance that vision. See how the housekeeping has been done to promote safety. See the signs and the displays. "This plant has gone two years without a disabling injury."

First comes the dream. Then you visualize that dream. Then you set some goals and you develop a program to make those goals a reality.

Can you see it happening in your mind's eye? Until you can you are not truly sold. Work on it every day.

Take a little quiet time early in the morning just before you roll out of bed and think about the dream--the dream of a totally safe environment where every worker is truly dedicated to working safely. Now commit yourself to doing what needs to be done that day to make it all a reality.

Get ready to sell safety. If you are truly sold yourself, then you are ready to begin selling others.

Chapter 3

HOT BUTTONS

I WAS LYING IN BED AT ABOUT 4 A.M. THIS morning--in bed--that is where I do most of my lying. And I was thinking about you, the people who will eventually be reading this book. Who are you?

If you are like the readers of my book titled *The World's Greatest Safety Meeting Idea Book*, Book one in this publication, then you represent just about every level of management and supervision.

I've talked to some top leaders from major corporations and I've talked to secretaries in tiny firms where they were saddled with the responsibility of holding a safety meeting.

They all bought my book and read it hoping it would contain some magic ingredient that would help them to somehow conduct a better safety meeting. Most of them reported that they found what they were seeking within the pages of my tiny book.

I certainly hope and pray that somehow this work too

provides the answers you seek to enable you to sell safety to the people that you work with. If nothing else, I hope that it leaves you with this one idea: Safety must be sold. Nothing happens until somebody sells something.   And when it comes to selling safety, you are the salesperson!

Finding That Hot Button

There is an old story about a second lieutenant in an infantry platoon and he was just out of officer's training school and still wet and dripping behind the ears. The Army had just come out with a life insurance policy and the 2nd lieutenant was assigned the job of selling the enlisted men on the idea of buying the life insurance.

He called the men together and told the fellows what a marvelous investment the insurance was, the incredibly low premium for $10,000 worth of insurance, and what it would mean to their families. He tried patriotism, love, fear--he tried it all--and not one man bought the insurance. Finally, a tough old drill sergeant called the lieutenant aside and told him he was going about the selling all wrong.

The lieutenant was really upset with the sergeant and with the men, but in desperation he finally said to the sergeant,

"OK, sergeant, if you think you know so much, you try it!"

Again the sergeant called the men together and he said simply, "Men, in just a few weeks we are going overseas and we will soon be in combat."

"Now if you buy the insurance and you get killed, then the government gives your folks $10,000. Now if you don't buy the insurance and you get killed, the government doesn't have to give your family anything."

"Fellows, who do you think the government is going to send into combat first?"

Every man signed up for the insurance.

Now in selling you might say that the sergeant had

discovered the right hot button to sell his men. And that is my present dilemma. And that is why I was lying awake in bed this morning thinking about you, the reader, and who you are and at what level you are trying to sell safety. Do you work with managers, supervisors, line people or everyone?

I'm sure you've heard the expression, "Different strokes for different folks."

I don't know exactly what that means but I'd guess it refers to different people's taste in art. Some like modern art; others prefer the old classics. Perhaps it refers to swimming. Some like the back stroke and others are content to dog paddle.

In any event, it refers to the fact that we have different tastes, different dreams, different goals. Different things turn us on . And we have different hot buttons. We often buy the same things for different reasons.

4 Hot Buttons That Work

In my earlier writing years I believed that there were four major reasons that people did things:
 * money or the fear of losing money,
 * romance, love, sex
 * health or self preservation,
 * recognition, glory, pride.

Working from that group of four, I could generally provide the motivation for my fictional characters. And when I wrote non-fiction articles, I could usually find a way to use these "motivators" to slant an article for a particular magazine or specific reader.

If you'll glance through the commercials of a magazine, you'll soon discover that most magazines are slanted toward a specific hot button. Some advertisements appeal to your desire for more money. Others appeal to romance or health and self preservation. Some automobiles are sold strictly on your need for recognition, as are some whiskeys.

Now, how can you sell safety by calling on these four hot buttons?

As I travel around this country and other points of the world and visit plants and refineries and mining operations, I see how others sell safety and I see people pushing these powerful hot buttons everywhere I go.

Sometimes the only way the top management can really be sold on safety is through their pocketbook.

Often organizations pay "lip service" only to safety. They hang up a sign of commitment. And after that, it is business as usual.

The Money Hot Button

When I work for major corporations, they often have me sign a consultant's confidentiality contract. It means that I will not tell secrets out of school. For that reason I might not fill in all of the details you'd like to know about some of the incidents I refer to. I hope you'll understand.

At one client's firm down South, a 21-year-old worker was inspecting something on the machine she was operating and her hand was caught in the machine and she was pulled on into the machine and crushed to death.

The victim was a single parent and the plant manager visited the family of the woman. He tells about the little

18 month old son of the woman sitting in his lap and pleading with his young eyes, "When is my mommy coming home?"

The cost of the workman's compensation claim will amount to approximately $116,000. Then there was life insurance payment of $25,000. The plant functioned at about 20 percent for a week following the accident. All of the workers attended the funeral.

Workers refused to work on the machine involved and others like it. Morale hit bottom. And now months later productivity is still suffering at that plant.

Let's take a look at that accident and let's take a look at the hot buttons. How do we sell safety to that corporation?

Our first hot button is money or the fear of the loss of money.

They tell me that the average corporation in America makes a profit of about 5 percent on sales.

A million dollars in sales produces a profit of $50,000. Just to cover the cost of the funeral, insurance and the workman's compensation alone, that fatality cost roughly $150,000.

It would take $3 million in sales for just that part of the cost. In many states the company might also face a claim or a lawsuit for liability. In many instances, this could often run the cost of the accident to a million dollars for payment of the claims alone. Incidentally, at 5 percent profit, a million dollars demands sales of $20 million.

We haven't talked about the cost of lost production at the plant. In fact, we haven't talked about many other things either.

The Hidden Cost Of Accidents

Here are some of the hidden costs involved in an accident. My thanks to H. L. Boling of Phelps-Dodge for this material.

* Cost of retraining replacements in job.
* Cost of lost production through less experienced employee replacement or area shutdown because of emergency.
* Loss of a positive productive attitude and morale.
* Medical costs.
* Cost of investigation (production people)
* Cost of replacements (hiring, physical, drug screening, safety training, etc.)
* Loss of employee loyalty.
* Cost of absenteeism.
* Loss of a good, reliable employee.
* Cost of added state and federal inspections.
* Cost of overtime coverage.
* Loss of company image.

At a Safety Association meeting in Texas, I had the honor of sharing a platform with Wynne Stewart of Orange, Texas. Wynne is a true safety professional and a star of a video tape series called Take Two For Safety, produced and distributed by DuPont Safety Services, and also of the safety series titled Safety Seconds, produced by Howell Training Corporation of Houston, Texas.

At one point in his powerful presentation, Wynne said that it had been estimated that the real cost of an accident was some eight to ten times the actual cost of Workman's Compensation payments and medical expenses.

Safety just makes good sense. And a great safety program can be a wonderful bottom line investment. Safety doesn't cost--it pays. And if top management doesn't buy into a safety program, they just aren't being realistic or cost-conscious.

A safety program might not bring in cash over the counter tops, but it will enable an organization to keep more of the cash it does generate in sales. Money spent on accidents is profit lost.

If you want to sell top management on safety from a hard-nose-bottom-line-dollars-and-sense viewpoint then get your hands on all the statistics you can garner. Gather some clippings on jury verdicts on industrial injuries.

Get some statistics on actual medical costs for injuries. They will probably amaze you as they do me.

Find out what your organization is paying for accident insurance. It is generally based on accident experience and so every accident results in higher insurance costs.

Remember, knowledge is power. The more facts you have, the better equipped you will be to answer objections when you get into the actual selling process we will be showing you later in this book.

Perhaps you might think that I'm putting a little too much importance on money right now. After all, you just can't put a dollar value on suffering or on a human life.

True. But the fact is, there are many people in corporate life who are blinded to everything but the bottom line.

I have read some pretty good arguments for the fact that the management by objective phase that swept American business in the 80's demanded that managers produced results every reporting period, be it a month or six months or a year, and that there was really no tomorrow, just today. If you didn't produce today, then there would be no tomorrow for you with that organization. And because of that short-term thinking, research and development suffered.

One of our major competitors, Japan, on the other hand, thought on a much longer-term basis. They think in terms of 5 years and 10 years and even longer.

Safety programs often do not pay off in a day or a week or even a year and yet quite often the results are rapid.

If your organization is loaded with bean counters, then you'd better have the beans on the table for them to count.

With employees, money can be an important motivation when it comes to safety. Unsafe workers can lose their jobs. And an injury can disable a worker to the degree that he/she cannot be gainfully employed. Safety makes dollar sense to everyone at every level.

Love As A Motivator

Let's go back to our four basic motivations. Romance and love is our next motivator.

I'm often amazed at the love and concern that workers feel for one another.

The empathy that workers feel for one another is so strong in some cases that they feel the pain of the injured party and suffer the loss. When a worker is killed on the job, there is often a long period of mourning among workers.

Certainly the love of one's family is a powerful reason

for workers to work safely.

I have met and talked with enough owners and chief executive officers from large and small organizations to be firmly convinced that most of them truly have a feeling of concern and love for their employees. Sometimes, some of them have a peculiar way of showing it, perhaps, but I truly believe that love can be a strong, determining factor in selling safety.

I hope that it is a strong force in your life and your motivation. If you really care for and care about and seek to know and understand the people you work with and the people you strive to serve, then to me that is loving and love can pull you through an awful lot of trials and heartaches.

That Self-preservation Motivator

Self preservation and health are our next hot buttons.

Anybody who will tell you that workers want to get hurt because they are lazy will tell you a lot of other things too.

I don't believe that people really want to get hurt; that is, not anyone in their right mind.

Now, I'm not implying that everyone you meet in this business is in his/her right mind.

I once investigated a claim where I became convinced that the man had intentionally put his leg on a railroad track so that the train would cut it off.

He did it and then applied a tourniquet. He hopped to his car and drove himself to the hospital and then he hired a lawyer and sued our railroad.

I became obsessed with that case and spent months piecing the man's entire life together, shred by shred.

In the trial, a doctor stated that the man suffered from Osteo Myelitis and that he had recommended amputation of the leg just a few days prior to the alleged accident.

The man claimed he was walking down the street and his foot became caught in the wooden planking over the railroad tracks. He claimed he screamed and waved his arms at the engineer of the oncoming train but that the engineer ignored him and the train passed over his entrapped leg and severed it and the engineer did not even have the decency to then stop the train and come back and give him assistance.

As near as I could put the thing together, I believe the man planned the whole thing. I think he hid behind a signal box as the train approached. Then after most of the train had passed he scooted himself toward the track with his leg going onto the rail and a wheel then passed over the leg, cutting it off.

The jury did not believe the man and found in the railroad's favor.

In a couple of other instances I met with professionals who made a living getting hurt. In both instances I was able to have them arrested and they plead guilty to offenses and were jailed.

These are rare, rare instances drawn from the thousands of claims that I handled over a twenty-five year career.

Oh, there were obvious suicides, many of them. But very few employees try to kill themselves on the job at least in a manner that is made to appear as an accident.

Most accidents that result in injuries are really accidents. True, some people seem to be accident prone, but most of these have psychological problems.

Most people have a really strong desire for self-preservation. They do not want to get hurt and they do not want others to get hurt.

Safety can be sold by appealing to people's desire for self preservation.

"Obey the safety rules and stay alive."

Corporations and their officers also feel a strong desire to keep their organization alive and well. Losses incurred from accidents can act as a plague on the financial good health of an organization.

A great safety program is like a powerful preventive medicine in an organization.

Recognition As A Hot Button

Our fourth hot button or motivator is recognition. People just love to be recognized. Corporations love it too. And so do I.

A while back our United Parcel Service delivered to me a package from the American Bookdealer's Exchange in LaMesa, California.

It was a beautiful plaque announcing that my Three Robot series of books had been voted "The A.B.E. Best Self Published Book of the Year in the Children's Category."

It is a beautiful walnut plaque with a clear plastic cover and the text was typeset on parchment -like paper.

I purchase such plaques for much less than $15 each in quantity. In fact, the entire award probably cost less than $15 including shipping, but to me, it is priceless.

My children's books and my work with children and schools to help kids build a positive self image is my hottest hot button.

I wouldn't trade that award for a thousand dollars or ten thousand either. As I said, to me it is priceless.

Recognition is a hot button that should never be overlooked in selling safety. Establish a program of rewards and recognition.

I have a friend at one of the largest public relations firms in America. Their firm goes out of its way to win recognition and awards for their clients. In fact, they go so far as to enter the various work that they do for each client in a variety of competitions. Often there are so many categories available that there exists practically an "everybody wins" environment.

With enough prizes and enough competitions, it just takes a little ingenuity and persistence to come home with some sort of a first prize for a client.

Then much ado is made in presenting the award to the client. Electronic flashes explode, a story appears in the local press and the client is thus reassured that the enormous fee that this top P.R. firm charges them each month is money well spent with the best.

Does all that sound silly to you? Well, most of us are very vain creatures and the truth is that far too many of us get far too little recognition or awards in our lifetime and for that reason a little award now and then goes a long, long way.

So now you just might have a better idea of what hot buttons are.

It is too soon to start pushing them yet though. First we'd better determine whose button we want to try to push first.

Where does safety start? From the bottom up or from the top down? Or does it start in the middle and creep both up and down?

Safety Begins With You!

Take an index finger and point it out. Point it up. Point it down. Now take a good look at your hand. I first saw a great speaker named Zig Ziglar give this demonstration. When you point your finger at somebody take a good look. Generally you have three fingers on that same hand pointing right back at yourself.

Like I said before. In the game of safety you are it. No matter who you are or what you do, safety begins with you!

Chapter 4

SPEAKING FOR SAFETY
AND FOR SUCCESS

E'VE TALKED EARLIER ABOUT THE fear people have of public speaking. I hope you have already done some of the things we've suggested.

Many managers feel dread making a simple presentation or proposal to a small management group.

Now I'm going to tell you something you just might not like to hear. I sincerely believe that you cannot become a truly great safety salesperson until you learn to speak well. You must learn to organize your ideas and present

SAFETY!
WOW!
...THAT GUY KNOWS HOW TO COMMUNICATE!...
...I CAN CERTAINLY UNDERSTAND HIM!...
....HE MAKES SENSE!...

them in a manner that brings conviction. And you must learn to speak with the top brass of your organization and with every level of management and employee in your organization in an effective manner.

Remember earlier in this book when I told you about the phone call I received from a secretary at a major corporation? She said that now and then the top safety man of their organization would visit their safety meetings but he was arrogant and ineffective.

Perhaps that same fellow was humble and dynamic when he was making a presentation to the top brass but when he spoke to the troops, he had a superiority attitude that turned the people off. Who knows? Maybe he was just scared and overly defensive.

Probably the reason he visited their meetings only occasionally was that he dreaded the occasions and found ways to avoid them.

How would you rate your ability to speak in public? How are you at making formal proposals? Do you feel equipped to walk into a board room and sell an entire safety campaign?

Steps To Proficiency In Speaking

Over the past twenty-five years, we figure that I have given over 4.000 professional presentations. Who knows just how many non-professional presentations I have made. There were a lot of them, believe me.

In high school, I was such a basket case of low self-esteem that I could not stand up in front of the class and read a simple paragraph. As the saying goes, I couldn't lead a group in silent prayer.

I was always a joker and I loved to tell people stories on a one-to-one basis but when it came to standing on my feet, I clammed up with fear.

Then in 1960 I signed up for a public speaking course put on by the Gabriel Richard Institute, sponsored by the Christophers. Perhaps you have heard of the Christophers. Their motto is "It is better to light one little candle than to curse the darkness."   I was terrified when I walked into that first class but there was some comfort in the fact that everyone in the class appeared just as terrified as I.

A dozen weeks later I was participating in a city-wide speech contest. I believe that I took third place in a field of three.

As I recall it, first place went to a Hispanic who could barely speak English.

The course gave me the courage to make a speech to my boss asking for a raise and reciting all of the reasons why I was entitled to it.

That day I received a $25-a-month increase. Not too long after that I was promoted.

Take Experience Where You Find It

Probably the best speaking experience I ever received was as Monday night chairman for our local Alcoholic Anonymous group. On Mondays we would often have new visitors who had decided over the weekend that just maybe they were now qualified to join our organization.

I felt like a missionary and I wanted so desperately to share the joy that AA had brought into my life and so, as chairman, I would conduct that meeting with real gusto.

I don't know just how many lives were changed

cause of my efforts, but I do know that it was one of the most rewarding experiences I have ever had.

Later, my wife Ruthie talked me into volunteering for the first Leila Hospital Follies in our community.

A hospital follies is a unique experience. A professional theatrical director comes into your community with music and costumes and a rough script and in the matter of a few days, he or she rehearses local talent and other hopefuls into an organized cast that performs for an audience of several thousand.

Since it was the first such program in our community, few men volunteered and being desperate for bodies, I was given a spot in nearly every number.

I opened the show as M.C. and within 30 seconds someone came on stage and shot me and I fell dead. The show was loaded with such blackout skits and I was in many of them. I sang with a trio and danced with a chorus. I was often going off stage with one group, running behind the stage as I tore off one costume and put on another and then I'd come back on stage from the other side.

I was awful. I couldn't sing. I couldn't dance and the show was a semi-disaster but we raised a lot of money for some hospital equipment that saved lives and they have had bigger and better hospital follies each year since then.   The first follies was my last follies but that one follies had done its job. I was hooked. I knew for certain that I liked the sound of applause.

A Mentor Changed My Life

My next experience with public speaking was when our railroad hired a Notre Dame professor named Herbert G. True, Ph.D.

Herb changed my life. He was a top-rated professional speaker. He wore a referee's costume and used slides.

He absolutely blew my mind. He was funny and he whizzed powerful exciting new ideas past my mind so quickly that I couldn't catch half of them.

We began a friendship that afternoon that continues today. I started writing speech material for Herb and then one day I decided that I'd like to become a speaker myself.

Why am I reciting my life story for you in a book about selling safety?

Because I want to show you that until I learned to speak effectively, nothing important in my career really happened. Public speaking was the key to nearly all of the success I've had in my career. It doubled and tripled and quadrupled my earnings and my influence and unless you are willing to pay the price demanded to improve your speaking skills, you should not expect to find the success you are seeking in the field of safety.

Toastmasters Helps

Once I decided that I would learn to speak effectively, I joined our local Toastmasters' club.

Toastmasters is an international organization that has touched the lives of millions.

Located in most cities in America, the clubs generally meet weekly and members have the opportunity to get up on their feet and speak.

Members receive speech manuals with a series of challenges and they work on such things as vocal varieties, gestures, speech structure, and many, many other things.

More than anything else, a Toastmasters' club gives you the opportunity to set some goals and get on your feet on a regular basis.

I started right in with a goal that within one year I would be making professional speeches. Most Toastmasters have no desire to speak professionally. They simply seek to improve their ability to speak publicly.

As a part of my plan, I overdid everything. For vocal varieties I whispered and I shouted. For gestures I threw things on the floor and I physically pulled people out of their seats. I volunteered every week to do a seven minute speech and most weeks I was given this opportunity.

Before the year was up, I landed an opportunity to speak at the Michigan Safety Conference in the railroad section. I received a standing ovation and our vice president was in the room that day.

That speech was one of the determining factors when I later sold our company on giving me my own department to use my talents to prevent injuries and improve our employees' attitudes toward the company.

My ability to speak in public changed my job and my life. I learned to walk into a small gathering of employees to tell a joke and to sell a safety idea.

I learned to stand in front of the top officers of the company and to sell an idea.

I read every book I could get my hands on that had to do with selling or public speaking. I started giving speeches at Lion's Clubs and Rotaries and Kiwanis Clubs. I led the children's singing at a Christmas party.

I made up my mind that I would never attend a meeting without at least saying something. This was not my nature at first. I would have preferred sitting safe and silent but I forced myself to speak up and I did my darndest to say something intelligent that added to the meeting.

To Sell -- Speak Up

There. That's enough. I think I've made my point. Nobody sells anything until they speak up.

The most powerful skill that you can develop for success in your career is your ability to speak.

The second most powerful skill that you can develop is your ability to shut up and listen.

Speaking is not a gift; it is a learned skill. It is something that comes with practice and study.

To learn how to speak, you must get up on your feet and sound off at every opportunity.

Listen to tapes on a daily basis too. Listen to the speeches of great public speakers again and again.

After a dozen hearings you will begin to notice things you overlooked before.

I'm still seeking and learning new things everyday. After twenty-five years as a professional public speaker I am still experimenting and growing.

If you don't know where to start, then start with a speaking course.

Do not, let me repeat that, do not take a course where you do not have at least one opportunity every class to get on your feet and speak.

Join a Toastmasters' Club and volunteer and participate at every meeting. Set some definite goals and stick to them. Go right on through the formal speeches. And have the courage to be a little far out.

Whisper and shout and throw things on the floor and try something new each session.

Don't play games with yourself. Everyone has a degree of fear when it comes to public speaking. That is the reason why you will be such an outstanding, successful safety person as you master this skill.

You will be way ahead of the crowd as you develop your ability to communicate effectively.

Speakers are leaders, and safety speakers sell safety at all levels. They prevent accidents and they save lives.

Chapter 5

ADDING ON THE BENEFITS

THE SCALES OF SELLING. HAVE YOU EVER heard the expression "stacking the odds in your favor?" Or what about "piling it on.?"

For a moment I want you to envision in your mind the scales of justice.

Picture the goddess of justice with scales in her hand and there is a balancing scale with two trays. On these trays one is to place the evidence in a case. The goddess of justice is blindfolded. Her own prejudices must not enter into the evaluation.

Now I want you to imagine that on one of the trays we have already placed a number of factors that will enter into your efforts to sell safety.

That tray holds a weight we will call "the status quo."

SCALE
BENEFITS

Another, "It isn't in the budget." And how about, "We're not doing so badly?" Let's add a little "Indifference," some downright "Laziness" and a bit of "Bad past experiences."

Add whatever ingredient you might think of that might stand in the way of your selling your safety program.
Ok, have you stacked the scale against yourself? Fine.

Now you know just what kind of a sales job you have ahead of you.

It is now your job to present evidence that will dramatically outweigh all that we've piled up on that tray. We must present so much positive evidence and testimony that we will overwhelm the opposition.

Selling is the simple process of making the prospect want something so badly that they will gladly give up their hard earned money or their previous beliefs to receive the services or products or benefits which you offer in return.

Selling -- Convincing Others Benefits Are Worthwhile

When you sell safety, in reality, you convince people that the price they must pay in time and effort and commitment is well worth the benefits they will receive from the reduction of accidents and injuries and all that goes with disaster.

Every year I'm invited to make presentations for top sales organizations. One of the points I always try to make is that most potential buyers are not concerned with features. Buyers are concerned with benefits.

Sell The Benefits

For instance, a buyer of a safety helmet isn't concerned or thrilled with the exact density of the material in that helmet. That is a feature. Those who will be wearing a safety helmet are concerned that it will keep a falling object from bashing their brains in. That is definitely a benefit.

It is good to mention features but every time you speak of a feature, you must follow up with the benefit which that feature provides.

I teach salespeople to repeat in their minds again and again the expression, "It has and that means. It has and that means".

It is another way of answering the question, "So what?"

Years ago I knew a safety glasses salesman who carried a glass eye in his pocket. He would ask prospects, "Would you like to get your safety glasses today and wear them, or would you rather get a glass eye?"

It has--"that means".

Our safety glasses will provide the protection to prevent an eye injury. And that means you won't be buying one of these glass eyes later on.

Assume Responsibility For Results

I'd like you to develop a set of broad, broad shoulders because I am about to ask you to bear a heavy, heavy load.

I'd like you to assume a great deal of responsibility in this process of selling.

I'd like you to acknowledge the fact that from now on,

whenever anybody does not buy your idea or your program or your suggestion on whatever, the reason that they did not buy is your fault, not theirs. There are no more stupid, idiotic, bull-headed, closed-minded, bug-eyed ignoramus in this world. There are simply the ill-informed and unenlightened group of prospects out there that you haven't done an adequate job of presenting to. You simply have not as yet presented your case for safety in the proper manner to them as yet. But you will. You can lay odds on it, you will.

When people say no to you, they are simply saying, "You have not as yet presented sufficient evidence to tilt the scales in your favor." And this is your signal to lay it on and even take a different approach to that same goal.

Testing Your Understanding

Now let's see how much you've learned about features and benefits. I will name the features; you name the benefits. My new cordless phone has a 10 number memory and that means... My deluxe 20-inch stereo color TV has a 28-key remote control and that means... Your 6 head Hi-Fi stereo VHS, VCR with MTS has an on screen display and that means... This all-new, 7-quart, 16-piece electric wok set has a non-stick interior and that means...

I think you get the idea. Features. Benefits. Yes, selling is discovering what people want, what benefits they are seeking and then just giving it to them.

Selling is putting enough evidence on the scales to tilt the prospect's thinking over to your point of view.

Chapter 6

SUBCONSCIOUSLY SPEAKING

MANY READERS WILL PROBABLY NOT accept what I am about to say. It will be beyond their current level of understanding. Frankly, it is beyond my total understanding too, but that does not keep it from working.

I'm talking about using my subconscious mind on a conscious level. I use my subconscious mind to solve problems. I've done it for many years and most of the time the technique works.

When I am working on a book or an article or a speech or whatever and I get stuck on something and the idea I need for the solution I am seeking eludes me, I simply consciously turn it over to my subconscious mind for an answer.

LISTEN TO ME, HUBERT.... THIS IS YOUR SUBCONSCIOUS BEAMIN' AT YA!.... THINK VISUALIZATION!.... THINK INJURY-FREE!! SUCCESS!...
DO NOW!
URGENT!
THE SAFETY DIRECTOR
QUIET!

I tell my subconscious exactly what the problem is and I ask for a solution and I then promptly forget the problem.

Creative Use Of The Subconscious

Years ago I wrote a fiction serial for a magazine called *Archery World*. I had a fictional character I called Charlie Angus and Charlie was a walking disaster.

Month after month I would take Charlie through one adventure after the other and often I would write him into a position of impending doom that even I could not rescue him from. Whenever this occurred, I would simply turn the challenge over to my subconscious just before I went to sleep at night. Almost always, the next morning I would awake, go up to my writing room, put my hands on my old typewriter and write Charlie out of his dilemma. Nearly always it worked.

You see, the subconscious mind works for you 24 hours a day. When you give it a challenge, the subconscious works on it constantly while you consciously go on to other things. It is like a computer churning away for you seeking the right solution.

Identifying Our Prospects

Now you might recall that I shared with you the fact that I was lying awake at four o'clock in the morning recently trying to figure out just who the reader of this book might be.

I was concerned with what level and what degree of authority they might be functioning from. Well I recently turned that challenge and concern over to my subconscious mind and early this morning as I climbed out of bed I had one of those flashes that in the field of creativity we call an "A-HA!"

Frankly, I think an A-Ha is just a charge of excitement that you feel when the subconscious mind is making a conscious delivery.

This morning the answer to my question came to me. "It makes no difference where the reader is. A great safety movement can begin at any level."

Now at first exposure that might not appear to you to be a life-changing, earth-shaking statement. "It makes no difference where you are in your organization right now. You can make a difference. You can be the instrument of change for the better in your organization. You can be the driving force that will prevent accidents and injuries and save lives."

The statement might not seem that powerful to you but to me it was the answer I was seeking. It solved my problem and once again my subconscious mind had come through for me. I came to realize and believe that what I am saying in this book can be used effectively by anyone at any level in an organization.

When I spoke for a dozen different audiences at Exxon Company, USA at Baytown, Texas, my hosts were Jeff McClure and Herman Williams. I really discovered how safety crosses all lines and barriers. These fellows are shift workers at the refinery and yet they have as much clout as anyone I have ever met in the safety profession. It was obvious throughout our visit that their total commitment to safety was shared by everyone we met with, from the plant superintendent to the fellow sweeping the floors. Both of these men were on special assignments from their regular jobs to devote their full time to safety.

It is visits like this one, where we met with people from all levels of labor and management, that convince me anyone can make an important difference anywhere when the commitment is strong enough. It was a real joy spending time with these people. Their spirit of safety is catching.

Safety Begins With You

A great safety movement can begin with anyone.

You can make the difference, and you will if you put your mind to it.

So while you're at it, why not put all facets of your mind to the project, both your conscious mind and your subconscious. It is a fantastic tool.

Do you realize that you can actually program your mind for success?

You can program yourself to be happier and healthier and a lot more successful than you have ever imagined.

Long before I found any success at all as a writer, I was a successful writer in my own mind.

And long before I found any recognition as a speaker, I programmed my subconscious mind to find ways to success for me.

Using Positive Affirmations

I use daily affirmations to program my mind and right now I have told my mind that I am the #1 professional speaker in the world in the field of safety. I tell myself that fact a number of times every day. I repeat that statement again and again and I close my eyes and visualize myself speaking at safety meetings all over the world.

I visualize editors of magazines calling me for quotes on safety matters. I see myself working for all of the major corporations and associations in the world.

One thing about the subconscious mind: it doesn't know if you are telling it the truth or not. If you keep on feeding the data in, it will accept it and it functions on the data it receives.

How am I doing with this #1 professional speaker in the world in the field of safety campaign?

I'm beginning to believe it and to accept it as a fact and so are others.

The major corporations and associations in America are calling me for speeches.

I've had calls from half a dozen safety publications in the past 30 days for interviews or permission to use something I have written on safety.

Any successful venture first starts as a dream or an idea in someone's head and you can most definitely become the #1 force in safety in your organization. After all, there is probably no one else around with that dream.

Start today with a dream. Now turn it into a definite goal. Visualize it as an accomplished fact. Start telling yourself that you are the strongest force in your entire organization in the field of safety. Tell it to yourself early in the morning and late at night.

Begin a lifetime quest for self improvement. Turn off the TV and start to read and to learn your craft.

Remember, the road to the top is not that difficult because there are very few who are willing to pay the price for success.

Serving Is The Key

The key to success is serving--serving others--and that is the true key to happiness in this world, too.

You can make a difference in this world and within your organization in the area of safety. You can be a shaker and a mover who makes great things happen.

Visualize it. Write it down. Start an intensive continuing learning program. Make a commitment, an uncompromising commitment to safety.

In Hawaii, I met a man who is one of the most outstanding safety people I have yet encountered.

His name is Pat Conroy and he is manager of risk control for King and Neel Inc. in Honolulu.

Pat is responsible for the safety programs of some five hundred firms in Hawaii and he takes a personal interest in every one of those organizations.

Pat's background is with the United States Air Force, where he was selected as top safety person by the Air Force.

I studied Pat for about a week when I was in Honolulu doing safety seminars and a banquet speech in the construction industry. I was trying to pick out just one thing that made Pat such a super star. I know about his outstanding record, how he has cut the number of injuries in nearly every firm he has worked with, but I was trying to discover the reason why he was so successful.

Finally it all boiled down to the word "service." Pat was not in it for the money or the glory or for anything else. He simply wanted to serve his clients.

That seems to be Pat Conroy's mission every day and it works.

Service really is the key to improving your safety record. It also happens to be the key to enjoying your work. Pat Conroy loves what he's doing.

Chapter 7

YOU'VE GOT TO HAVE A GIMMICK

ALWAYS A LADY.

Many years ago I saw a Broadway play called *Gypsy*. The play was based on the life of a famous lady of the burlesque theatre named Gypsy Rose Lee.

In one of the most talked about musical numbers of Broadway theatre, a group of tough looking strippers do a number in which they explain to Gypsy that to succeed in burlesque strip tease, a girl had to have a gimmick.

Gypsy decided that she would dress, walk and strip in a very lady-like fashion and in burlesque at that time, it was indeed a unique gimmick.

I believe that to sell safety you also need a gimmick. In fact, you need a series of ongoing gimmicks to keep safety fresh and alive and on the minds of every worker every day.

The misadventures of Joe No-No, number 1.

I'm not sure that I like the word gimmick. It sounds a bit dishonest or something to me. But safety is tough to sell unless you can find a unique manner in which to promote it.

Joe No No -- The Bad Example

As I mentioned earlier, when I worked for the railroad, I suppose the best gimmick I developed was the role of Joe No No.

Joe No No was the fictional, stumbling, fumbling idiot who had broken every safety rule we had. We finally fired him just to make it clear that you simply could not act that way and remain alive or remain on the job.

Every year I attend a half a dozen trade shows looking for gimmicks.

I love to find inexpensive items which can somehow be used to promote the idea of safety.

Just recently I spent four hours at an exhibit in Chicago and I must have looked at more than 10,000 different items.

I have a friend named Pete Bol and Pete and I attend these shows together. We love to explore new ideas.

Sometimes the exhibitors will give us a sample or two or we might actually buy a sample if it really appeals to us.

I found two things that I could not resist. One was a hologram. A hologram is an image created by illuminating an object with laser light. All of the three dimensional characteristics of that object are recorded when the laser light reflects from the object to a piece of holographic film. The film is then specially processed to enable ordinary white light to recreate a most realistic three dimensional picture. You've no doubt seen a hologram in the form of an eagle on a Visa credit card. Well, I found a hologram of a human eye. Somehow I believe this might be used to prevent an eye injury. The idea is hibernating in the back of my mind.

De-pin Idea Is Born

The other thing I found was a dozen safety pins pinned together. The sales rep explained to me that safety pins were sold by the gross, that there were twelve pins of various sizes pinned together and that was considered one item.

To purchase pins from that company, I'd have to buy a case which was fourteen gross. That is fourteen gross of a dozen pins. A gross, as you probably recall from school, is 144. Fourteen gross comes to 2,016 sets. With twelve in a set you multiply 2,016 by 12 and you get a grand total of 24,192 pins.

Now what would anyone in their right mind do with 24,192 pins? Well, who said anything about anybody being in their right mind? I said that great safety sales people have to have a gimmick. Well, they have to have guts too. I ordered fourteen gross of a dozen safety pins. I had, what I believe to be, the foundation of a great safety gimmick.

I returned to my office the next morning with my one little set of a dozen safety pins and the realization that I'd soon receive that package of pins.

I told my subconscious mind that we had a challenge. Later in the day the idea flashed into my conscious mind.

It said, "Safety De-Pins on Me."

I made a rough card about the size of a business card and wrote out that idea. "Safety De-Pins on Me."

I showed it to a dozen friends during the next day and they all wanted to keep it. I discovered that nobody can ever find a safety pin when they need one and so they wanted the pins.

I knew I was on the right track.

Next I worked on a different project and it was based on the idea that we must look out for one another if we wanted a safer world to live in. I looked at my pins and the card and I changed it to say, "Safety De-Pins on Us."

Now I had a card and a way to use the pins. We could distribute them at safety meetings to all attendees.

A Business Card

I'd use it as a business card. I could quickly go through a couple of thousand of these--and yet I was not satisfied at all.

I told my subconscious mind that this safety pin con-cept could be a whole lot more and I challenged myself and my mind to make it better.

I started to play the game, "What If."

What if we gave employees the cards with De-Pins on them and encouraged the workers to wear one pin on their shirt or blouse or jacket or whatever on Mondays for the next month.

Monday would be De-Pin day. And if someone asked them why they wore De-Pin they could answer. "It's to remind me that safety De-Pins on us."

Now I didn't spend 35 years working with employees

...at
COMPANY NAME
OR LOGO HERE
SAFETY
DE-PINS
ON
US!

DE CARD
NAME
DEPARTMENT
PHONE

SAFETY DE-PINS ON US!
YOUR INFORMATION HERE

DE-PRIZE

without realizing that this idea would not work unless you gave the employees some reward or some reason to wear that pin on Mondays.

I decided to come up with an incentive award for wearing the pin and explaining correctly why it was worn.

I figured that the safety committee could hand out ball point pens as a reward.

I started playing with the idea in my mind. Monday is De-Pin day.

You wear De-Pin and you win the pen. After a couple of repetitions it became -- "You wear De-Pin and you win De-Pen."

I decided to buy ball point pens that read, "Safety De-Pens on Us."

Well and good. But not great.

People will do just so much for a ball point pen. Why not something else?

Why not a drawing for a grand prize among those who won De-Pen?

I came up with De-Card. When you wear De-Pin you win De-Pen. And you fill out De-Card to be eligible for De-Drawing for De-Prize.

We made a sign to hang on a really great compact stereo with CD player; then I added a half dozen CD's. The sign read "De-Prize."

De-Pins. De-Pens. De-Card. De-Drawing. De-Prize.

Cost? A quarter or so for pins. A half dollar for each pen. A few hundred dollars or so each week for De-Prize.

Certainly less than the cost of just the medical treatment for a fairly minor injury.

A Growing Incentive

One safety director I know believes in sweetening the pot each month. When his people work a full month without an injury he awards De-prize. When they go two months he doubles up and awards two prizes. Three months bring three prizes and there is nothing he likes better than awarding twelve prizes on the twelfth month of injury free reporting.

Another safety person I know gives cash prizes, increasing them in increments of $25 each month when the entire company works without a lost time injury. In the second month he makes a private deal with the supervisors so that they receive double the amount in a second drawing.

How did it work? He went from 40 lost time injuries to none.

Costly? Not really. You see, this man represented an insurance broker and at the end of the twelve month period he had the joy of giving the client back a $150,000 rebate on their insurance policy.

The Idea Grows

I showed my "De-Pin" idea to a safety director for a major corporation.

He gave the cards and pins and the idea to the top managers at a meeting and he called me yesterday. The chairman of the board of his corporation wanted 30 cards and sets of pins for their board of directors meeting.

I showed it to another organization and they called for permission to write up the whole campaign in a newsletter that goes out to 4,500 safety people.

I showed it to my son Dan and he asked me for a box of pins, the artwork for the cards and sign, the phone number of the pen company.

Now some people will look at the pins and the card and say, "That's corny," or "That's really stupid," or maybe they will scoff and say, "Is that the best you can do?"

They will never ever give you a better idea. They will simply try to shoot you down.

Just remember, the purpose of a gimmick is to remind people to work for safety on a daily basis.

How do you sell safety? Any way you can to everyone you meet, every day.

You sell safety with De-Pins and De-Pens and De-Cards and De-Drawings and De-Prizes and whatever else it takes to get people's attention and remind them that truly, safety De-Pins on Us!

CHAPTER 8

BEAN COUNTING AND SELLING SAFETY

HAVE A CONFESSION TO MAKE. I HAVE never been overly fond of two groups, accountants and lawyers.

At one time I had a boss who was both a C.P.A. and a lawyer. He was the most obnoxious man I have ever encountered. His name is available on request.

For a long time I was convinced that accountants had no emotions. And I still firmly believe that many lawyers have no scruples.

So much for my prejudices. I told you this only to give even greater credence to what I am about to suggest. Certainly, I would never suggest that you have anything

Show 'em Numbers...

at all to do with a lawyer. It is the accountant I have in mind.

To sell safety in a "bottom line" business climate, you will need to become handy with numbers as well as with statistics, costs and projections.

Saving Dollars Makes Sense

If you cannot sell your management on becoming involved in safety and preventing accidents and avoiding deaths and injuries because it is the right and the only decent thing to do, then, just maybe, you will be forced to take out your calculator and your computer printouts and prove that safety not only makes good sense but it produces bottom-line profit dollars for your organization in the form of savings.

The horrendous cost of medical expenses added to the costs of workman's compensation and liability insurance coupled with the exorbitant fees charged by lawyers makes accident prevention one of the best investments your organization can make today.

I have been known to poke fun at accountants and call them bean counters, but after a number of experiences speaking for accountants, I've discovered that they often make warm and wonderful audiences and on a one-to-one basis they are pretty remarkable people.

I still don't like lawyers, but that could change, maybe.

From Accountant To Safety Director

Just recently I spoke for an organization and when I had a few moments with the director of safety, I asked him that question which often produces a remarkable response. "How did you happen to get your job?"

I sat back and listened. He'd graduated from college as an accountant and had gone to work in the accounting department. One job led to another and then one day, out of the blue, he was offered the job as Director of Safety. He was an excellent manager and they felt he could do the job.

He more than exceeded their hopes. And I asked him about how he kept track of their results.

"Do you have a computer program to keep track of how you're doing?" I asked.

The question worked every bit as well as the fabled "open sesame."

He reached into his drawer and showed me a stack of reports and statistics that would make your hair curl.

I asked him about keeping track of costs and it was all there--month by month, year by year, department by department.

He had it all at his fingertips--a comprehensive track on the whole company and just what was happening when and where and to whom and that led to a pretty good answer to the why of accidents.

Who? What? Where? When? Those answers come fairly quickly following an accident but when you can get down to the why and discover the real why to an accident or a series of accidents, then just maybe you can take the action that will prevent that next accident.

Tracking Accidents To Prevent Them

At the National Safety Congress I talked to hundreds of safety people from organizations of every size and they represented a wide variety of businesses.

One fellow told me that he had developed a computer program that enabled him to track just about any why that could come up. "I can track an accident down to the specific tool an employee was using at the time of the accident," he told me. "I can track it down to the foreman in charge." He explained that often by studying data, he could pinpoint a problem and zero in on it to prevent a future accident.

In Hawaii, my friend Air Force Technical Sergeant Greg Hansen is a true safety professional and he combined his safety expertise with his genius for computers. Greg's goal was to reduce the time Air Force safety people spent on paper work so they could spend more time in the field where the real safety action is.

By using computer technology, Greg eliminated a lot of the time consuming red tape involved so people can get on with the business of saving lives.

Numbers Represent People

One warning: Never, never forget that those numbers in those computer reports represent people. They are a recording of torn flesh and blood and pain and suffering. Please, never become a desk reporter. Don't become an uninvolved bean counter. Get out there in the field every week and press the flesh. Shake hands, slap shoulders. And most importantly, listen.

Whenever your safety statistics start to show signs of trouble, the first statistic to look at is the one that tells you how many hours you've spent in the field with others who are involved with people.

People can blow a lot of smoke in written reports but when you take the time for some real hands-on visiting, you will be rewarded with a much better feeling for what is really happening.

Numbers can work wonders in your safety program. They can be turned into charts to clarify exactly what progress you are making in your organization.

They can show you where the money is going, where and when and how too.

But remember, the why often boils down to people and attitudes and too often the real reason for an accident doesn't show up in a statistic. You have to do a one-on-one to dig for the real problem.

Chapter 9

SAFETY ON CAMPUS

LAST NIGHT WAS FANTASTIC. I SPOKE for a packed room of students at Lake Superior State University located at Sault Ste. Marie, Michigan, in the upper, upper peninsula--so upper that as I spoke, I could look out the window and see the magnificent International Bridge to Canada.

The audience might be classed as a tough one. You could call it a hard sell. There weren't a lot of laughs in the right places and I didn't say all of the things they might have liked to hear but the evening was a wonderful success.

The feedback from that audience was excellent and there was a lot of laughter and participation once we got comfortable with one another.

CAMPUS SELF-SERV
PUFF STUFF
"SWEET CHEW"
CIGARETTES
CHEWING TOBACCO

Tobacco On Campus

At one point I brought up the subject of using tobacco. I had done a bit of research, as I waited for my room assignment, at the campus store and I discovered that half of the male students who were purchasing tobacco were not buying cigarettes. They were buying chewing tobacco.

I'm sort of death on tobacco myself because I have watched friends die from lung cancer and from emphysema. And 42 years ago I licked my own three-pack-a-day habit.

I've seen young people with their gums eaten out and with cancer of the mouth too from chewing tobacco and so I simply said that with all of the evidence we now have on the harm of smoking and chewing, I could not understand how any young person with a grain of intelligence could continue the habit.

I didn't preach. I just stated as opinion. And after that talk two students and one of the parents came up and assured me that as of that meeting they were quitting smoking for good.

Trend Toward Chewing

I have done a little research now that I noticed the number of students buying chewing tobacco. I learned that it is quite popular on a national basis on college campuses.

A Center for Disease Control (CDC) survey of about 20,000 people found that less-educated people who also tend to be of a lower social and economic status, are more likely to be smokers than high school grads or people with at least some college credits.

Education Levels And Smoking

Dr. Lois Escobedo of the Atlanta-based CDC stated that "There has been some progress in reducing cigarette smoking, but the study shows most of the progress is limited to the well educated."

Among 18-34 year olds surveyed, 41 percent of the people who didn't graduate from high school were smokers.

By comparison, 34 percent of the high school grads smoked, and only 19 percent of the people who had more than a high school education smoked.

Surprising Statistics

Now, here's the survey that really raised my eyebrows. A Pennsylvania State University study found that one in five college men chewed tobacco, almost double the number who smoked.

Of the 5,894 college students surveyed, 22 percent of the men chewed tobacco while only 13 percent said they smoked. Of the women surveyed 2 percent said they chewed and 16 percent said they smoked.

Elbert Glover, Director of the Centre for Tobacco Research at Penn State and head of the study said, "People see smokeless tobacco as a safe alternative to smoking. The very first hazard people think of with smoking is lung cancer."

Still, a 1986 Surgeon General's report said smokeless tobacco causes cavities, gum disease and oral cancer. It is also believed to be as addictive as smoking.

Glover fears that an epidemic of oral cancer, a disease that typically doesn't become evident until its victims are in their mid fifties, will erupt in a decade or two when the current generation of chewers moves into late middle age.

Somebody Sold Something

What does all of this have to do with selling safety? Well I submit to you that there is an entire industry out there that simply refuses to lie down and play dead.

And the studies I've just cited and my own observations have convinced me that the industry has somehow done a remarkable job of convincing our college students that it is A-OK to chew.

A recent trip to New Orleans convinced me that cigars are the new trend and a lot is being done to convince the young that a #25 inported cigar is the nearest thing to heaven that they might experience.

What does it matter how people take their tobacco just so that they keep the industry alive and thriving?

Imagine--22 percent of our male college students have developed an addiction to chewing tobacco and I was absolutely unaware that this was going on. Were you?

Safety comes in many forms and I'm concerned with the youth of this world. Certainly we are all aware that smoking causes lung cancer and heart problems.

Evidently it is time to launch an educational campaign so that even our better educated population will understand that if you stick with it, tobacco will get you no matter what way you choose your poison.

Chapter 10

THE SIX HATS FOR SELLING SAFETY

'M SURE YOU'VE HEARD THE EXPRES-sion "He or she wears a lot of different hats."

We all wear different hats, I'm sure. For instance, I'm a home owner. Now and then I put on my home-owner hat and attempt to change a light bulb or cut the grass.

I'm the president of Growth Unlimited, Inc. and so at times I wear the president's hat. I'm a father of four, grandfather to five, a former husband, driver. At my home up North I seem to be groundskeeper. And so the list goes. Author, speaker, consultant, waste basket emptier, garbage taker-outer, chief cook and bottle washer.

In selling safety I'd like to suggest that you consider wearing six hats when you try to sell a major project.

The Greeter

The first hat you must wear is that of greeter. I like to use a hard straw hat with a brim for this job. Picture a circus barker with a cane standing out in front of a tent saying just the right words to lure the customer inside.

A greeter's job is to get the person or people you want to sell to into a relaxed, comfortable, trusting frame of mind where they will be open to your presentation.

The greeter endeavors to set up a situation where you have an individual's complete, undivided attention. Somehow you get everything out of the way and clear the deck. The greeter talks just 20 percent of the time and listens, listens, listens. If you had an hour for your entire presentation then you'd spend about 5 minutes wearing this greeter's hat.

You might have to take that party away from his/her office or telephone to a restaurant or a coffee shop or whatever to set up the occasion for the sale.

Once you've done this, it is time for your second hat.

The Detective

Actually, you will have been wearing this second hat for quite a while prior to this sales presentation. The second hat is that of a detective. To illustrate this role, I use an old battered Sam Spade hat pulled down over one eye.

The detective must discover just what the prospect wants. What are the needs? What turns that particular prospect on? Is it recognition? Do they want to win an award? Is it money? Are you dealing with a bottom line bean counter? What about compassion? Does this party care about people?

How does this person's boss feel about safety? Many projects are sold simply because a party feels that their boss wants this to happen.

The better you are at your detective work, the better your chance for success.

Let me digress for a moment and explain something about these hats you will be wearing. They work in succession. If you fail to do the job that is required in a certain role, then there is no need to move on to the next.

If you have failed as a greeter, then the detective and the rest of the gang can just stay home because your chances for success are strictly minimal.

If you can't get some undivided time to present, then you probably won't do a good job in any of the following roles. If you fail to do a proper job as detective, then you won't know what track to take in the rest of your presentation.

As a detective you will be listening 80 percent of the time. You should spend twenty minutes in this role and you must dig in and identify some genuine problems and concerns. Search for clues as to how your prospect feels about his or her job and his or her responsibilities.

Many times people say no to safety programs because they feel that they will not have time for such a project.

Sometimes they are afraid of the cost.

Perhaps they have been involved in projects in the past that have failed. A great detective discovers the prospect's "hot button." The more you can learn while you are wearing your detective's hat, the better job you can do in this next role as a demonstrator.

The Demonstrator

As a demonstrator I tie a red bandana around my forehead a la Willie Nelson. Sometimes I carry a sign on a stick like a demonstrator of the 60's.

As a demonstrator I lay out before the prospect all of the features and benefits of my proposal.

Sometimes we have a tendency to see things only from our point of view. That is why your detective role was so important. You've just gathered some valuable information in your investigation and now is the time to put that information to use.

Make your presentation to appeal to your prospect's point of view.

Every time you mention a feature of your product or program, be certain that you mention a benefit.

"It has and that means" is a great way to do this. "It has a tracking feature and that means that we will always have a handle on just how we are doing."

Develop your presentation beforehand so that you can tick off a dozen features and benefits that will appeal to anyone and then stress those benefits that will appeal to your prospect based on what you have learned about that prospect.

A demonstration should be a 50-50 proposition when it comes to talking. Let your prospect participate in the demonstration. Get that other party involved. Count on about 10 minutes for your demonstration.

When questions come up, answer them but avoid talking costs until later.

The Verifier

Now it's time for your verifier's hat. I wear one of those

old eye shades that accountants wore some seventy-five years ago. This implies a person who gets down and really checks out the facts.

A verifier backs up everything that the demonstrator says.

It is time to bring in your heavy ammunition. It is proof time.

This is where you bring out your graphs or your charts. It is time to lay your testimonials on the table. It is nitty-gritty time.

If it is a bean counter you're talking to, then bring out the data based on other people's experiences.

Bring out whatever proof you can to show that what you are saying is the truth. If you have a letter of support from a superior in your organization, produce it.

When you know that you must produce verification, then you will soon amass a wealth of proof for your claims. A verifier talks about 80 percent of the time and does the job in about 10 minutes.

The Debugger

Now we bring in the heavyweight. We call this next role the debugger.

A debugger gets all of the bugs out of the deal. A debugger wears a Congo hat and carries a bug spray can.

Debuggers answer objections. They talk about the cost of things. They use the word "investment" instead of price.

Debuggers ask closing questions such as, "Can we go ahead with this project right away?" or questions that give the prospect the choice of yes or yes as a reply. "Would you like to start this today or next Monday?"

When prospects say, "I want to think about it." Debuggers ask, "Just what feature of this program do you want to think about. Is it the validity of the facts I've just presented?" And if the prospect says no, then the debugger continues on down through all of the things the demonstrator demonstrated and the verifier verified. Finally he asks, "If it isn't any of those things, just what is there left to think about?" and he again goes for the close, "Don't you think it would be wise to go ahead with this project right away?" And he nods his head fully expecting the prospect to nod back. Debuggers do about 50 percent of the talking and hopefully do their job in about 10 minutes.

The Dreammaker

Now we are ready for our final hat--the dreammakers hat. Back in the late 60's and the early 70's there was a television series called "The Millionaire." The lead character was a lawyer named Michael Anthony. He wore a black overcoat and a black Homburg hat.

Michael Anthony was the representative of John Bearesford Tipton, an eccentric millionaire whose hobby was discovering people in need.

Michael Anthony's job was to knock on people's doors or ring their bells and at exactly the right moment in their life when all hell was breaking loose, he would announce that he was in possession of a certified check for one million dollars made out to the party answering the door. It was arranged so that the check would be tax free.

Now how would you like to have Michael Anthony's job? Do you think you could close a sale like that?

Well, I want you to visualize yourself wearing that

black Homburg and knocking on doors with that million dollar-check in your briefcase.

Dreammakers do about 80 percent of the talking and take about 5 minutes.

When you've worn those other hats properly, you win the right to put on that Homburg and play the role of the dreammaker.

You are ready to make people's dreams come true. You'll make this a safer, happier world. Yes, working with your prospect, you will prevent those accidents and injuries and fatalities because you know and I know that great safety programs produce fantastic results.

Objections

"But I'm not selling that kind of a program," you say.

"A six hat presentation just won't work for me." "Ours is a different situation." "I'm dealing with all kinds of people and groups, the board of directors, top management, job supervisors, foremen, truck gang, digging crew, or just my boss."

Sure, we are all dealing with a different group everyday, perhaps.

Dealing With Time Restrictions

And just who ever gets a full hour to make a presentation?

Perhaps you will have to make your entire sales presentation in just 20 minutes. In that case, just divide the times we've suggested for each phase of the sale by 5. Greeters take one minute. Detectives get 4 minutes. Demonstrators have 2 minutes; verifiers 2 minutes. Debuggers have just 2 minutes and the dream maker does his or her job in one minute.

Once again, these time frames are suggestions only. The important thing is to get your prospect comfortable so he/she can listen to you. Determine their needs and their hot buttons. Show them how your program or project will benefit them. Back up your claims with verifiers. Then get the bugs out of the way. And finally, make that dream come true.

Some people will interrupt you and take you off track. But when you take the time to fill in the data required to wear these six hats effectively, you will have an arsenal that will allow you to defend yourself against all concerns and to assault those nonbeliever's again and again until you win the victory of a great safety program.

Those times that you give to each stage of your presentation will vary, of course. Don't move on to the next role until you feel confident that you've done the job. The same applies to the percentage of the talking and listening you'll be doing. The important thing is that you stay on track and retain control. Flexibility is always a great asset when you're making a presentation. Stay loose. Keep moving toward your destination with confidence.

So now you have the six hats for selling safety. I hope you wear them in good health.

Structure Helps Identify Weaknesses

Once I discovered these hats, I was able to immediately identify just where I was at any given time in a presentation.   When I failed, I could generally go back and see where my data bank was lacking.

Once I knew what I needed, I could go back and try again.

Maybe I lacked some statistics. Perhaps I needed a testimonial letter from someone on how the program had worked for them.

Maybe I just missed the boat on what made a prospect tick.

All I ask is that you try the hats. They will feel a bit uncomfortable at first. You will no doubt stumble. But now you have a road map to follow and you have stations to stop off at along the journey. You have check points, a time frame to work within. And I hope you feel deep down inside your gut that you have a worthy destination.

Safety people save lives. Safety programs make a difference.

Chapter 11

PERSISTENCE

O BOOK ON SELLING ANYTHING WOULD be complete without a chapter on persistence.

The Words Of Winston Churchill

In fact, if I walked away from this book with just one message burned deeply into your subconscious mind, then let it be the message that Sir Winston Churchill gave to a class at a girls' school years ago.

The story goes that Churchill was to be the honored speaker at a banquet, and as often happens, the program dragged on and on late into the night and Churchill had not yet been called upon to speak. Finally when he was introduced, he stood up and with all the passion he could summon for the occasion, he said simply, "Never, never, never, never, never, never, never give up. Never give up. Never give up."

That was his message to that class.

That was his message to the people of Britain too that turned the tide in their war with Germany.

The Calls Successful Salespeople Make

I've seen some research on the number of calls a sales person makes on a single client to make a sale. I've used this study in other books I've written on selling but I think it deserves repeating right here.

Fifty percent of the salespeople in the world make one sales call on a prospect, and if that prospect doesn't buy, they never call on him or her again; 18 percent make two calls; 7 percent make three calls; 5 percent make four calls; and 20 percent of most sales forces make five or more calls on likely prospects. The statistics go on to say that 20 percent sell 80 percent of all that is being sold.

Another study shows that 80 percent of everything that is sold is sold by 20 percent of the sales people in this world. In other words, most organizations pay 80 percent of their salespeople to produce 20 percent of their sales. Quite often they do not pay them very much though and not for very long for in the sales profession the law is "Produce or Move On." Those who sell in the top 20 percent are generally well paid and their income is often supplemented with prizes of trips to Hawaii for them and their spouses.

Now why did I bring up that 80-20 figure on sales calls and on salespeople? Because they go together. The sales people who do most of the selling are those who persist and make that second and third and fourth and fifth call on a prospect.

One of the major factors in making sales is persistence

and if you hope to become successful at selling safety in your organization, then you must develop your ability to persist.

If a kind word doesn't work, then find a big stick and vice versa.

If you can't sell an idea at one level, then try another. Quite often a subordinate will tell you, "I could never sell my superior on that idea." When you hear that, just ask, "Would you mind if I tried?" Often such a question will bring action.

When people realize that you are not about to give up, they often give in.

The Importance Of Explaining

So often the real key to selling a good idea is simply a proper explanation.

Far too often people have given up on a great life-saving idea long before they took the time necessary to explain the idea and really sell that idea to the person who might take some action and make it happen.

Nothing happens until somebody sells something and no great idea is implemented until somebody first takes the time to explain the idea and its benefits to somebody.

Often selling safety is simply a matter of educating somebody.

It really doesn't matter how many times they knock you down, just so that you get up each time. The world is just full of wonderful, upbeat stories of people who have overcome poverty and hardships and handicaps of every nature and gone on to success and greatness.

Facing Rejection Builds Character

I firmly believe that if you haven't faced a great deal of rejection and defeat in your lifetime you have been somehow deprived of an element that will lead to your reaching your true human potential.

Remember, the business world is spinning around faster than ever before.

An idea that was not practical yesterday might seem brilliant tomorrow.

An organization that feels it just can't afford major expenditures on safety one day might greatly change its tune following a fatal accident. It's a sad but true fact but often it takes a tragedy and a major loss in litigation for a bean counter to become a believer of the simple truth that safety pays.

Hang in there one more time, and don't be too quick to leave the office in defeat when your idea or your program has been rejected.

I've seen people get their way in offices and make sales just because they wouldn't leave.

A Blind Trade

Sometimes you have to trade to get your way. I remember one day when I had to slow down a fast train to get some photographs I needed.

The superintendent said no. I hung in there for a half an hour and wouldn't leave his office. Finally he made me an offer. "Art," he said, "I may need a favor from you someday."

"You've got it!" I said.

"Ok, I'll slow down that train for you, but I want you to sign an IOU for one big favor."

I signed the note and forgot about it. About six months later a matter came up that I felt very strongly about.

I had turned a claim down and felt I'd done the right thing. And then the superintendent asked me to drop by his office.   He had no jurisdiction over the matter whatsoever but he asked me about it.

I got pretty hot under the collar about his sticking his nose into my business and I told him so. "I turned the claim down and that is that." I said.

And then he took the note out of his desk. It was the IOU I'd signed.

"Art," he explained, "I caught a lot of flack over slowing that train down for you but I did it. I can see your side of this matter but I can see the other guy's too and I need him on my side right now. I want you to pay that claim for me. It isn't much money and I think it will be honest for you to pay it too. It's just a judgment call. How about it?"

I looked at the IOU and I thought about it for about an hour but I paid the claim.

Maybe It's You

People do different things for different reasons and for different people.

Quite often the reason people will not buy your idea is not your idea at all. Often it is you.

Let someone else sell the idea for you when you run into a stone wall.

Often the secret to persistence is the wisdom to try a slightly different approach. That is one reason why it is important that you keep a record of your actions. When people say "no," write down the reason If you cannot overcome an objection and you believe that the objection is a real one, then go out and find a way to answer that objection effectively that next time.

Never feel ashamed that you were turned down; that is, if you were prepared and you did your best. A rejection at least shows that you asked for the sale.

The only time to feel badly is when you've quit.

So there you have a lesson on persistence. Churchill said it so well that I would never try to improve on it. "Never, never, never, never, never, never, never give up. Never give up. Never give up."

Chapter 12

DESTINATIONS

AT A WEDDING I ATTENDED, ONE TIME as an usher, the bride stood at the back of the room. The music was playing, the procession of flower girls and attendants had all gone down the aisle but the bride would not budge.

I was at the back of the aisle and I asked her why she did not go down the aisle. She gave me a funny look and said, "The groom is not there yet, waiting for me."

I explained to her that when she started down the aisle the groom would get the signal to walk forward and by the time she got to the front of the room he would be there waiting .

Her father really looked relieved when she finally took my word for it and, sure enough, by the time she got to the front, the happy groom was there with a big smile waiting for her arrival.

Afterwards, we kidded about it and I told her that if she were an airline pilot she probably would not take off unless she received word from the destination airport that they had the unloading dock ready for her plane.

Destinations: The Bumper Car Ride

The Importance Of Beginning

So often when we go to sell an idea or a project we cannot possibly have all of the factors that will come into play in line. That is why I encourage you to develop an attitude of flexibility.

Have you ever had the opportunity to drive a bumper car at an amusement park? The idea is to drive your car around the arena but in reality the real idea is to just have a lot of fun and perhaps get rid of some of your aggression at the same time.

The cars are equipped with rubber bumpers all around them and the idea is to bump into one another to prevent their progress.

It is an ever-changing obstacle course and the challenge is to simply somehow bump your way to your destination as you impede others along the route.

I like to look at most projects as a sort of bumper car derby.

When I run into an unmovable object, I simply back up a little and try a different approach. Now if I waited until the path was clear before I began my journey, then I would never get moving.

If I was unwilling to take a few bumps and lumps, then I wouldn't have a hope for success.

They tell me that an airline pilot is seldom exactly on course toward the final destination, but that he periodically makes adjustments along the route.

In anything worthwhile that we try to accomplish in life, we must expect to get knocked about and thrown temporarily off course.

Expect A Detour

As columnist Russell Baker put it so well, "The shortest distance between two points is always under construction."

We must expect detours; we must expect resistance; and we must learn to live with constant change.

Yesterday was one of those beautiful, wonderful winter days in Michigan. We had a couple of feet of snow on the ground and the sun was shining without a cloud in the sky.

I had a couple of speeches booked at Sault Ste. Marie, a trip of about 320 miles.

It was Sunday and my first talk would be on Monday evening at Lake Superior State University.

I checked the weather reports and there were clouds and winds up to 25 mph in the Upper Peninsula. I decided to travel on Sunday and as I crossed that fantastic Mackinaw Bridge, I could see the snow blowing on that solid sea of ice below.

The minute I pulled onto land, I was greeted with gusts of wind that blew the piled snow across the highway.

I checked and, sure enough, the airport was closed and so I had planned well in deciding to drive.

And the next morning as I looked out my window, I saw a blinding snowstorm.

I was to speak that night and again the next night--this time for the Chamber of Commerce--and then return home and be in Grand Rapids, Michigan, for a seminar on Thursday afternoon.

Already my mind was working on the logistics of that trip.

If the roads were clear, I would try to get in a hundred

miles or so of driving on Tuesday night after my program.

There is a rule in the speaking business: "Travel as soon as you can to your next destination for you never know what tomorrow brings."

Depending on the weather and how I felt, I would move on toward my next destination.

I said, "toward my destination."

In great weather it took me 6 1/2 hours to make that trip and I had no intention of driving that long at night. But, weather permitting, I would make a start. A hundred or a hundred and twenty-five miles would be a great start on my journey and there were a number of comfortable motels along the route.

Begin Your Journey Now

Don't wait until you have all of the questions answered before you begin your journey. Develop the habit of flexible thinking.

Great managers never have all of the answers. But they seek out all of the best answers they can find and then they make a decision to act. Then once that decision is made, they plow ahead full speed.

As you travel down the road, you will discover others will not always be in the right place waiting for you with open arms as you approach. The important thing is that you know where you are going and that you head in that direction with   confidence.

Chapter 13

CLOSING THE SALE

THIS COULD VERY WELL BE THE MOST important chapter in this book by far.

A Jigsaw Puzzle

I'm afraid that it is a bit like a giant jigsaw puzzle in structure. The last time I counted there were 16 separate components required to make sense of all of this. And yet, as I have presented these ideas to audiences, from Hawaii to New Hampshire, I have been led to believe that I am onto something very important. Something that can and will save lives. It has produced many thousands of signed personal commitments to safety and to positive interaction. So, please, bear with me. I think you will be rewarded for your persistence.

Let me begin by telling you that I have had the honor of

visiting a great number of plants throughout the United States over the years. More recently, I have visited the plants of some major corporations and these are organizations who spare nothing when it comes to safety.

I visited organizations that were having twice as many injuries as their state's average. And I have visited the plants of some safety super stars.

I spent some 35 years with one organization watching it go from the worst in the nation to the best in safety and more recently I have had a burning desire to learn what it is that separates the safety super stars from the also rans.

My Start In Safety

My first job that involved safety was in the General Claims Department of the Grand Trunk Western Railroad. I was a mail boy and one of my duties was to pick up wire reports at our telegraph office and to write up the new injuries and accidents in our day book and our alphabetical books. This was years ago before the invention of the ball point pen. I had the old style wooden pen with a nib point.   In fact I had two pens and two inkwells. One inkwell held black ink and I used that pen to write in the names and occupations of those injured and the locations of the accidents. The second inkwell contained red ink and I had a second pen for that one and with that pen I often wrote the word "dead" next to the injured parties name.

This was a time before automated railroad crossing gates or flasher signals at most grade crossings, and it was not unusual for us to have a fatal accident nearly every week. In fact, when we did have a crossing accident between an auto and a train it was often a fatal and quite often an entire family was wiped out in an accident. Families were larger in 1948 and I've written up accidents when as many as 8 people were killed. And there were days when I had to write up more than just one fatal accident in a single day. Tragedy was a way of life on the railroad in those days.

Hold Up Your Hands

We did not have a large personnel department back then. In fact, the son of a former general manager was in charge and his main duty was to record the names and social security numbers of employees. There was no psychological testing, no urine tests, in fact, many employees received no physicals at all.

Back then there were often shanties in the yard where yard crews might warm their hands by a pot belly stove. Hoboes and "boomers", that is, brakemen who traveled from one railroad to another to work for a few days or a few months, gathered there. When a yard master needed a few new men he would go into that shanty and announce that he was hiring. He'd say, "Hold up your hands fellows." And the men would hold up their hands.

When he spotted men with a few fingers missing he would know that they were seasoned brakemen and he'd hire them.

It was not at all unusual to shake hands with a railroad employee and if they had a few fingers missing then you knew that they had worked as brakemen coupling cars in the yard. Coupling devices were crude and often resulted in injuries.

Visiting The Kinston Plant

In January 1990 I had the rare privilege to speak at the DuPont Kinston Plant in North Carolina. I did five programs for all of their employees and had the opportunity to tour their plant and visit with a number of their workers.

John and Libby Newsome were my hosts and they provided a very special kind of North Carolina hospitality. Their total commitment to safety exemplified the spirit of the whole DuPont team.

I met with Bob Mussat, their Site Safety Manager, and found the kind of safety person every plant manager prays for. Bob loves his job and he shares DuPont's total uncompromising commitment to safety.

The Kinston Plant holds the world's all time record for safety. I understand that they went 12 years and 11 months without a serious injury. That involved some 66 million 645 thousand plus exposure hours from March 26th, 1964, to February 10th, 1977.

They are still doing a tremendous job there and I observed that every worker seemed involved in their safety program.

The day before I arrived at their plant, they had an accident in which a worker who was pulling a heavy load on a cart was injured as the cart went against the guard and swung over crushing his little finger against the handle of the cart. Part of his little finger was severed.

I met with the man for he was back to work the next day.

As I talked with those audiences I asked the people this question. "How many of you could feel the pain that that man felt when his finger was crushed?" And nearly all of them raised their hands and nodded.

And I asked them how many of them felt a sort of mourning over this horrible accident? And again they all responded by nodding their heads and raising their hands. And it suddenly struck me how different things had become in the years since I first started working for the railroad.   From a climate where people just seemed to take it for granted when a man had a finger or two cut off, to a time when a couple of thousand people were deeply, personally concerned when a man lost a part of his little finger.

A War Story And The Buddy System

Years ago, I was a combat rifleman in Korea. At that time the main line of defense was about at the 38th parallel.   There were hills in this area that we continued to fight over and the fighting was intense. We lost whole battalions in taking these hills and often the hills would change possession several times in a single week.

I often ask the members of an audience how many of them were in the service. And then I ask those who were in the service how many of them were in combat. And generally there are a few such people in every audience. I ask those who were in combat how many of them had a buddy?   And all of them always raise their hands.

In combat conditions G.I.'s need a buddy to stay alive.

When we were on those hills out in front of the main line we might be attacked at any moment. And we stayed in bunkers which were glorified fox holes. Generally we had two men in a bunker. And when darkness fell we would generally try to get some sleep. We'd take turns and if I was the first to sleep then I would literally turn my life over to the care of my buddy. In essence I would say, "I'm going to sleep for a couple of hours now, buddy, and I don't want to get bayoneted while I'm sleeping. If there is trouble I don't want you bugging out without me. I expect you to wake me up and to take care of me."

And when my buddy woke me he would then turn his life over to my care and keeping. He would expect me to stay awake for the next two hours on guard to protect his life from the enemy. Buddies watched out for one another on attacks too. They covered each others flanks. When I was hit by mortar fire during an attack my buddy screamed out, "Medic! Medic!" and a medic came and plugged me up so I didn't bleed to death.

Now will you believe that I am somewhat prejudiced in favor of the buddy system? I'm alive today because I had a buddy.

Just hold that thought of the Buddy System in your mind for a while. I assure you that all of these components will come together for us in time and that each of them is necessary for the whole.

My Husband Is Going To Divorce Me

One morning when I was working as a railroad claim agent in Battle Creek, Michigan, I received a phone call from the train dispatcher to notify me that there had been a fatal crossing accident some 30 miles from my home.

I immediately drove to the scene. I talked with the train crew and scoured the area for witnesses. I learned that a man had driven his automobile up to a railroad crossing where the flashing lights were flashing and the gates were coming down. He sat there waiting for the approaching train and before the train arrived, a woman driving in the same direction as he, came up behind him, without slowing down, ran directly into the rear end of his auto, punching it through the lowered crossing gate and onto the track where it was immediately struck by the engine of the oncoming train.

The man was killed in the accident and as I talked with witnesses it soon became clear what had happened. I took statements on a disc recording machine and finally I located the woman who had caused the crash, at the scene. I asked her what had happened and she got a terrified look on her face and replied, "My husband is going to divorce me." I tried to take a different approach. "Where were you going at the time?" I asked and she replied, "I was coming into town to see a lawyer but it was just 6 o'clock in the morning and his office was closed so I was driving home." "And what happened?" I asked. And again she repeated, " My husband is going to divorce me." She had no idea of how the accident had occurred. She wan't even aware of the accident.

Now I think you will agree that that woman was pretty well wiped out by a personal crisis in her life.

We All Have Personal Problems

Nearly everyone in my audiences seem to agree that quite often we are all pretty well shaken up by some kind of a personal crisis.

For instance you find some funny looking cigarettes or a strange white powder in your teenager's dresser drawer. Or maybe your husband or wife tells you that they aren't going to divorce you.

Maybe, like the people in my audience last week, you have been working up to 80 hours a week for the past four months recovering from a disaster.

Everyone seems to agree that not everyone is hitting on all of their cylinders every moment that they are at work. Now put that thought on hold for now while we move on.

Disasters Initiate Safety Programs

In my travels to different organizations and in my conversations with many top safety people I have learned that most great safety programs are developed following disasters. In other words, you first have to get pretty bad before you can get pretty good.

Government rules and regulations demand that every organization gets involved with safety to a certain extent. OSHA and the various State Agencies make you tow a certain line. But there are many other things a corporation can do to more than simply comply with government regulations.

Engineering

When an organization gets really serious about preventing injuries and saving lives, they often call in safety engineers.   Some engineers I've met seem to believe that they can engineer out all of the possibilities for injuries in a system.

Equipment

Then there are those who promote safety equipment. They have a guard to protect you from almost anything.

Education

Trainers believe that education is the answer. With

sufficient training a person can be taught how to avoid all injuries. Some trainers believe that. For instance, you can include in training the ways of lifting to avoid back problems.

Enforcement

There are the enforcers too who feel that safety rules and the enforcement of those rules is the answer.

Ergonomics

Ergonomy is still a thing in the field of safety today. Ergonomy is the study of energy. Many of today's injuries or disabling physical conditions in industry are caused by repetitive motions. We find this with data process people who enter data into a computer all day.   Tennis elbow is another such injury. And there are corporations who believe that ergonomy will eliminate all injuries from out work places.

Environmentalists

Environmentalists are having their say in safety too. They are trying to make the work place safe from an environmental point of view.

So who is right? What is the answer? I think they are all able to help cut down the number of injuries and accidents.   Everything I have mentioned helps.

Safety Teams

Safety teams that involve management, supervisors and the non-salaried workers are a powerful force in building a safety program, too.

Dale Gray, former Manager of Environmental Health and Safety at Ford Motor Company headquarters in Dearborn, Michigan, told me about the fantastic teamwork they have developed between labor and management in the field of safety at Ford. "Art," he told me, "when you attend one of our meetings, you won't be able to tell who's from labor and who's from management. We both share the same goal and that is to make Ford a truly safe place for all of its employees."

I am discovering that those organizations that take the time and spend the money and provide the leadership are succeeding in cutting down the number of accidents and injuries.

I have also found many of them plateau. That is, they reach a certain standard of excellence and then they fail to get better. They peak, so to speak. They run into an invisible wall and they cannot seem to penetrate that wall. They use incentive programs and safety drives. Then they go back to plan one and start all over again. Yet, time and again, they seem to hit that wall that blocks them from perfection.

What did I learn from the superstars who penetrate that wall again and again? I will tell you in a moment but first let me add a few more components to this puzzle.

We've All Got Problems

It was just about on our thirtieth wedding anniversary when my wife, Ruthie, came home from work and said, "Honey, I have a lump."

At first I thought she was talking about me.

Unfortunately that was not the case.

I told her not to worry, a lot of women have lumps and it was probably nothing and quite often it was not serious. She immediately made an appointment with a specialist.

The doctor did a lot of tests and finally told us that it was malignant. He said that he would do a mastectomy and that as long as the cancer had not spread to her lymph system that the surgery would take care of things. I remember him saying that she could get a special bra and that no one would know about it but me. He said that she could live a long and happy life.

They did the surgery in December of 1984 and discovered that the cancer had spread to Ruthie's lymph system.

For six months Ruthie went through hell with chemo. Then the symptoms disappeared and we thought we had made it.

Three years later Ruthie came home and announced, "I've got another lump on the other side."

We got in the car and drove directly to Cleveland Clinic.
They are supposed to have one of the best cancer centers in the world.

The doctor did a biopsy and told us that, yes, it was malignant but that it was a very small lump. He suggested an operation called a lumpectomy. They removed just part of the breast.

Again the symptoms were not there and we went for three more years.

Ruthie had tests all along the way, but nothing showed up.

Then Ruthie began to feel sort of listless. She had some stomach pain and then she discovered another lump.

Again it was cancer of the breast and they did a mastectomy on what was left of the breast. They did all sorts of tests on Ruthie.

A few weeks later our local doctor called us in for a consultation. The results of all the tests were in and the body scans showed 5 spots on Ruthie's liver.

"What does that mean?" I asked the doctor when we talked privately.

"It means that we are in stage three." He explained. And then he added. "There is no stage four."

The doctor said that without chemo, Ruthie could be expected to die in less than six months. "With chemo," he said, "she might last longer. Chemo will not cure her but it might prolong her life some. How much we have no way of knowing."

Ruthie elected to take the chemo and it was pure hell.

She lost her beautiful hair. After a couple of months she lost her appetite and she could hardly eat. She started losing weight and all the color left her cheeks.

It got so bad that she looked like one of those victims of war who are starved and have suffered for years in a prisoner of war camp.

One day she sat down and told me, "Art, I don't think I am going to make it."

Ruthie was a terrific fighter and all throughout this up 'til then she had been brave and full of hope for a recovery. She had lost hope.

I expected it might be only a matter of weeks after that.

Then one day I received a phone call from a safety professional over in Chicago. He had purchased our video tapes and in one of the tapes I had talked about Ruthie.

He explained that he had had a terminal illness and the doctors had given up on him and he had met a nutritionist who he had worked with and he had saved his life. Then he told me that his mother had had cancer and that same doctor had made her well. He gave me the nutritionist's name and phone number and said that I might call him.

Perhaps you already know this, but when there is a terminal illness involved people are ready to grasp for straws. Because of this, there are a great deal of frauds and unscrupulous confidence people who prey on the ill with promises of miracle cures.

Generally the solution to your medical problem is yours if you just pay your life savings to the presenter.

I did not know the fellow who called me but I made a call to the nutritionist immediately.

"She can't eat." I explained to him. "She is wasting away."

The doctor listened patiently and then he said to me, "Art, I can get her eating within two weeks. That is no problem."

"And what about the rest, doctor?" I asked.

"I think I can help her" he promised.

And then I asked the magic question. "Just how would I go about paying for your services." I asked.

To my surprise he replied, "I'm not concerned with that. I just want to help."

As a nurse, Ruthie knew a great deal about her condition. She had been interested in nutrition, too and when she talked to the doctor they were able to communicate very well.

Ruthie began a diet of grains and fruits and supplements that I could never hope to understand. She went to great extremes to follow the doctor's orders.

And then something wonderful happened.

Within a few days Ruthie began eating. The color had returned to her cheeks. And within a couple of months, when they did a body scan on Ruthie, the spots on her liver were gone.

Ruthie regained her weight and her hair grew back rapidly.

We began to celebrate.

I told her that I wanted to take her on a nice vacation and that I wanted to take a different vacation every month.

Then another miracle happened. I began to get bookings all over the United States and Canada at locations that everyone dreams of for vacations.

We went to Hawaii twice. We flew to Florida and Disney World. We visited Opryland and had several trips to visit the kids in California.

I'd speak for an hour or two at a location, then we would just enjoy ourselves.

We rode a boat in the channel downtown in San Antonio, Texas and soared in a helicopter in Maui. It was fantastic.

Then in September of 1992, I keynoted the Safety Conference in Spokane, Washington.

Ruthie did not go shopping in Spokane.

The conference was fantastic. I spoke in the Opera House which had been built for a world's fair. Two thousand people attended my morning session each day.

Ruthie seemed worn out.

Following the conference we drove over to Couer D' Alene and we had a magnificent suite at the big lodge there.

Ruthie didn't even want to drive through the hills there.

We went home early and Ruthie went to the doctor.

The cancer was back in her liver. By December it had spread to her spine in several places and she was now bedridden.

Again the cancer spread to her chest.

And then it spread to her brain.

My daughter, Amy, a registered nurse came home and tended her until the very end.

Ruthie died on June 26, 1993.

I tell you about my Ruthie, not because I want your sympathy.

Ruthie has been gone awhile now and I've gone on with my life.

I tell you about her because her story is the story of so many people.

I'm not any different than any other man or woman.

I'm sure that you will agree that there were many times during this period that I was a #1 candidate for an accident.

There were many, many times when I was not myself. Many times that my mind was not at all on what I was doing.

So often, when I had investigated accidents and someone had been injured because of a stupid action, I had asked myself this question, "What in the world was this fellow thinking about? Was he crazy?"

And so often the answer was, "He was thinking about his wife, or his kids, or the bills he couldn't pay.

"He was thinking about the funny cigarettes he'd found in his 9 year old's dresser drawer....or maybe the gun."

We all have problems, big problems.

We are all vulnerable.

We all have moments every day where our minds are on other things, not safety at all.

And that is why we need others who will take care of us in these moments.

We all need sister's and brother's keepers.

That is why our positive interaction program is necessary.

Can you see why this makes sense? I hope so.

Signing A Contract

Let me ask you a personal question. Have you ever purchased life insurance or bought a car on time payments?

Did you ever get married? Have you ever signed a contract?

Sometimes I do programs for salespeople, those who sell insurance or cars or whatever. And as someone once said in sports, "The game isn't over until the fat lady sings." A sale isn't really made until the customer signs the contract.

We call would-be salespeople who don't get signed contracts "visitors."

When you put your signature on a piece of paper you are generally pretty serious about the subject.

com
xxx
John Ha

My Bicentennial Speech

In 1976, I became rather popular on the lecture circuit with a Bicentennial speech. Part of it was entered into the Congressional Record in Washington, D.C. by a U.S. Congressman. And part of that speech was printed in Success Magazine. About 50 other publications ran parts of that speech and over a hundred professional speakers asked for and were given permission to use parts of my speech in their talks to audiencesall over America.

A Man Named Tom

Mostly what I tried to do in that talk was to make our founding fathers come alive as real people. One segment talks about the time a young fellow came running into a meeting. This fellow Tom was well known to the group and respected too. He was a licensed architect, a licensed engineer, he farmed 7,500 acres successfully and still found time to practice the violin for 3 1/2 hours each day. And he'd mastered four languages and spoke them well. All this and he was not yet 31 years of age.

This fellow named Tom had a piece of paper in his hand as he entered the meeting room and some of the other men asked him, "What have you got there, Tom?

And Tom replied, "I've just been up all night writing down all of the things we've all been agreeing on."

And they said, "Read it!"

And Thomas Jefferson proceeded to read to that audience the Declaration of Independence. And when he finished he took the paper and pen and he walked over to one of the men and said, "Just put your John Hancock man in that room. And in that document they pledged to one another their lives, their fortunes and their sacred honor.

And because they had signed that document many gave their lives and many lost their fortunes and their families, but none lost their sacred honor. And because they signed that document and stood behind it we are now living as free people in one of the greatest nations in the world.

What Makes The Difference?

Now, what is it that I discovered by talking with so many workers from so many plants?

I found out that most of them looked alike. They seemed to be working in clean plants too. And most of them had safety programs involving engineering, equipment, education, rule enforcement, environmentalists, back programs, ergonomists and all the rest. And the good ones had total involvement by all levels of management and supervision and by the unions and the workers too. But what was it that made the difference?

Positive Interaction

More and more I am running into the phrase "positive interaction." As I understand it, it means that when you find an unsafe condition or when you discover someone working in an unsafe manner then you immediately call it to their attention in a positive way.

That means that you do not walk up to someone who is not wearing their safety helmet and say, "Hey, stupid. Put on your helmet!"

What you do say is something like this. "Hey, Charlie, you are too important a member of our team for us to lose you. Will you please put on your helmet? We care about you!"

In other words, you do it in a friendly way, with a positive approach.

I recently heard of an accident where three workers stood idly by and allowed a worker to have an accident that they could have prevented. They didn't want to get the fellow mad at them for butting in. And that man, although still alive, is totally and permanently injured as a result of the accident that followed.

Many workers are hesitant to call violations of safety rules to other worker's attention. In fact, many supervisors hesitate or look the other way to avoid a conflict.

What If?

OK. Now, granted most of us do not work in combat conditions, but most of us will agree that we are not all functioning at 100 percent all of the time. And most of us really need a buddy to look out for us at one time or another.   What if everyone in your organization started being a buddy to everyone else?

What if we all gave each other permission to intervene in a positive way when they see us doing something that just might lead to an accident or an injury?

A Written Commitment

And what if we made the kind of written commitment that we make when we sign for a marriage license or for a car loan or for an insurance policy? What if we signed the kind of declaration towards safety that our founding fathers signed toward a free nation and independence?

I wrote such a document. I suggest that top management sign it first. And then supervisors. And then every employee.   And I suggest that the various documents be copied and given to all who sign and that such a document be framed and displayed in each work area.

What I discovered in talking with superstars who have cracked that invisible barrier that prevents you from reaching true excellence in the area of safety is this. Most of them have a written commitment to one another in this regard.   Most of them have signed on the dotted line.

And when I asked those people at the Kinston DuPont plant how many of them could feel the pain that man felt when he lost the end of this little finger they all raised their hands. And when I asked them how many of them felt a sense of mourning, again they raised their hands. They all felt a sense of loss and a sense of failure. They were all the buddy of that injured man. Their commitment to one another and to safety was so great that the accident really hurt them inside their guts.

Total commitment to one another's safety--that is the key.   That's what my *Declaration of Inter-dependence* is all about. Take a few minutes to read it over.

Now, take your pen and put your John Hancock by the X.

Then get your management team and your supervisors and everyone of your employees to do the same thing.

Making It Work

Recently, in North Carolina, I had the honor of speaking for the assistant managers of the direct marketing division of Sarah Lee.

Their leader, Mike Ernst was one of the most enthusiastic team oriented people I have met in a long time and when I showed him my Declaration of Inter-dependence, he went for the idea immediately.

We agreed that when I read the declaration to their audience, I would call him up and he would put his "John Hancock" on the document.

Then after Mike agreed to the commitment publicly he signed the document. I then asked the members of the audience how many of them were ready to make such a total commitment to safety. They all raised their hands and then applauded that idea.

The folks at DMD, Sarah Lee are really organized and within an hour they had taken the declaration out and had it blown up to 22"x34" and had it mounted in the lobby on an easel and they attached three pens on strings.

I was really thrilled when I saw the lines of employees wanting to personally sign that document and make their own total commitment to safety.

In Baton Rouge, Louisiana, Steve Merritt followed up on a presentation that I had made with his maintenance workers at the Exxon Company U.S.A. refinery by presenting the Declaration of Inter-dependence to their employees and they all lined up to make this commitment to one another.

You Make The Difference

Try it! Will it work? That will depend, in good measure, on you and on the enthusiasm you project when offering this concept. Of course, I'd love to come into your organization and make a presentation of this declaration to your management team. Then I'd like to do it to your entire organization.

tion to your management team. Then I'd like to do it to your entire organization.

The time has come for an uncompromising commitment to safety. As your people make this commitment and truly become their sister's and their brother's keepers, I truly believe that we will have a safer world.

More on positive interaction to come. Don't miss the follow-up material in section IV of this book.

After making several hundred live declaration presentations we've discovered many new presentation ideas we'd like to share with you.

Now, here's our Declaration.

For Canadians we created our personal pledge to safety and to positive inter-action.

I hope you'll implement this program at your site soon.

In Session

Declaration of Inter-dependence
(c) Art Fettig, 1998

When in the course of human events it becomes necessary for an organization and its members to make a total uncompromising commitment to safety for its future growth and for the good of all employees.

And whereas, we do hereby resolve that we will do all in our power, every moment of every day, to make safety a value which we hold dear and integrate into our planning and in the fulfillment of our goals and activities.

Therefore, we do hereby declare and acknowledge our dependence upon one another. For the practice of safety is both a personal and a mutual obligation.

We state our commitment in this verse titled, *"Our Sister's and Our Brother's Keepers."*

We are our sister's and our brother's keepers.
for safety calls for our uncompromising commitment,
to one another, and to safety, too.
I promise I will positively interact when I find you
performing in an unsafe manner, and I expect
positive interaction from you on my behalf,
when I go wrong.
We are human you and I, and accidents and injuries occur,
when we forget or just react wrongly
not doing what's right and reasonable for our own safety.
We are our sister's and our brother's keepers.
Trusting in one another, for a safer world

And for the support of this declaration, we mutually pledge to each other our lives, our futures, and our sacred honor.

For information and permission to use the Declaration, contact:

Art Fettig, 1 800 441 7676

A Personal Pledge To Safety And To Positive Inter-action

(c) Art Fettig, 1998

Acknowledging the need for a total, uncompromising commitment to safety, recognizing the truth that we are human, we acknowledge our dependence on one another, for safety demands that we truly become our sister's and brother's keeper and the practice of safety is both a personal and a mutual obligation.

There-fore I promise to let my co-workers know that I value and appreciate their safe actions. When I observe them doing something unsafely, I will communicate my concern and positively inter-act in a caring, tactful, respectful and honest manner.

In return, I hereby give permission and request that all of my co-workers and managers inter-act in that same positive manner with me.

I promise to accept that praise and concern for what it is, an expression that my friends and co-workers care.

Let us draw our inspiration from the words of that great Canadian , Terry Fox, who said,

"Somewhere the hurting must stop. I'm determined to take myself to the limit for this cause."

For   information and permission to use this pledge contact: Art Fettig, President, Growth Unlimited Inc. 36 Fairview Ave, Battle Creek Michigan 49017
Phones 1-800-441-7676 or 616-965-2229

𝕮hapter 14

← →

FIVE TIPS FOR POSITIVE INTERACTION

1. IF YOU OBSERVE SOMEONE VIOLATING A safety rule or working in an unsafe manner, positively interact. Be a sister's and a brother's keeper. Remind them that they are important and you don't want to see them get injured.

2. Expect some flack now and then. Remember, people have personal problems. Be patient but be firm. Remind them that you'd expect them to positively interact with you under similar circumstances.

3. Don't go on an ego trip. This is no "gotcha" game. When you approach positive interaction with the right attitude then people will appreciate it.

4. When others call your unsafe conduct to your attention then thank them. It is sometimes difficult to take

criticism, but remember, positive interaction saves lives.

5. If you try a positive interaction approach and it fails, then call the situation to your supervisor's attention. Again, do this in a positive, not a negative way. After all, our goal is to prevent accidents and injuries and to save lives, not to get others in trouble.

Be a sister's and a brother's keeper. Use positive interaction every time you see someone working in a dangerous, unsafe manner.

Chapter 15

MOVING TARGETS

FOR YEARS THE BILLBOARD HAS BEEN A popular, effective means of advertising and advertising is certainly an important tool for selling.

Nearly every organization I visit uses billboards of some kind to sell their safety message. The problem is this. Many of them hang up a new poster every six months at the same old location and expect miracles.

If you pay attention to the large billboards you will notice that they are ever changing. And you will also note that many advertisers move their messages from one billboard to another.

At the DuPont Kinston Plant I observed that they had a number of safety posters on easels and they tell me that they move them about as moving targets to catch your attention.

People often learn to ignore a poster that is always at the same location with basically the same message.

Years ago when I was first trying to learn the speaking craft, my mentor, Herb True, suggested that I just keep throwing exciting new ideas up in front of an audience allowing them to take a hold of whatever concepts appealed to them.

He suggested that I never let an audience get settled in. "Every time they think they know where you are going, Art," Herb told me, "pull the carpet out from under them."

I think the same concepts work with posters.

Find a cartoonist in your organization and have her or him draw you colorful posters that use the same powerful concepts you find in other posters only have them customized with your logo and perhaps characters which your people can identify with.

The following illustrations should spark your imagination. We've got a lot more poster ideas we'll share with you later.

Many plants have their employee's children color our posters. Then we have the kids sign their work.

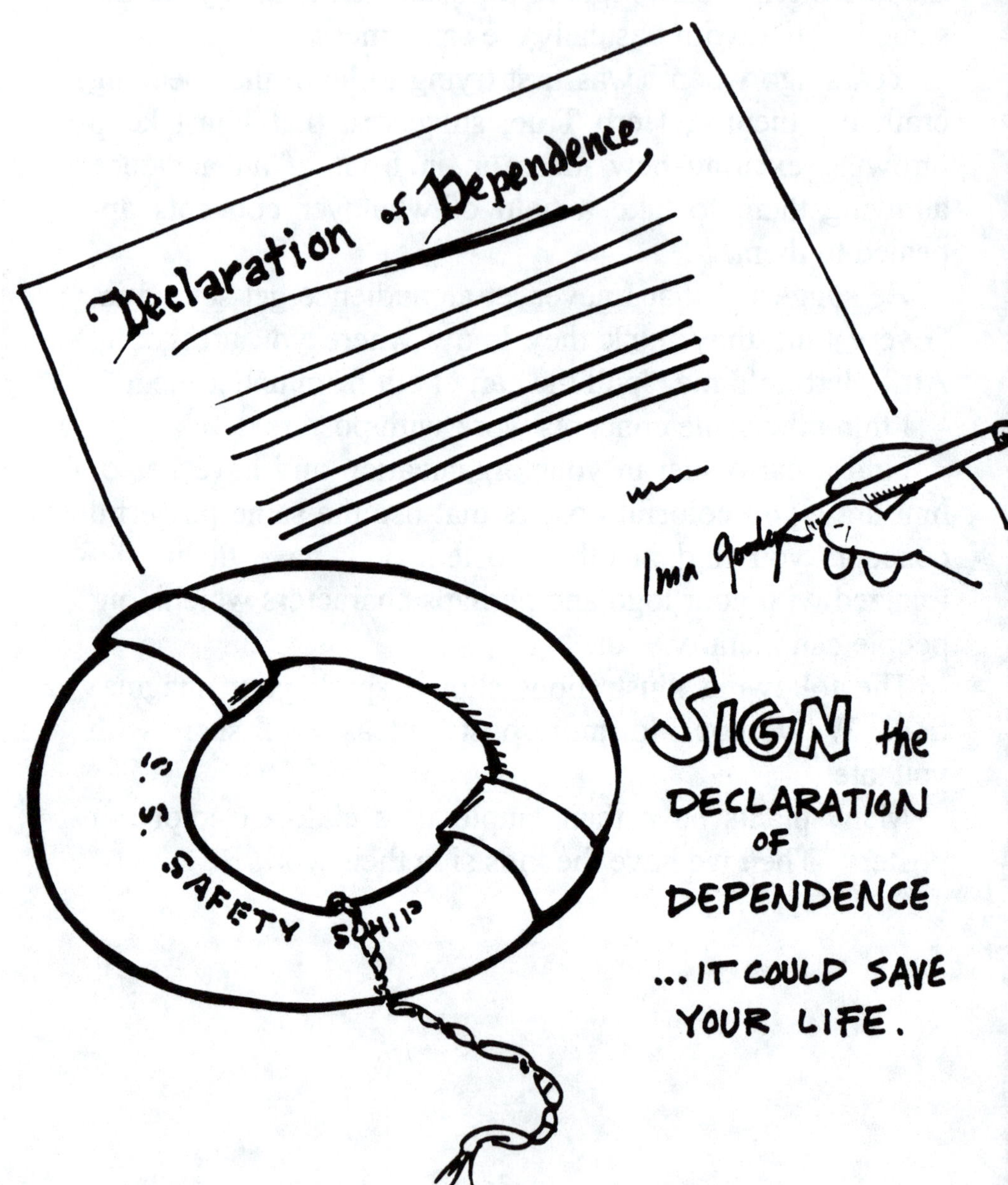

Declaration of Dependence
Ima Goodguy
SIGN the DECLARATION OF DEPENDENCE
...IT COULD SAVE YOUR LIFE.
S.S. SAFETY SHIP

GIVE YOUR FELLOW
WORKER THE RIGHT
TO USE POSITIVE INTERVENTION
WHEN THEY SEE YOU WORKING
UNSAFELY.

CAUTION: HEAVY
WAIT! STOP! CAN I HAVE A FEW WORDS WITH YOU?
...IF YOU SPOT SOMEONE WORKING IN AN UNSAFE MANNER--
POSITIVELY INTERVENE
...be a Brother's and a sister's keeper.

Chapter 16

A STEP AT A TIME

FORD MOTOR COMPANY'S CHIEF EXECUtive Officer Donald Peterson, who retired in 1990, had a management style that will be a model for chief executives for years to come.

Peterson hired W. Edwards Deming, a quality master who taught the Japanese the secrets of statistical process control.

Peterson became Deming's personal champion and dramatically boosted the quality of Ford's cars.

Deming taught Peterson the philosophy that became the driving force behind everything that Peterson accomplished, continual improvement. The theory is that every worker should try to improve, day by day, and never get discouraged.

That philosophy changed the fortunes of Ford Motor Company.

That philosophy can change your life, too--the theory of continual improvement, a program of daily growth.

Don't expect to make one magnificent sale which will herald a new era of safety within your organization.

There is an old Chinese proverb that says, "The journey of a thousand leagues begins with but a single step." Selling an attitude of safety is a lifetime quest. A program of quality must often be sold to just one worker at a time. So too with safety.

It will not happen if you stay at your desk. You have to get into the arena. And you will meet your critics and detractors.

Ignore Your Critics

Always remember the words of President Teddy Roosevelt,who once said, "It is not the critic who counts; not the man who points out where the strong man stumbled or where the doer of deeds could have done them better. The credit belongs to the man who is actually in the arena, whose face is marred with dust and sweat and blood...At the best, he knows the triumph of high achievement; if he fails, at least he fails while daring greatly, so that his place shall never be with those cold and timid souls who knew neither victory nor defeat."

Feedback Helps Us Grow

At Growth Unlimited, Incorporated, we thrive on feedback.

If this book helped you in any way, please drop us a

note and let us know. If you feel it let you down, let us know that too. We are always seeking to improve our products.

The most important concept that I can leave you with is this: Ideas without action are useless.

Unless you try these ideas, they will not work for you. You must put them into action. Sometimes you will fail and sometimes you will think you have failed when you have succeeded.

Often you will not see the fruits of your labor for months or years to come. Persistence is the key to selling and the best way to overcome discouragement is with renewed efforts.

I wish you success and if I can in some way help, just give me a call.

Art Fettig, 1-800-441-7676

Fax Number (616) 965-4522

Email artfettig @voyager.net

Website www.IMASource.com

BOOK Four IV

the Quest Continues

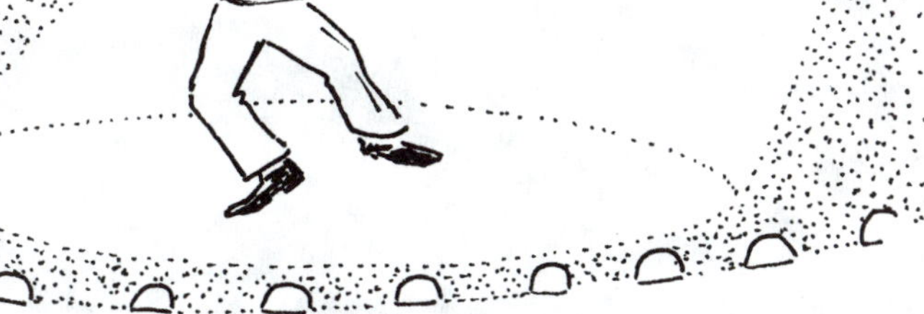

Chapter 1

THE QUEST CONTINUES

THE FOURTH BOOK IN THIS collection is one that I have looked forward to for a long time.

It gives me the opportunity to gather some of my favorite material and present it to you the reader. For instance, my story on Sue Satterfield is one of my favorites because it shows how one person can solve an environmental problem, and with nothing but a strong and positive attitude, create and implement an immediate solution.

All my life I have tried to capture things. First I captured ideas in print in the form of articles published for dozens of different magazines. Then I often took those same articles and put them together in my early books.

Some ideas I captured in smaller booklets.

Then the tape recorder came along and we created audio tapes and audio albums.

My good friend and associate, Terry Porchert, came into my life and became my video producer and we've now captured many of my best stories and speeches on video tape. In fact, we did an inventory recently and learned that we have over sixty different videos at this time.

In *The Quest Continues*, I have the opportunity to upgrade many of the articles which first appeared in our newsletters.

Then there is the story about my Tap dancing experiences. It is true that at 66, although I had a dream about it for over a quarter of a century, I finally got around to taking tap dance lessons and in past years I have stopped shows in fancy hotels in Atlanta, Georgia; Nashville, Tennessee; Las Vegas, Nevada; and even in my own home town.

Maybe that says something about my own quest. My goal is to touch people's lives and in the safety field my continuing quest is to provide the means to help others prevent accidents and injuries.

We talk about our continuing quest for the Golden Goose Egg, that is our name for Zero Injuries.

It is an elusive target, but that does not dampen our enthusiasm in the pursuit.

One firm I worked with made the statement that there are no such things as accidents. That since they can be prevented they should not be called accidents.

They believe that every would-be accident can and should be anticipated and prevented.

That is a pretty lofty goal and yet, I guess they are probably close to right.

Recently, a friend of mine asked me to write a little contribution for her new book on the subject of luck.

My favorite saying is that *luck is simply when preparation meets opportunity.* If that is correct then if we ever attribute a great safety record to luck, then we must also celebrate all of the preparation that went into the process.

I think that it is lucky for me that you are reading this right now. I spent nearly 50 years preparing to write this material and that might be considered a lot of preparation, but the fact that you are giving me the opportunity to share my thinking with you is very flattering to me.

Perhaps we are both lucky that this is happening.

I'm not certain that I will go beyond that fiftieth year in the safety field. Maybe I've done my job and it's time for me to set this aside and spend the rest of my writing and speaking career spreading good humor and joy.

In any event, I certainly hope that in some way my work has and will inspire others to continue the quest for that golden goose egg. Zero injuries. Zero pain and suffering. Zero heartbreak.

Let me pass this baton on to you, the reader. Take it and run a good race. I wish you a lifetime of victories.

Chapter 2

I'LL TAKE CARE OF THAT!

AS SAFETY PEOPLE WE MUST REAL-ize that we must be made of special stuff. How often have you walked into a situation that just isn't right and yet, because there were others who should have taken the responsibility, you simply pretended to not be aware of the situation?

Certainly we are all guilty of this and that is why the story I am about to tell you is so important, especially today is these challenging times.

Sue Satterfield is a real "Southern Woman." That is the first thing she made clear to us when we met her in Atlanta, Georgia. Georgia Power Company had hired me to do a series of programs for their supervisors and foreman.

My wife, Ruthie, and I first met Richard Satterfield

and his wife, Sue, in April and we returned in October for a second session. They were fantastic hosts on the first trip and so we decided to spend a couple of days visiting the beautiful foothills of Northern Georgia together.

We visited the Hiawassee fairgrounds on a Saturday and then in the evening we attended a Country Music show. We guessed that there were some five thousand people in the auditorium which was packed. Luckily we found four seats together in the rear of the giant hall. As we walked inside the auditorium I was hit by the hot, stale air. A group was on-stage singing their hearts out and the audience response was really flat.

Sue sat down, sniffed a bit and said out loud for us all to hear, "This air is foul." And, of course, we all agreed. "I'll take care of that!" She said confidently. Sue stood up and went to the rear of the hall where the fellow from the Lion's Club, the program's sponsor, sat at a table. "This air is foul in here." She said to the man.

He explained that he was alone at the desk and there was simply nothing he could do about the situation. "We've got to open up some of those side doors", Sue said, and again the man explained that he could do nothing about the matter.

"I'll take care of that!" She said, and she walked over to a fellow sitting on a chair at the rear of the hall. "We are going to let some fresh air into this hall." She said. "Will you help me?"

Actually Sue said, "Will you *hep* me?" However I

am a Yankee and so there is just no credibility to whatever I report as southern talk.

The man at the rear of the hall stood up and joined Sue as she walked over to the side of the hall and, with the help of two other men, slid up one of those big steel sliding overhead doors.

You could feel that sweet smelling Georgia mountain air rush into the huge room. A moment later a second door swung up and more air rushed in.

Then Sue walked over to the far side of the hall, with her newly enlisted crew, and wham! Another door sailed upwards and then yet another.

Now she had a great system of cross ventilation going. It was heavenly.

Five thousand people who had been sitting there suffering with the lack of oxygen and whatever other elements people suck out of the air supply, now began to inhale deeply.

It was like magic. The musicians on stage began to perform better. The crowd really got into the music, now that their survival was no longer in jeopardy. They started in clapping and stompin' and that turned out to be one of the most wonderful Country Music shows that we have attended in a very long time.

After they opened the fourth door, Sue calmly walked back to her seat with us and said proudly, "We took care of that."

Can you imagine five thousand people were willing to just sit and put up with really stale air and not one of them made an effort to do anything about it? It took a "real southern woman" named Sue.

Oh, how the world needs more people like her. How many times have we all suffered in silence rather than take the necessary action to make this a little better world?

As safety people we must have the gumption, the courage, the wisdom, and the take-charge spirit that Sue Satterfield displayed at the Hiawassee County Fairgrounds recently.

Georgia Power has invited us back again and this time Sue promises that we are all going Country Dancing. Well, she didn't exactly say that but, after four goes at it, that is what I finally understood that she said. It isn't always easy for me to understand because, as I said, Sue is a real "Southern woman and a fantastic person."

Chapter 3

A LIFESAVING MEETING

I SPEND MANY HOURS A WEEK READing and doing research for my writing and speaking assignments.

Whenever I am visiting an area that is new to me I often read what I can about that location.

When I was asked to keynote the Governor's Safety, Health and Wellness Conference in Alaska I thought it would be a good time for me to invest in James A. Michener's book titled, *Alaska*. I am so glad that I did.

Michener has always been one of my favorite authors. He died recently. His first book, *Tales of the South Pacific*, captured my imagination.

In his book, *Alaska*, I discovered a fascinating story that I tell to audiences whenever I have the opportunity.

James Cook was a rather young naval officer in the British Navy when he was first made Captain of his own ship.

It was in 1778 and up to that time a British warship could leave England with a crew of 400 sailors and expect to have 180 dead by the time that the voyage was over. Sometimes the toll reached the appalling figure of 280 dead.

With those kind of losses it took a bit of imagination and often brute force, to enlist a crew for such a voyage. No doubt you've seen scenes in movies like, *Kidnapped*, where recruiting crews would go into a tavern and beat the customers over the head with clubs and drag them onto the ships.

I suppose the next morning when the victim came to, someone would be there with a handshake and say, "Congratulations! You made a wise career move. You have just joined the British Navy."

For just a few moments I hope you will use your imagination as we picture ourselves aboard Cook's warship as he assumes his first command.

Cook is up on the poop deck standing tall as he addresses his assembled crew.

"Men," he begins. "They tell me that on an average voyage I should expect that about half of you will die."

Captain Cook looks down at his crew and measures off about 180. "That means that everybody from about here over will die."

There is a wave of fear passing over the assembly and they begin to listen more intently.

"Now if we have really rough seas and bad weather then perhaps 280 of you will die." Again Cook measures the group and sections about 2/3 of the group. "About from here over." He says.

Again there is more murmuring and signs of even greater concern and fear.

Looking very solemn and pausing for impact he finally continues, "However, men, I have come up with some rules for your safety and health. If every one of you will follow these rules then none of you must die on this voyage."

There is a general sigh of relief and Cook senses it as he says, "How many of you will listen to the rules?"

Four hundred hands go up. Let me ask you the reader, would you be interested? Of course.

Captain Cook then went on to the list of rules.

First.   Keep your quarters clean.

Second.   Wear dry clothes whenever you   can.

Third.   Follow our rule of one watch on, two off, get plenty of rest.

Finally.   you will each day consume your portion of wort and rob.

"Say what?" The excited crew called out.

"Wort and rob." Cook repeated. "Wort is a mixture of malt, sauerkraut and whatever vegetables we can throw into the pot. Rob is a mixture of lime and orange juice."

As you know, British sailors became known as Limeys, because, each day, they had to consume their portion of rob.

The crew, to a man, agreed to follow the rules and as a result Cook was able to eliminate the scourge that had taken hundreds of thousands of lives on ships throughout the world.

Scurvy was the cause of all those deaths and Cook's list of safety and health rules and their daily applications changed the course of naval history.

Captain Cook became a legend in his own time and he brought fame and fortune to the British Empire.

Cook and his crew charted unknown waters. He sailed to Alaska and Washington and to Hawaii and beyond.

Certainly, this must have been one of the most important safety and health meetings of all time because these rules were implemented throughout the British Navy and then by navies all over the world.

Chapter 4

SOMEWHERE THE HURTING MUST STOP

AS I STOOD IN GALE-FORCE WINDS coming off the ocean, I read these words in Harbourside Park in St. Johns, Newfoundland recently, and I was impressed with their significance in the field of safety. Appearing on a plaque honoring Terry Fox, the young man who tried to run across Canada wearing an artificial leg, the complete text of that plaque reads,

> "SOMEWHERE THE HURTING MUST STOP.
> I'M DETERMINED TO TAKE MYSELF
> TO THE LIMIT FOR THIS CAUSE"
> *Terry Fox*

Terry's cause was cancer research and the plaque, on which the words above were inscribed is found at the point where Terry began his cross-country run.

With an artificial leg replacing his own, removed because of cancer, and suffering other cancer related complications, he ran a distance of 3,339 miles. In Thunder Bay he was forced to stop and later died in a hospital there. Terry took himself to the limit and, in doing so, raised over 24 million dollars for cancer research. In essence he gave his life for that cause.

"Somewhere the hurting must stop." I used that quote in the closing session of the Newfoundland's Safety Council meeting, where I had the rare treat of being both the opening keynoter and the closing speaker.

Terry Fox's words seemed to be exactly the right challenge to that group as they headed home to face the task of implementing the ideas they had learned during their two day conference.

Subsequently, I had the privilege of addressing 800 maintenance workers for General Motors in Defiance, Ohio. Terry Fox's words were appropriate again as I challenged them to make a personal commitment to safety by coming forward and signing our "Declaration of Inter-dependence." One of their co-workers had recently fallen to his death while several other GM employees had been killed in accidents during 1990.

My challenge to them was to make a personal commitment that this would be the time and place where "the hurting must stop." And that's my challenge to each of you reading this book.

Let the hurting stop here and now with each of us, and like the inspiring story of Terry Fox, let each of us be determined to take ourselves **"to the limit for this cause."**

In our situation.....the cause of preventing accidents and saving lives.

**Let each of us take ourselves to
the limit for this cause...Pre-
venting accidents and saving
lives.**

Chapter 5

TODAY'S CHALLENGING TIMES

IT'S A JUNGLE OUT THERE. HAVE YOU heard? Have you noticed first hand that these times they are a changing? Somebody else said it so well, "The only constant today that you can count on is change." But how is change affecting your job in the field of safety?

Most days I talk with at least a half a dozen safety people from all over America. Some have a hundred people they must look out for. I talked with a friend the other day who has ninety-thousand. Some head large safety departments and a few work at safety just part time for small shops. They all give me the same message. "These times they are changing."

Some of my safety friends tell me that their jobs have been changed. Some report that they have been assigned additional duties. And some of these same friends tell me that their budgets have been cut.

More work and fewer people to do the work with. More challenges and less money to use to meet those challenges.

Some report that there is a lot less emphasis on safety and a lot more on simple survival. One fellow summed it up this way, "When the going gets tough, safety goes down the drain."

Perhaps I sound a little bit depressed. After all, I am supposed to be motivating these safety people and they seem to be demotivating me.

I believe that right now, today, in America, Safety people need a stronger stomach than ever to stay in the safety field. They need to make the greatest commitment of their lives.

If you work for a corporation or an organization that has claimed that SAFETY IS OUR #1 PRIORITY in the past, then perhaps you'd better look out. For safety is often a priority they hang up on a flag pole for people to salute just during the good times. Safety just might be a luxury that is mistakenly considered too costly during troubled times.

Whenever I run into that word "priority" when it comes to safety I get a little nervous. Because priorities change. I like to think of safety as more than just a priority. Safety must become a value with organizations and with people inside those organizations.

A value is something we hold dear. Something which becomes a part of us. Safety must become something that is at the forefront regardless of how things happen to be going that particular day.

The slogan "Safety Pays" is a true one. Injuries and accidents are so costly and they can never be measured on the bottom line.

And so the challenge to everyone in safety today must be HANG IN THERE!   HANG IN THERE, TOUGH!

If you don't have the stomach to live with tragedy, or even more important, if you don't have the internal fortitude, or to put it another way, if you don't have the guts to stand up and fight for safety and the very lives you were hired to protect, then just don't come back from lunch today. Don't come back to work tomorrow. Find another spot that demands less of your commitment.

Safety really isn't for everybody. But, if you do HANG IN THERE TOUGH! Then learn to live your profession with a passion. It is the only way to go.

Chapter 6

WHAT DO WE DO?

THE OTHER DAY I ANSWERED THE phone and it was a wrong number. The party on the other end said, "Well , while I have you, what do you do?" I told him briefly that I wrote books and gave speeches.

"About what?" He asked.

I explained that I talked to Safety Leaders and management teams all over the U.S. and that I often go to plants and talked with managers and supervisors and groups of workers, often at safety rallies and banquets.

The fellow persisted. "And what do you talk about to all those people?"

I knew the fellow was calling on my toll free 800 number so I was paying for the call so I tried to cut it short.

"About attitudes." I replied.

"Attitudes?" He asked.

"Sure attitudes." I replied. "We find that when people start looking out for themselves and for each other that the number of accidents and injuries drop."

"So how do you get them to look out for each other?" He asked.

I was beginning to wonder if this fellow was really a wrong number after all. He sounded like an investigative reporter, or maybe someone from our competition.

"There are many times in all of our lives when we let our guards down, and then accidents happen. We convince people that it would be a good deal if they had someone looking out for them. Then they come forward and sign up for safety. They also promise to look out for one another and they give each other permission and request that the others look out for them when it comes to safety."

He didn't respond. For a second I thought I had satisfied him, but then he asked, "Does it work?"

"Sure it works." I said.

"Who have you tried it with?" He asked.

"With GM people. With Exxon in Texas, Louisiana, and California. With Du Pont people. With people in Alabama, Georgia, Illinois, Indiana, Michigan, Oklahoma, New Hampshire, Florida, New York, Alaska and Hawaii. With people all over the United States and in Newfoundland, Nova Scotia and Toronto and railroaders, power people, construction workers....."

"Hold it." He said, "I get the idea. And thanks."

I said, "Wait a minute, I've told you everything

about what I do. What do you do?"

"Do?" He said. "I don't have anything to do. I'm retired. So I just sit here and dial 800 numbers to see who answers."

Chapter 7

SAFETY & PARADIGMS

A FEW YEARS BACK I DISCOVERED A futurist named Joe Arthur Barker and he really turned on my creative thinking juices. A half a dozen friends had already told me about the great video titled *DISCOVERING THE FUTURE* and when I visited my good friend Roger Shaw over at General Motor's plant in Muncie, Indiana he was good enough to let me watch the video there.

I went right from there to a bookstore and purchased Barker's book titled *FUTURE'S EDGE, Discovering the New Paradigms of Success.*

One of the definitions of a paradigm comes from Willis Harmon of the Stanford Research Institute. He defines the paradigm as "the basic way of perceiving, thinking, valuing and doing, associated with a particular vision of reality."

As I watched the video I immediately let my mind race ahead and apply what I was learning to the safety field.

The best example from all that I saw came from the Swiss Watch Industry. In 1967 the Swiss dominated the watch industry. They produced 65% of all the watch movements and brought in from 80 to 90% of the profits. They continued to improve their product and had a wonderful research program. At that time the Japanese had just 1% of the world market.

Swiss researchers came up with a breakthrough in watch movements called the electronic quartz movement. They presented to the Swiss manufacturers who looked it over, asked, "What is it? It cannot be a watch movement because it has no gears and no main spring." And then allowed their researchers to showcase the useless invention at the World Watch Congress in 1968.

Today the Swiss have less than 10% of the world market. A company named Seiko in Japan now has about 35% of the world market. Some 50,000 of the 65,000 Swiss watch makers have lost their jobs.

The Swiss thought so little of the electronic watch movement that they didn't even bother to patent the invention.

Now, the paradigm in which the Swiss did their thinking actually destroyed most of the business.

They thought a certain way. They held a fixed set of beliefs.

Of course the logical question is this, "What beliefs

are holding you back in the safety field?"

Although the concept did not come from Barker's book or his video, I picture paradigms as little boxes within which we live.

When a new idea is presented to us that does not fit in comfortably with our current set of beliefs, then we reject it. It makes us uncomfortable.

I did a lot of driving after viewing that wonderful video and I started thinking about the different people I had encountered in the past 50 years involved in the safety field.

A couple of experiences came to mind. In each instance I felt very much like banging my head against the wall because I was so frustrated. I simply could not understand the other person's way of thinking. I felt it was gross stupidity, indifference, near criminal stupidity.

I did not understand what was happening. I was simply presenting concepts that would not fit within the other person's current paradigm.

One example involves a top, top safety official with a major union. In fact, this man was responsible for the safety of hundreds of thousands of workers.

One day the man called to advise me that they would not allow me to speak at a major joint session of union and corporate safety leaders.

"You are a menace to have on our property," he explained to me quite bluntly.

I, of course, asked him why he felt that way.

"You have been telling our workers that they should

take responsibility not only for their own safety, but for their fellow workers as well." He said. "The fact is, the corporation is entirely responsible for the workers safety. They should provide a fail-safe environment where a worker cannot get injured regardless of their conduct."

I tried to get the man to expand on this feeling and he went on to say that, "even though a worker breaks a safety rule, or rules, he or she should not have to pay for this with an injury."

I reminded the man that ten of his Brothers had paid with their lives the previous year. "And many of those fatal accidents could have been avoided if the workers had just done a better job of looking out for themselves and if their Brothers and Sisters had been looking out for them."

Again he repeated that this was not their job, that the total responsibility for safety was with the corporation and not the worker.

Can you picture a guy locked in a little box and he would not allow his thinking to explore any idea that would not fit in the box? Well, I can because I talked with him.

Now let's put the shoe on the other foot.

Not long ago I talked with a safety director who had a different set of ideas. His safety paradigm sounded exactly like this. "We do everything that is humanly possible at our plant to make it safe for the worker. "But, Art," he explained, "we have a bunch of yo-yo's at our place, and you just can't tell some of these people anything. It is as if they wanted to get hurt and no matter what we do, they keep getting hurt."

That man, too, is locked in a box. He knows he cannot change things so he has given up trying.

As I was travelling along I-69 enroute to Indianapolis the other day my mind went spinning as I thought about all of the different sizes and shapes of paradigms that are out there in the safety field.

I've run into safety people who believe ergonomics are the hope of the future. That everything else is obsolete.

Surely you've met engineers who believe that they can engineer out all possibilities of injuries, provided they can have enough time and enough money to accomplish the job.

Have you ever met the equipment problem solvers?

Or the engineers?

What about the training specialists who tell you that if they can just have your employees for enough hours for enough weeks that they can train your people so thoroughly that they will never be injured again.

And then we come to the human behaviorists. The behavior modification specialists who think that they have the key.

Can you see how easy it is to get boxed in? How your own background and your own experience can possibly blind you to new ways, new discoveries, new possibilities that might provide one more piece to the continuing puzzle called worker safety.

I see it clearer now. I still believe that our approach

to winning worker commitment to safety and to positive interaction will help with all of the other necessary approaches to safety.

I never did promise anyone a rose garden. Safety is an ever changing ever challenging process.

As I dig deeper into the matter of paradigms I find that my safety observations are a bit superficial, still we have our own unique paradigms, prejudices, hang-ups, limitations, whatever. The secret to keeping fresh and excited about our job and our mission of safety is to make a genuine effort to keep on growing every day and to attempt to keep our minds open to new ways of preventing accidents and saving lives.

Take a good look at your own thinking process. I challenge you . Don't end up as an unemployed Swiss watch maker, scratching your head and wondering how you missed the boat when it came to quartz movement.

Open up your mind to exciting new possibilities. That's the hope of the future.

Chapter 8

MILLIONS FOR DEFENSE

L AST WEEK I TALKED WITH A RAILROAD superintendent. He told me that they had spent one million dollars that day in claim settlements. "The problem." he said, "is that a big chunk of that is a settlement for a back injury and this employee is back working and could claim another back injury tomorrow and we'd be right back where we were before the settlement."

Sound familiar? Well as Paul Harvey says, "Now here is the rest of the story."

Although the superintendent admits they spent one million dollars that day and it was just a part of their annual spending, nevertheless, he said that they did not have the personnel available to get involved with a more intensive safety program.

For some reason people have the money for medical

expenses, for workman's compensation payments and for personal injury settlements. They have the time to appear in court, and to give depositions in lawsuits and to answer the reams of interrogation and yet they can not afford the personnel to conduct a program to prevent all this needless aggravation and expense.

Personally, I believe it is a matter of selling. Somewhere,, someone has badly failed to sell the idea that safety really pays. Perhaps top management simply feels that injury and accident are inevitable and that the laws of chance cannot be altered. Of course, this is pure hogwash.

Another major point in figuring the cost of safety is when employees develop safe habits their safe attitudes are reflected in better quality, high productivity, and less absenteeism.

When employees see that the organization that they work for cares about their safety and welfare then employees care more about the organization.

Chapter 9

←——————→

SUPPOSING

BACK IN 1926 WHEN CHARLES A. LINDbergh flew U.S. mail runs between St. Louis and Chicago, he often became bored on calm days when the weather was no challenge. To kill time and to keep alert he played a mind game called "Suppose."

Suppose they could refine a new kind of gasoline, a lighter fuel with less weight so that they could carry more. Suppose he could buy one of those new type Wright-Bellanca planes just coming into production. Maybe he could then fly St. Louis to New York.

Supposing he could fly all night like the moon. He could break the existing records across the country. He could span continents. Supposing he could even fly from New York to Paris.

For years now I have played a game called "What if." I can remember staying in an inexpensive hotel in Chicago and walking down Michigan Ave. at Grant Park looking across the street at the Conrad Hilton Hotel dreaming about some day landing that early morning speaker spot at the National Safety Congress.

And one day in 1976 I received a call from a fellow asking me to visit the National Safety Council's office in Chicago. He wanted to talk to me about speaking at the Congress. What a thrill it was speaking for thousands of the world's top safety people.

Supposing...Yes I played that game of "what if" or "supposing" or whatever you want to call it for twelve more years. Supposing they asked me to do it again. And in 1988, it was at the McCormick Place and once again I was the early morning speaker.

Supposing they asked me to keynote the Governor's Safety Conference in Alaska? In Hawaii, In Washington? In Newfoundland? In New Hampshire and New Jersey and what if....just supposing.

What if G.M. called? And Upjohn, and Westinghouse and DuPont and Exxon? What if Power Companies from all over the U.S. called? What if I was invited to Bermuda, the Virgin Islands, Nassau, Malaysia?

What if I wrote a book on safety and thousands of safety people bought it? And what if I wrote another and another...just suppose.

And what if in time I'd give speeches in all 50 of these United States and in more than half a dozen

Canadian Provinces - what if, all of that...just supposing.

Would I then be satisfied? Let me answer that for you because I've had all of those dreams and they've all come true, but the game goes on. I'm still playing that game.

What if I could write one article and it could touch one person's life and supposing that person did one thing that would prevent a serious accident....

Or, what if, just supposing, I could give one speech that could inspire two people to fight a little harder for their safety programs and....

Just suppose if YOU could speak at the early morning session at the National Congress. What if I could inspire YOU and a few more just like you to dream?

What if I could inspire you to join the ranks of Charles A. Lindbergh and a lot of other pioneers?

Supposing I could persuade you to play the game "what if" or "supposing" or whatever you want to call it? What if I could get you to dream big, wonderful challenging dreams?

Well, just suppose if.........

Chapter 10

BIKING

I'M LEARNING A LOT FROM PEDALING MY new bicycle around the neighborhood. You just can't coast uphill.

The same is true in the Safety Profession. No matter how hard you try you just simply cannot coast uphill.

What I've also learned by being around the safety profession since 1948 is this. In the safety profession you simply cannot coast, period.

I must have heard at least a hundred safety leaders confess to me, "Art, we were doing so good that we just eased up a bit and it all seemed to fall apart." In other words they tried coasting.

Safety is something that demands a constant, all out effort. You have to keep pedaling just as if you were going uphill no matter what the terrain might appear to be.

I must confess that I am bike minded recently. Just a week ago I went to a neighborhood garage sale and over in the corner I discovered an old Firestone, balloon tired, two wheeler. It looked a bit tarnished but the tires looked good and I even took it out for a road test.

The brakes worked fine and maybe it did need a little oil, but I paid the man $15 and loaded it into my van.

I discovered that the bike was mostly chrome and in excellent condition so with a little effort I had a bike that glistened.

Then I set the seat up higher and raised the handle bars and now I am exploring the neighborhood every morning.

Another thing I have discovered is that Battle Creek, Michigan is a hilly city. When I coast down the hill from my house to the river it is practically effortless. In fact, I have to hit the brake several times to slow down so that I can deal with the traffic on the road at the bottom of the hill.

Going back up is another story. I can manage it for a bit, but then I must surrender to the hill and walk my bike up the rest of the way.

At a few other locations I have learned to gain enough momentum on the way down the hill so that if I start pedaling right away I can pedal all the way up the next hill.

I guess that with experience I will learn that with every ride downhill I can expect that there will be another hill to climb just down the road a bit.

So it is with safety. Some people get a bit of a coast with spring and summer. Then the snow comes and there are a dozen different ways a worker can get injured in winter injuries.

In spring, many workers do things that subject them to off duty injuries such as softball games and water skiing.

Life is a series of hills and valleys and unless we become planners then the uphill challenges sometimes overcome us.

What am I learning with my bike? The same lessons that I keep relearning a dozen different ways each day.

Life is a challenge. It really does not get easier. We have to face the reality that coasting is a luxury that carries with it a penalty. With every down hill coast we must expect an uphill climb down the road.

A great safety program does not allow for coasting. We must keep making that all out effort every day, every moment if we hope to become and remain champions.

Chapter 11

LEARNING AT NOTRE DAME UNIVERSITY

EVERY SEMESTER I DRIVE OVER TO South Bend, Indiana and make a one hour presentation in the business class of my good friend and mentor Herb True, Ph.D.

In addition to becoming a famous professional speaker, Herb has continued to teach at Notre Dame.

Following my talk, many of the students claim that my one hour presentation had a greater impact on their lives than any of the classes they have taken in their entire education process.

While I find that extremely difficult to believe, I still love hearing it.

What is the message I present that has such an impact?

It is really quite simple, I tell the students that they have greatness within them. That they are here for a purpose. That each of us has a mission, a talent, a special calling. And if we fail to answer that mission, to use that talent to fulfill our calling that something that should be done to make this a better world will remain undone for an eternity.

I suggest to the students of Notre Dame that they find a job that they can become passionate about.

During my presentation many of the students laugh and then many cry and I give them special poems to help them.

It isn't much, really, but many of the students have never thought about becoming passionate about their work or about an obligation to make this a better world.

Every time I give that presentation at Notre Dame, I feel better about myself and better about the future of this nation and this world.

On my drive home I always find myself evaluating my own talent, my own performance and I ask myself what can I do this day, this week, this year to make this a better world. And as I find the answers, I find that I continue to be passionate about my work.

Chapter 12

PURPOSE

RECENTLY I TALKED WITH A SAFETY manager with one of the major petroleum corporations. "I've been reading your safety books, Art," he said, "and I just realized that they aren't about safety at all. They are about success and happiness."

He then went on to tell me what a major impact I had had on his life. Of course, he was absolutely right. My safety books are not really about safety. But if you do read them and apply the ideas in them, then I guarantee you will have a lot more success and happiness in the safety field.

This book is not about safety either. Not really. It is about success and happiness too.

I seldom find anyone who is unhappy about their work who is doing a great job. Usually the unhappiest people in the world are those who do their work poorly. You find great zest in people when those people are doing outstanding work.

I find it kind of fascinating to be working on a book to help people do a better job in the 21st Century. Frankly, I never expected to be around in the 21st Century. I have always considered it beyond my life cycle. Yet, feeling as I do today, I now no longer doubt that I will be around; I now feel that I will probably be doing what others believe to be working.

I haven't really done any work for a couple or more decades now. What I do I would probably do without remuneration if it was necessary. (Don't pass that around please, a lot of people pay me a great deal of money to do what I am now doing.)

The fact that what I am doing is play did not come about by accident. It is all part of a carefully contrived plan, believe me. I set out to make my work fun, and the better I got at what I was doing the more fun it was.

When I got to the point in public speaking that I succeeded every time I tried, then I set new standards for myself.

Once in my career I received twenty-seven standing ovations in a row. At that point I realized I was telling the audience exactly what they wanted to hear instead of what they should be hearing.

I changed my personal goals, instead of winning a standing ovation, I set out to create some kind of behavior change in at least one member of that audi-ence. I set out to touch just one life every time I gave a talk.

Once I set the goal, then I found there was far greater joy and satisfaction in my work. Instead of having members of my audience coming up and saying, "You were great!" I began to hear them saying, "Thank you."

It was as if I had given them a special personal gift with my talk. After a few years I finally discovered what it was that I was giving to each audience. I was giving each person that great gift of feeling better about themselves. I told them, "There is greatness in you." Fortunately many of them believed it, often for the first time in their lives.

And many of them went out and discovered that greatness I was talking about. They honed their talents and they set out to use their talents for the good of all humankind.

Remarkable things have happened to people and many of them say that turning point in their lives was when they attended one of my programs or read one of my books.

Does that mean that I am someone special and that you should hold me in special esteem? No, it means that you are someone special and you should hold yourself in special esteem.   Again, my message is the same message that I offer to everyone that I meet. **There is a greatness in you. You are somebody special. You will do great things in your lifetime.**

It would be nice if you held me in special esteem. I'd like that very much, but I hope you begin to see the greatness in everyone you meet. If you can be the instrument that puts them in touch with their own greatness, then so much the better.

Recently I spoke for middle and senior management people who work with major petroleum firms and for a number of power organizations each year.

I asked the members of this particular audience this question. "How many of you believe that you could hold your jobs five years from now with the knowledge and skills you have today?"

No one raised their hand. I was not satisfied yet. I thought I'd try again. Maybe they were just being cool and not answering.

"Lets put it another way," I suggested. "How many of you think you will have to acquire new knowledge and master new skills just to survive?"

This time everyone raised their hands. Everyone.

I thought I'd try one more question. "How many of you believe that your employers will supply you with all the knowledge and all of the training you will require to survive?"

Once more no one raised their hand.

"Great, " I said. "Then all of you know that you will have to do much of your own learning, and somehow acquire new skills without the benefit of your employer. After all, I have the feeling there will be more and more downsizing in the years to come. Downsizing and out-sourcing . So as we move into the twenty-first century, we must accept that school is never out for the professional."

A number of years ago I wrote a book titled *Positive*

Parenting. I had a psychologist write the introduction for me and she told me of an experience she had on the day she received her Doctor's Degree of Psychology.

At the graduation ceremony, an aunt of hers came up and embraced her and congratulated her. Then she said, "Isn't it marvelous? You will never have to read another book."

School is never out for the professional.

Today, more than ever, if you are not learning something new, then you are falling behind. Change is happening at such a rapid pace that it is impossible to just stand still any longer. Today we are either moving forward or falling behind.

What do I hope to accomplish with this book?

First, I hope to remind you that the safety field is a very special place to be. It can be exciting, challenging, rewarding and sometimes heartbreaking.

Quite likely you will not remain in the safety field all of your life. If you are on the fast track then in your working career you will probably have several different employers. You might completely change your field two or three times.

That is what is good about the information in this book. While it is true that it will serve you well in the safety field, it will also serve you in whatever line of work you fall into in the future.

My own personal plan is to keep growing until the day I die. Yes, I hope to be of service until my dying day.

My one hope is that this book will help you to find

more fun and satisfaction in your work.. If you find enough, then it will no longer be work for you. It will be fun and when it is, I know you will have achieved a new level of excellence.

Life is a constant state of climbing higher. I hope you learn to enjoy it at every level you reach.

Chapter 13

LAWYERS AND LITIGATION

THIS MORNING I WAS READING A FOUR page legal contract regarding the reproduction and sale of a series of video tapes we have created.

There were a number of clauses that I did not really understand and so I sent the contract to a few people whose opinion I really respect. They were just as confused by the contract as I was and they suggested that I hire a lawyer and take his or her advice.

Many years ago I made the decision that I would avoid lawyers and litigation at all costs. I firmly believe that lawyers represent themselves first and foremost and the rights and interests of their clients are way down the list in their order of priorities.

This is a sad, cynical, but far too true conclusion.

A couple of years ago the Michigan State Chamber of Commerce hired me to give a speech to a group of young people selected by their communities as real winners. They were the cream of each area and those young people who might be expected to serve as mayors, legislators or such in the future.

In one segment of my talk I did some humor about lawyers, I attacked the legal profession and the speech was greeted with unbound enthusiasm.

Later I received a number of invitations to speak at local chamber meetings and each caller requested that I expand my attack on the legal profession.

I declined all of the invitations. "Once is enough," I insisted. "I've got it out of my system."

As you start your challenging journey into the 21st Century I would strongly recommend that you avoid lawyers and litigation at all costs.

I have observed again and again that lawyers have a way of making the possible, impossible.

Instead of bringing people together they wedge them apart. Clarifying turns into complicating. Simple negotiating turns into all out war-fare.

Over the years I have found that most of the time people can be brought together and disputes can be settled in a friendly manner if you keep the lawyers locked outside of the room.

Now if you happen to get arrested for murder then you may feel free to ignore my advice.

There might be a few other instances in your lifetime that might prove me wrong, but as far as for me, I will do everything in my power to avoid lawyers and litigation.

Lose out now and then? Sure I will. Get hornsnickeled in a deal once or twice? You bet. But the anger, the hate, the loss of respect and reliance on my fellow man and woman that I will avoid will more than compensate for the monetary loss that I might incur.

There is a story going around that at one of the leading American universities they are now using lawyers instead of white rats in the laboratory experiments. They find that there are a lot more lawyers than white rats and that people conducting the experiments do not get emotionally attached to the lawyers.

There I gave you one of the stories. If you want half a dozen more, just call me. But, No! I will not do an anti-lawyer speech for your local chamber of commerce. You do it.

Everybody will love you, except the lawyers.

And they will sue.

Chapter 14

A PASSION FOR SAFETY

I'M NOT SURE JUST WHEN THE WORD "Passion" became so important to me when it came to safety.

Perhaps it was the time that I actually buried the body parts left behind in that Kalamazoo railroad yard.

Somehow that event seemed to represent all of the horror I had witnessed in my twenty-five years in the general claims department of the Grand Trunk Railroad Company.

I think back now on the first day in that department. It was February, 1948 and I had been hired as a mail boy. Part of my duties included the filing of papers and at times the retrieval from the rows of file cabinets lining the office walls.

It was shortly before noon when claim agent Mike

Prus introduced himself to me and requested that I pull a certain file covering an accident involving a speeding train and a school bus.

"Just get the file," Mike explained to me, "and check to see that all twelve photos are in the file." I located the file and the photos were in an envelope near the top of the file. Back then photos were black and white, but that didn't lessen their impact on my mind and my stomach.

The photos showed the mutilated bodies of young students that had been killed in that tragic bus-train collision.

I took a deep breath and counted the photos. One, two, three. It was horrible making my way through that mess, but somehow I managed.   Ten, eleven, and finally twelve.

They were all there all right. I put the photos back into the envelope and then put the file on Mike Prus's desk. "They were all there." I said.

"Welcome to the General Claims Department," he said. "Now you can go to lunch."

I left the office and right now I can not recall if I ate or not. I did notice that when I returned to the office that everyone was looking at me.

Later I learned that this was a regular initiation ritual for all new employees and that many of them never returned from lunch. It was a screening process. You had to have the stomach for this kind of work.

Then, some twenty-five years later, there I was in the early morning at that railroad yard with a couple of sticks, digging a hole in the ballast and endeavoring to bury the remains of that employee triple amputation, sick once more and saying to myself, "No more, no more. I can't just investigate accidents and handle the claims any longer. Somehow I've got to help prevent these accidents."

Call it a mission, call it a passion, call it what you want to call it, but that desire has grown in the twenty five years since then and more and more I find that I must do what has to be done to make this a safer world.

How would you find the passion? I think it must start with a spark and it must be nurtured. It needs feeding and fanning and like a fire it must be tended and kindled and given the environment to grow.

This book is about a number of things, but my goal is to encourage and feed your passion for safety.

It must have been a worthy master for me, for after fifty years I doubt that I'll abandon it. In fact, I suppose that I will continue my passion until there is no way I can serve it.

I only hope that my passion for safety will somehow rekindle a greater passion for safety in your life. I have found it is contagious. Perhaps together, we might start an epidemic.

Chapter 15

X-FACTOR

DID YOU EVER HEAR ABOUT THE X-Factor? I'm sure it has been given a lot of other names.

In high school I learned that X stood for the unknown.

What does the X-factor have to do with safety and with success and with the 21st Century? Well, I like to suggest that it means everything. It means the absolute difference between simply surviving and really thriving.

The X-Factor to me is that magic ingredient that separates the top winners from the rest of the pack.

Over the years a number of authors and other researchers have set out to discover what it was that was responsible for a few folks soaring to the top of their field; while others who appeared equally dedicated, equally talented seemed to just sort of wallow around in semi-mediocrity.

Over the years I've heard a wide range of answers. One that keeps coming up is the element of luck.

"I guess I was just awful lucky," you might hear the winners say, but then I heard the best definition of luck ever. It said, "Luck is when preparation meets opportunity."

In other words, the luckiest people in the world are those who have paid the often painful price of continuing preparation and who are always alert for opportunity.

You'll find that most lucky people are not only prepared and alert, but they are also courageous. They act when the time is right.

Then when they have outstanding success the rest of us stand by with envy and say, "That lucky stiff."

Another X-Factor that most successful people subscribe to is that of setting goals. "Unless you are headed somewhere in particular, you rarely get there," they say.

Jet jockeys sometimes call the X-factor, " The right stuff."

A casual observer might think they are referring to what some people call guts. Guts or grit or courage. Others might think it is just acting macho.

Actually there is much more to it than that. The

right stuff does include courage, but there is a lot of other good stuff included too. The good stuff includes intelligence, the ability to absorb huge quantities of technical information, a big serving of self-sacrifice, the ability to absorb pain, a passion for adventure and much more.

Frankly, I must admit, I do not know several of the other ingredients necessary.

That is the problem with honing in on X-Factors. Just when you think you have isolated one another pops up.

What if we tried to isolate the one factor that would apply to great safety people? What would it be?

First let me admit that I have been wandering around the safety field since 1948. I've spoken for thousands of safety people all over the United States and Canada.

I've been in their homes, in their plants and spent hundreds of thousands of hours talking with them. I've stood long hours exhibiting at state and national safety conferences.

Believe me, I have been observing successful safety people for nearly fifty years now and in all that time I have met the good, the great, and the bad. Yes, the ugly, too.

I've met doctors, lawyers, engineers, accountants, nurses, and people with genuine degrees in safety. I've met some who talk as if the people that they work with were a bunch of sheep and they were the chosen shepards.

I've met a few who despised their jobs and the

company they worked for. I've met thousands of safety team members that have just caught the spark for safety. I've met many just burning up with the passion for safety and I've met the burned out too.

What was the X-Factor that I discovered? It was love. Great safety people felt good about themselves. Great safety people really cared about the well being of the people that they work with too. Sometimes they cared so much that they would get a fellow fired and sent down the road just to keep him from getting killed.

What do you think that the X-Factor is in safety?

See if you can identify the really great safety people in this world. When you do look them over really good and then make a list of your own.

Once you get a list, then make up your own set of goals to go with them. See if you can't become just like the real winners, The world can certainly use a few more great safety people. Believe me.

Chapter 16

MOTIVATION

IN THE GREAT MUSICAL, *FIDDLER ON THE Roof*, Teve, the philosopher explains a summary of total beliefs when he says, "Life is like a fiddler on the roof trying to eke out a simple tune while simultaneously hanging on to the roof to keep from falling."

When I studied human behaviorist, Alexander Maslow's, *Hierarchy of Needs*, I learned about motivation and why people do things. Maslow explains with a pyramid. At the base of the pyramid are the survival needs, such as food, shelter, clothing and sex.

The cave man and cave woman were kept pretty busy just filling those basic needs. After all , that was where most of the action was. Eventually the cave man got smart and said to himself, "Himself, it would sure be nice if I could get my food shelter and clothing without getting all scratched up. And the same with sex. Some of those women fight back and get pretty ugly.'

And so man climbed up the second step of the pyramid of needs and that was the need for safety. Now let me explain, before we go any further that whenever one of the needs that is lower on the pyramid is threatened or not filled then the lower need becomes the real prominent motivation.

Once the safety need is met, we move up to man's need for acceptance by his peers. He wants to be one of the guys. A woman wants to be accepted too. With acceptance we move up to the need of self-esteem. We want to feel good about ourselves and what we are doing.

At the top of Maslow's pyramid comes what he calls self-actualization. I like to think of self-actualization as the point where you have discovered your special talents and you have taken the time and effort to sharpen your talents, to hone you skills and you commit your time to using your gifts for the good of mankind.

It is singing your song and letting that special music inside you come out.

Once someone said that the greatest tragedy that could come to a man is for him to die with his song unsung, with his music still inside him.

Now what I believe Teve was saying was that we are all fiddlers on the roof and we are all trying to make beautiful music on our violins, but life is not easy and we must take care of all of our other needs. So we spend most of our time just hanging onto the roof for survival.

If there is one thing I have learned in my years of striving to make beautiful music in my life it is this: You can't make beautiful music unless you have the courage to take chances and let go of the roof.

I also learned that you will fall off the roof now and then and sometimes you get hurt and you'll feel a lot of pain.

But I've also discovered that it is worth it.

If you hope to soar then you have to let go. This is a book about letting go and soaring with the eagles.

Chapter 17

AN UNSAFE ENVIRONMENT

I'D LIKE TO TELL YOU ABOUT A COMPANY I worked for in October and early November of 1951. During about a three week period a remarkable 97% of our company's employees were either killed or seriously injured on the job in the regular performance of their duties.

Tragically, thousands of others who were working for a competing company were also killed or injured as a result of the company's performance.

I can remember well, standing near the job site waiting for my time to go into action watching the parade of litters carrying out the dead and mutilated bodies of my associates.

Sound like a war story? It is. The job site was Korea and the Company was Able Company, Seventh

Regiment, 1st Cavalry Division, US Army, and my job classification was combat rifleman.

On November 7th, 1951 I was, fortunately, wounded seriously enough to be evacuated to Nara, Japan for surgery.

The thousands of others who were killed were soldiers of the North Korean Army who were killed in our daily battles for a hill named Old Baldy and on adjacent hills.

I can remember the morning the Republic of Korea (ROK) soldiers came up on our hill and gathered up the bodies of the enemy dead. They put them into a huge pile of several hundred dead and poured gasoline on the bodies, lit a fire, and departed.

When the enemy on the adjacent hill saw this they hit us with every mortar and artillery shell in their arsenal it seemed.

Why am I telling you this true war story? Because I want you to realize what a truly hazardous work site is.

When you see your fellow workers falling dead all around you, then you suddenly realize that this is not a good place to be.

I don't know what environment you, and the people you serve work in, but after surviving that experience in Korea, personally, everything else seemed like a piece of cake.

Chapter 18

TAP DANCING

IT WAS TWENTY YEARS AGO, MAYBE twenty-one or two and I was in my forties. I guess my daughter, Nancy, was twenty, That would be about right. I had a booking to do three early morning speeches in the grand Ballroom of the Conrad Hilton Hotel in Chicago., for the National Safety Congress.

They would cram a couple thousand people in that room for my sessions and I was dedicating every spare moment of my crowded life to preparation. As a professional speaker, I had become quite well known for my unusual, memorable closes. I had planned to use my popular "people" close which I did with a musical background playing.

Then on the second day I planned to use my new verse I had written titled, *My Brother's Keeper*. For the third day I had a wild idea. I wanted to learn a simple soft shoe dance to do to the music of *Bye-Bye*

Blues. I worked out words and the timing and in my mind I could see myself dancing on stage with my lovely daughter, Nancy, at my side.

In my imagination it was spectacular. About a month before the booking I took a deep breath and approached my daughter, Nancy with the idea. To say that she gave a cool reception to the idea would be a real understatement. After a few days of coaxing, plus the promise of a monstrous bribe, she consented to join me in the basement Rec Room, together with a tape player on which I had the proposed music.

As we got to the part where I had visualized the dancing, I cried out, "Now! This is where you come on stage in shorts and black tails, toss me a cane and a top hat and together we go, ta ta ta ta - tata - ta-ta-ta-tatatata - ta- ta- ta."

"Dad," she said in disgust, "do you mean ta ta ta ta - ta ta - tata?"

"Yeah!" I said. "Something like that. Just something that will look smart and absolutely show that I know how to do the soft shoe with you."

Nancy told me to shut off the music. She hated that music. It was old fashioned. It was stupid and it just wouldn't work.

"Well try to make it work for us." I pleaded.

I won't go into all the gruesome details, but we struggled with it for a full hour and the next evening we struggled even harder and finally after another hour of struggle, Nancy suggested that I sit down and listen to what she had to say.

"Dad," she began. "I love you and I think you have a wonderful talent for giving speeches, but a dancer you are not and a tap dancer you will never be."

Coaxing didn't work. Bribes no longer had any effect on her. Her mind was made up. I was a klutz. I didn't know my right foot from my left. I was positively hopeless. After two hours struggle, I was not one bit better than I was to start with.

She finally summed up the situation by saying, "And not under any circumstances would I be caught dead dancing with you in front of two thousand people on-stage at the Conrad Hilton Hotel."

I got the point. I was heartbroken. My dream was fading. I tried a half a dozen times to veto her edict without success. Eventually I gave up my dream and replaced the soft-shoe idea with a wonderful story.

Nevertheless that old dream of tap dancing remained in the back of my mind. and continued to haunt me. Every time I saw an old Fred Astaire or Gene Kelly movie, every video that shows Sammy Davis Jr., or Tommy Tune dancing brought back that dream and made me wish I might have done that wonderful close.

The years passed and I got older and grew an enormous pot belly and the chances I would ever fulfill my tap dance dream diminished with each added pound and passing year.

As I've shared with you before my wife, Ruthie contracted cancer and after a nine year battle, she died. At first, I mourned and found some solace in half gallon binges of ice cream.

Finally, I got sufficiently disgusted with my weight and physical unfitness, I went on a reconstruction program. In all, I guess I must have lost some fifty pounds or more and with it that ugly pot belly.

With that weight off, I felt so light that I felt like skipping. I felt like just flitting around. My feet were like feathers.

It took a while for the possibility to return to my mind, but one day I joined a senior center and when I checked the list of programs they were offering, I spotted one that said, "Tap Dancing for Seniors", and the instructor was Shari Rarick.

Imagine, Shari Rarick, the same wonderful woman who had taught our Nancy to dance so many years before.

I called Shari. "I see you are offering a tap class," I said, "I was wondering if I could take your class?"

"Certainly," she replied, "We'll take anybody."

Then for an hour each week I submitted myself to a session of complete humiliation. There were about twenty women in our class and me. The women were so cute flitting along so beautifully in time with the music and there I was stumbling around like a complete klutz.

If you are reasonably coordinated then I am sure it will be difficult for you to understand this, but my feet and my mind have a broken connection,

I'd visualize a step and see my feet going in the right direction in the proper sequence. Then as I tried to do this step, my feet, as if they had a mind of their own, would go off completely in a different direction. It made no sense at all to me and it was a source of great disappointment and frustration. At the end of the six week course I did not sign up for another term.

I had gone to Chicago and purchased a pair of patent leather tap shoes. Then one afternoon, I was looking for something in the basement and I discovered a miniature plywood ping-pong table just 3'x4' in size. On a whim, I took off the fixtures and brought it upstairs for a minor experiment.

I placed it in front of my television in the den and put on my shoes. Then for about a half an hour I tried the steps I had learned. Then I tapped my way around the board searching for something that might work for me.

I've played at playing the drums since I was a kid thirteen years old and so rhythms are not something new to me. I tried a couple of old beats and I soon discovered that if I did a step very much like running in place it sounded great. In fact, the heel and toe taps seemed to magnify everything and with a little practice I found that I could do a whole series of variations on that one step.

Within a week I had located a CD of Louis Armstrong and his All-stars doing a blazing rendition of *Tiger Rag*. My original goal, set over twenty years ago, was to do a slow soft shoe. But now that I had discovered this new step, I felt that instead of a sedate soft-shoe, I could set my sights much higher and go for a higher goal.

I practiced just the last one minute of Tiger Rag. Then I put it on a cassette tape several times for practice sessions.

One minute might not seem like a whole lot of time, but as Mark Twain used to explain; time is relative. it depends on whether you're kissing a pretty girl or sitting on a hot coal stove. I soon discovered that you can deliver a whole lot of variation on a running step in one full minute.

Describing a tap dance is a little like trying to tell how a melody goes with just words, but I will try to put a picture in your mind of just how the dance goes now after a couple of months of daily effort.

While the music starts out fast and just gets wilder, I start out slow, just tapping around like I've just discovered my tap shoes.

Then I begin to experiment and try them out a bit. At the end of the first chorus I double the speed of my steps and it's not bad. I do a couple of turns then I put my hands in my pockets and kick my feet out to the sides just sort of enjoying the experience.

There is a certain jaunt to the theme of the music and I seem to be caught up in the music. There is a break, I stop for an instant then the jaunt takes over and suddenly my feet are flying. My arms begin to swing in circles and I look a bit like a two bladed helicopter that is about to take off.

Again, there is a two beat break and I stop as I holler out, "Big Finish."

I now double the steps of my flying feet and my

arms are flying twice as fast now and as the song comes to an end, on the final five beats, I throw out exploding caps that accentuate the beats with Pow! Pow! Pow! Pow! Pow!

I guess you had to be there and I will never forget it because when I first did it in front of an audience of seniors, they went wild.

It was like an old dream coming true. It reminded me of something I'd heard recently about trapping monkeys.

In deepest Africa, when trappers want to capture a lot of monkeys they do not chase them from tree to tree. Instead they take about a hundred big jars out into a clearing. These jars have long narrow necks and inside the jars they put gooey nuts that monkeys love.

Then the trappers go out and drink beer all afternoon because they know that about six o'clock in the evening each jar will have a monkey with its arm stuck in it and the monkey will have a fist full of nuts. Unfortunately, the monkeys never do get to enjoy these nuts. All they had to do to win their freedom is let go of the nuts.

I know that in many ways I am a lot like one of those monkeys. Perhaps you are too. Now I'm not trying to sell you on Darwin's theory that we are all related to apes. Not at all. But I do think that we do take a hold of ideas, beliefs, thoughts that may not be necessarily true and often those beliefs can keep us from reaching our full potential.

These restricting beliefs can keep us from attaining

wealth and fame and yes, happiness too. We just don't let go.

For some twenty years I believed that never, no way would I ever become a tap dancer. Now I don't want to blame my daughter, Nancy, in any way for that belief. That was just her belief. There was no reason that I should have accepted it at all. I could have gone out that day and have gotten a second opinion or a third or a fourth.

However, I don't want to give the impression that I now know how to tap dance either.

I've simply got a little one minute close to my speech that looks pretty good, that is, if you don't know anything about tap dancing.

I never wanted to be a great tap dancer. All I ever wanted was twenty seconds of dancing that would make a point.

I got my dream, in fact, instead of twenty seconds, I got a full minute and that is the way it often is when we let go of those self restrictive, self defeating ideas that hold us back.

I'm still practicing that dance every day and I think it is getting better.   That's often the way it is. Practice might not always make perfect but it does often lead to improvement.

Since I learned that tap dance I've been using it to close many of my speeches, in fact, I've had standing ovations with that dance at Opryland, Las Vegas, Atlanta and several other locations with audiences as large as 2,000 people. First comes the dream.

Now I'm searching my mind for some of the other, self restricting ideas that I've been carrying around with me all these years. Who knows, I just might learn how to carry a tune if I really put my mind to it.

My first grade teacher just might have been wrong. Just maybe I'm not really a Johnny one note. If I dance then just maybe I can sing.

Chapter 19

BEHAVIOR MODIFICATION AND SAFETY

HOW WOULD YOU LIKE TO HAVE EVERY ONE OF YOUR EMPLOYEES SIGN A PERSONAL COMMITMENT TO SAFETY AND TO POSITIVE INTERACTION?

IN OTHER WORDS HOW WOULD YOU LIKE TO HAVE EVERY EMPLOYEE AS AN ACTIVE MEMBER ON YOUR SAFETY TEAM? DO YOU THINK IT WOULD MAKE YOUR JOB A LOT EASIER, EVEN FUN? YOU BET!!!!!!

At a safety conference held up north recently the Vice President of a major public utility made a remark that following the fatal injury on the job, many of the fellow workers of the deceased had revealed, "We knew he'd get killed someday, he was always taking chances."

In the twenty-five years I spent handling bodily injury claims and investigating injuries for a railroad, I was always amazed at how many times workers were seriously injured.

> **If you want to achieve what we call that golden goose egg signifying zero injuries then, I believe, you must find a way to change attitudes and modify negative, apathetic behavior.**

In my investigation I would find a couple of witnesses or fellow employees who would remark, "I knew he was going to do that."

When I asked them what they did about it, they would always reply, "Nothing, you just couldn't tell that guy anything."

A Silent Conspiracy

Just imagine people standing by silently watching their fellow worker killed or badly injured on the job. They believed that it was worthless to tell them that they were working unsafely and it might result in an injury. I've heard of something called a "Silent Conspiracy." Perhaps this is a silent conspiracy of unsafety

If you want to establish a great safety record. If you want to achieve what we call the golden goose egg signifying zero injuries then, I believe, you must find a way to change attitudes and modify negative, apathetic behavior.

When people learn to interact with each other in a positive way to prevent unsafe conduct, to prevent accidents and incidents and injuries, we call that positive interaction.

I've spent some fifty years in the safety field. I began in February of 1948. Since then I have written nearly one thousand articles, I've had 42 books or booklets published and I've made nearly 4,000 professional presentations in all of the 50 United States, in 8 Canadian Provinces and a number of foreign countries. I've worked for DuPont and Exxon and Mobil and the Air Force and Navy, AT&T, you name it and I've probably worked with the organization and what I am now going to say is the most important thing I have ever said in the safety field. It is the key , the essential key, to behavior modification, to positive interaction, and to my brother's and sister's program within an organization.

Please, please. listen up closely for just a moment. This is critical, this is essential and ignoring this will quite likely insure the failure of your program.   A positive interaction program will work only if you first have the participants' **signed permission.**

A positive interaction can and will work only if you first have the participants' signed permission.

Now the immediate reaction of most folks when you mention the word "signed" is for them to say, "Oh, our people won't sign anything."

Generally speaking, I would agree with you, but we are not speaking generally. I'm talking about something very special and it has a proven track record.

The signed permission for positive interaction is contained in a document we call, "*The Declaration of Inter-dependence.*"

It was modeled after our nation's Declaration of Independence, that document that was instrumental in creating what I believe is the greatest nation in the world.

You have already read about it several times in this book,. Please bear with me, this is critical.

In our Declaration we declare our inter-dependence upon one another for our safety. We acknowledge our own fallibility and state that we are human and vulnerable and that accidents happen when we let our guards down.

We agree to positively interact when we see others working in an unsafe manner and request and give permission to others to positively interact with us when they see us working in an unsafe manner.

There it is. It just might be insignificant to you on first glance, but think about it.

IS THIS BEHAVIOR MODIFICATION?
YOU BET!

Today more than ever we all have reservations about telling someone that they are doing something that might result in an injury. We've all been told to mind our own business We've probably been told much worse, too. "Bug Off!" or "Who made you boss?" "Don't get in my face, man!"

There seems to be a series of invisible walls that keeps us from communicating with one another. Men say they cannot communicate with women, women with men. Young people with older, older with young, workers with supervisors, supervisors with workers. Folks with more or less seniority, races with one another.

There seem to be dozens of reasons why people can't communicate with each other, even for their own safety and survival.

That is why most of the safety people who investigate accidents will tell you that repeatedly, when investigating a serious injury or a fatality, they will find fellow workers who will admit, "I knew he or she was going to do that."

When people get together and sign our Declaration they are driven by emotion and logic to admit that they are vulnerable, that they too have bad days and bad moments, that they need brother's and sister's keepers to look out for them for their own survival.

BEHAVIOR MODIFICATION
BY POSITIVE INTERACTION

They also agree to allow others to positively interact with them while they positively interact with others.

About 95% of the people exposed to our Declaration presentation, either at a live presentation or viewing the video, sign up for safety. At most of the plants I visit, I am told that I should not expect many of the workers to cooperate.

I was warned at a GM plant in Ohio that if 30% signed up it would be a miracle.

The plant manager was stunned when presentation after presentation we signed up at least 95%.

One power company showed our video to 10,000 workers and obtained 10,000 signatures.

In Canada we changed our document and called it, *A Personal Pledge to Safety and to Positive Interaction* the results have been the same. We get nearly 100% positive response.

Now don't make the same mistake that a few safety people have made with our Declaration. Some have felt that the instrument was adequate to change behavior and win the worker's support. It doesn't work by itself. Some trainers think they can watch my presentation and then do their own thing and make it work. So far, I've never heard of anybody doing it successfully.

Frankly, I do not know exactly why my presentation works so well. Every time I hand the first person in the audience a pen with my Declaration, I seriously wonder what the reaction will be.

So far, our results have always been positive. People listen to my talk, either live or on video and they want to sign up immediately. They are sold and they realize that it is for their own good and that is a good, loving thing to do.

Yes, you say, maybe they will sign it, but do they live up to it?

We have had excellent feedback from many of our clients. Here are a few examples.

I went into Phillips Petroleum in Odessa, Texas in January of 1994 and did a presentation of the Declaration with their employees. The feedback was very positive, and to date they have not had one reported loss time accident.

Here is another example, in the exact words of Ron Smith, the safety supervisor at Akzo Chemicals in Pasadena, Texas following a January 1993 presentation:

"Originally, some people were skeptical that one lone speaker could have much of an effect on the workers here. After the talk though we have seen the philosophy of "your brother's keeper" find its way into the different managers' talks concerning not only safety, but quality and production as well. How has this helped us in our quest for that "golden goose egg" of a TRC rate of 1 or less? Well, as of April 20, 1993 of a TRC rate of 1 or less? Well, as of April 20, 1993 we achieved 1,000,000 man hours without a LTI/AFW case. We have yet to have an OSHA reportable accident this year and the trend shows that we're still going in the same positive direction. With the level of increased awareness towards safety and others, I am becoming bombarded with positive suggestions to improve and/or enhance our safety program here. All said and done, I believe that your visit was beneficial in more ways than we expected and that is any way you look at it, very, very good."

Let me repeat the words of Mr. Smith, "With the level of increased awareness towards safety and others...." This is indeed behavior modification at its best.

Would you like that to happen at your organization? Would you like to have 1,000,000 work hours without a Lost Time Incident or OSHA reportable accident/ **Would you like people to come to you with positive suggestions for better safety programs?** Would you agree that this is behavior modification? Well look at this...

Here's our Declaration for you to examine again:

In Session
Declaration of Inter-dependence
(c) Art Fettig, 1998

When in the course of human events, it becomes necessary for an organization and its members to make a total uncompromising commitment to safety for its future growth and for the good of all its employees.

And whereas, we do hereby resolve that we will do

all in our power, every moment of every day, to make safety a value which we hold dear and integrate into our planning and in the fulfillment of our goals and activities.

Therefore we do hereby declare and acknowledge our dependence upon one another. For the practice of safety is both a personal and a mutual obligation.

We state our commitment in this verse titled, "Our Sister's and Our Brother's Keepers."

We are our sister's and our brother's keepers.
For safety calls for our uncompromising commitment,
to one another and to safety, too.
I promise I will positively interact when I find you performing
in an unsafe manner, and I expect a positive interaction
from you on my behalf, when I go wrong.
We are human you and I and accidents and injuries occur
when we forget or just react wrongly not doing what's
right and responsible for our own safety.
We are our sister's and our brother's keepers.
Trusting in one another for a safer world.

And for support of this declaration, we mutually pledge to each other our lives, our future, and our sacred honor.

If you'd like to preview a declaration video, just give us a call at 1-800-441-7676. The tape alone sells for $295.00.

Our Declaration video and our powerful safety meeting video sizzlers are described in the back of the book.

While we are talking about behavior modification, let me make a challenge to you. How about modifying your own behavior? Do it now! Pick up the phone and call us. Don't put it off.

That's 1-800-441-7676

Chapter 20

THE FINAL CHAPTER

THERE WERE A NUMBER OF TIMES when I seriously doubted that this book would ever see the light of day. Of course we've reached many thousands of safety people and through them, no doubt, millions of workers with our ideas over the years through our live programs, our books, our booklets, audio cassettes and many video productions.

Nevertheless, this particular collection of my work went through a number of detours on its way to you.

Fifty years is a long time to watch and ponder.

It has been a magnificent journey. And I was there at the right time to see what was and what is and what might come to be.

The value of human life had certainly increased.

Businessmen no longer considered the death or mutilation of a worker as the price of doing business.

We've come a long way. A long, long way. And yet, people are still getting killed on the job. This has certainly not become a fail safe world.

Safety has become a science.

And yet the human factor, the potential for human error is always with us. I haven't changed my basic opinion much in fifty years. I learned early on that people cause accidents.

My message has always been for the working man and woman. Look out for yourselves, look out for one another. Give others permission to look out for you.

Pretty simple. Doesn't take a degree or years of study.

The one thing I have relearned so many times is this, people are good and caring and loving and a lot more things if you only give them the chance. You can't scream compassion into someone's head. You have to teach it by your example.

The main cause of accidents is people, but the solution to the challenge of safety also lies within people. The more you can involve your people in your programs the higher your chance of success.

So that is my final message.

Get compassionate about the safety of your people. Get passionate about your job. Make your own commitment to preventing accidents and saving lives just like I made so many, many years ago.

I'll still be around for a while.

I've just packed my patent leather tap shoes for the

employees of a major computer firm near Seattle.

Tomorrow, I'm meeting with my new partner, Greg Brayton over in Coldwater, Michigan and we will be recording a couple of new songs.

You see I've started a whole new career as a songwriter and we recently released our CD with Greg singing my songs.

Yes, we've already done a couple of songs on safety.

And yes, I'll still be doing a safety speech now and then.

Fifty years is a long time but it goes by fast if you're having fun.

If there's any way I can be of service, just give me a call because giving service is what life is all about.

Art Fettig was born in Detroit, Michigan July 5, 1929. In 1960 he moved with his family to Battle Creek, Michigan, where he now resides. He married Ruthie, his wife of over thirty-eight years and she died of cancer , June 26, 1993. They have four grown children and four grandchildren.

Art Fettig began writing professionally in 1961 and he has thirty-five books published, including *How To Hold An Audience In The Hollow Of Your Hand*, *The Three Robots* series of children's stories, *The Platinum Rule* and *Love Is The Target.*

He began working in the safety field in early 1948. And spent thirty-five years in the railroad industry, working first as a claim agent investigating thousands of tragic accidents. Then, for ten years, he dedicated his efforts to preventing such accidents. His award winning audio visual programs on safety have been seen by millions of students throughout the United States and Canada.

During the Korean conflict, Fettig served as a combat rifleman in the United States Army. He was wounded in combat and awarded *The Military Order of The Purple Heart..*

He is the founder of Growth Unlimited Inc., a corporation dedicated to bringing positive living concepts to people.

In 1963 he began his career as a professional speaker and has made presentations in all of the fifty states, eight Canadian provinces, and several foreign locations including Malaysia and Hong Kong. He is now a veteran of well over 4,000 professional presentations.

Today, Art Fettig spends a great deal of time writing and speaking in the fields of safety and motivation. He is especially active in the power, petrol, and construction fields. He is often featured as a keynoter at major conventions.

In 1980 he was certified as a "Speaking Professional" (CSP) by the National Speaker's Association. Art continues to write and lecture on personal growth, positive attitude and change. Author of eight children's books, he is a frequent visitor to elementary schools where he speaks for students on "Saying Yes To Positive Living."

Art Fettig is featured in over fifty video programs on safety, sales, motivation, and positive attitudes. He is also featured on several audio cassette programs.

Art has the unique ability to reach people of all backgrounds and of all ages with his spellbinding messages. He's a popular convention keynoter and is in constant demand by major corporations to speak for all of their employees, including blue collar workers and top management groups.

Art Fettig may be contacted at Growth Unlimited Inc., 36 Fairview Ave, Battle Creek, Michigan, 49017. Phone toll-free at 1-800-441-7676 or (616) 965-2229. The Fax number is (616) 965-4522.

Or Email at: artfettig@voyager.net

Visit our Website for free weekly Monday Morning Safety Memo www.IMASource.com.

What do these companies have in common?

* Alabama Power	*Intel Corporation
* American Electric & Power	* Mississippi Power
* Central Illinois Light Company	* Nevada Power
* Consumers Power Co.	* Pennsylvania Electric
* Enron Corporation	* Texas Utilities
* Exxon Corporation	* Wisconsin Electric
* Georgia Power	

They've all hired Art Fettig

For a dynamic meeting. Many of them have had Art back again and again. If you want a powerful meeting at any level- top management-supervisors-safety, anyone in industry, including associations, call Art Fettig today.

A Declaration of Inter-dependence Is Art Fettig's Finest Safety Presentation Now it is available on Video

Some say it is the most powerful safety video ever produced. It wins a personal, signed commitment to safety from everyone who views it! Participants say it is the best safety presentation they've ever seen.
Catalog #DV-1 (Time 42 Minutes $295.00)

We've also produced a special Canadian version titled, A Pledge to Safety. Catalog #1086 (Time 60 Minutes $295.00)

Of course a live presentation has more impact, but we've captured all of the excitement of a live meeting. Show this exciting, inspirational video and then follow-up monthly with our short safety meeting video sizzlers. Just $85.00 per sizzler.

We've got follow up booklets too. Send them to your employee's home and bring this powerful message to the whole family.

DB-1 Declaration Booklet   Just $4 each
PS-1 Pledge to Safety Booklet   Just $4 each

SAFETY MEETING SIZZLERS!

What is a Safety Meeting Sizzler?

At Growth Unlimited Inc. we created a series of videos with the express goal of adding sizzle to your safety meetings.

Several years ago a client of ours faced the prospect of a three day training program for employees.

"We'd like to hire you to come in for each training session and do ten or fifteen minutes of high powered, really entertaining material about twice a day for three days. We'd like to," he explained, "But we don't have the budget. We'd like you to do this every three months, but instead we have an idea that just might work. How about coming in for a half a day and we'll shoot a series of fifteen minute segments with a great video crew. They can play those tapes at training sessions."

It sounded like a real winner to me.

So many times people had come up to me at state and national safety conferences and remarked, "I just wish I could take you home with me for a safety meeting with our employees."

And so often either my time or their budget was restricted so this could not happen.

My friend with the video project idea further explained the challenge. "We have a load of technical stuff we must cover in our three day program and our people will need pumping up every so often."

I went in and did the half day and it was all set up so that each segment I did could stand alone. The result of that day's shooting was our original series of 8 Safety Meeting Sizzlers.

Over the years, thousands of workers at plants all over the United States and Canada saw those videos and we received dozens of letters from safety people telling us how well those videos worked to improve their safety meetings.

One fellow wrote how he used one of our videos 46 times at safety meetings all over their system.

A woman with a Coast Guard station in Alaska told how she used our videos at her meetings and they were so popular that their workers were borrowing them to show to their families and at school meetings.

Recently, we had the opportunity to have three different audiences on three different mornings in Newfoundland and we were given complete freedom to video tape whichever segments we wanted to cover with these groups.

The results were more than twice as good as we had hoped for.

The audiences were fantastic. The meetings had a certain magic to them and we captured all that magic on videotape.

     The result is a new series of 24 Safety Meeting Sizzlers.

     We use the term Safety in describing them, however our customers are telling us that they are using them not just for safety meetings, but for meeting of all kinds including meetings on quality, on change, on productivity, on drug and alcohol abuse and in a number of other areas, all with great success.

     This series of 24 video is listed in detail on the following pages. We offer the entire series for just $995.00 U.S.

     Individually you may purchase them for just $85.00 each.

     Order five (5) of your choice for $340.00

     Order a dozen of your choice for $695.00

     Quite frankly, most of our customers order them all, and when they do they save over $1,000.00.

     If you have any questions about our products just give us a call at 1-800-441-7676.

#1089 Sharpening Your Ax Time 14:15 Learn to sharpen your skills to compete in the 21st Century. A great woodsman shows the way.

#1090 Good! Good! Good! Time 15:44 Secrets of the Princes of Serendipity. Overcoming adversity. A winner.

#1094 The Fiddler & Maslow Time 12:44 Learn why people do things, or perhaps why they don't. About motivation and successful living.

#1097 Squiggley Lines Time 10:15 All fun but gives you insight into the topic of safety. Discover Hot Buttons and how to push them.

#1098 The Philosophy of Fun Time 22:18 Learn to love work and discover how to have fun in any job. Watch your happiness soar.

#1100 Enthusiastic Arithmetic Time 7:02 Sometimes things just don't add up. Perhaps you are the only one with the right answer. How to handle it and win.

#1102 A Tribute to Safety People 7:45 A gung-ho, standing ovation tribute celebrating how safety people make a difference in this world.

#1103 Stuff Time 7:44 Do you have the right stuff. It is the essential ingredient for success. Learn where to find it and how to make it work for you.

#1107 Frank Sinatra Sweats Time 9:35 When Art Fetting is mistaken for Andy Griffith in Las Vegas he learns a powerful lesson from Frank Sinatra.

#1113 Persistence & Heroism Time 10:19 Canadian Rick Hansen inspires while a rejected poem teaches a powerful lesson on hanging in a bit longer.

#1116 Learning From Our Children Time 12:46 You mind is like a computer. Learn how to feed it good stuff and allow children to help get you on track.

> **"I've used Art's video since 1986. They really work with people at all educational levels. They provide powerful, entertaining punch in a short timeframe, with important results."**
> **Herb Everett, Westmark Hotels, Anchorage, Alaska**

#1117 Focusing on Safety Time 13:29 Learn how to focus on excellence and quality and productivity and to make safety an integral part of the process.

#1119 Interact To Communicate Time 5:19 A powerful waterfall demonstration that will stick in your mind. Get your message through to everyone.

#1120 Empathy and Safety Time 10:58 Using the verse, The Builder, you'll learn to climb into others shoes and see their point of view.

#1121 A Real Southern Woman Time 7:31 Ever feel that you alone cannot make a difference in our environment? Let Sue's example impact your future.

#1124 5 Tips on Positive Interaction Time 6:12 A perfect follow-up video to reinforce the Declaration of Interdependence.

#1125 My Brother Joe Time 8:50 The perfect video to enhance your substance abuse program. Tow returning veterans with an alcohol problem. One lives, one dies.

#1126 Sculpturing Greatness Time 11:31 Discover that greatness within your from Michaelangelo. Has touched the lives of thousands.

#1128 A Million Miles, Safely! Time 8:34 What can you learn from award winning drivers? Just Drive! Use this video with our booklet You Do WHAT While You Drive.

#1129 I-71 Time 4:30 A tragic truck-bus collision and a verse wins a personal commitment to not drinking and driving from 2,000 students.

#1130 Eagles & Chickens Time 10:48 Are you a chicken or an eagle? Learn to sear no matter what your situation or environment.

#1131 A Life Changing Disaster Time 11:33 Investigating a triple amputation changed Fettig's life. Learn how he committed his life to safety.

#1132 Carefully Taught Time 9:13 A lesson in prejudice. A visit to Hawaii taught Fettig about love and understanding.

#1134 Dis Time 8:45 What's Dis? Fettig discovered Dis one day and gained a strange new insight into the challenge of stress. Learn to handle your own stress better.

Just $85 each but when you buy in quantity you will enjoy some real savings.

Buy 5 for the price of 4.........................Save $85................Just $340.00
Buy 12 and you save $325.00...Just $695.00
Buy all 24 and you save $1,045.00....................................Just $995.00

A booklet that your people will read and act on immediately. They'll drive safer.

You Do WHAT While You Drive? A guide to highway sanity.

Thousands have already benefited from this powerful little booklet. Now you can share this driving safety message with your people. Ideas taken from an interview with drivers who have driven a million, two million and even three million miles without an accident.

Plan to purchase a copy for every employee.
DW-1 Just $4.00
Buy 500 or more for just $3.00 per copy.
With 5,000 or more we'll grant you a license to print your own. Call 1-800-441-7676.

Order Page

Art Fettig's Growth Unlimited Inc.
36 Fairview Ave., Battle Creek, MI 49017
1-800-441-7676 FAX 616-965-4522
E-mail: artfettig@www.voyager.net

	Price	Shipping	Number	Total
Declaration Video	$295.00	$ 3.00	______	______
A Pledge for Safety Video (Canadian)	$295.00	$ 3.00	______	______
Safety Sizzler Videos	$ 85.00 EA	$ 3.00	______	______
5 Tape Sizzler Special	$ 340.00	$ 5.00	______	______
12 Tape Sizzler Special	$ 695.00	$10.00	______	______
24 Tape Sizzler Special	$995.00	$10.00	______	______
Declaration Booklet	$ 4.00 EA	$ 3.00	______	______
Pledge for Safety Booklet	$ 4.00 EA	$ 3.00	______	______
You Do What While You Drive Booklet	$ 4.00 EA	$ 3.00	______	______
Winning the Safety Commitment Book	$29.95	$10.00	______	______
The DEAL (A $2,372.95 Value)	$1,195.00	$10.00	______	______

Michigan residents add 6% sales tax ______________

Total ______________

Please ship to:
Name_______________________________**Title**________________
Company____
Address____
City____________________**State**__________**Zip**__________
Phone__________________**Fax**______________________

E-Mail address____
 Please send me free newsletter e-mail.

Check or Money Order Enclosed______________________________

Bill me_____________________**Purchase Order #**_____________

Charge to my account:
American Express______________**Mastercard**__________**Visa**__________
Card Number__________________________**Expires**____________

Signature____
 (Signature required on all credit card orders)

SATISFACTION GUARANTEED: If you are not 100% satisfied just return merchandise in good condition, immediately, for a 100% refund.